George Townsend Warner

Landmarks in English Industrial History

George Townsend Warner

Landmarks in English Industrial History

ISBN/EAN: 9783337112158

Printed in Europe, USA, Canada, Australia, Japan

Cover: Foto ©ninafisch / pixelio.de

More available books at **www.hansebooks.com**

LANDMARKS IN ENGLISH
INDUSTRIAL HISTORY

LANDMARKS

IN

ENGLISH INDUSTRIAL

HISTORY

BY

GEORGE TOWNSEND WARNER, M.A.

Sometime Fellow of Jesus College, Cambridge
Assistant-master at Harrow School

LONDON: BLACKIE & SON LIMITED
NEW YORK: THE MACMILLAN COMPANY

PRINTED AT
THE VILLAFIELD PRESS
GLASGOW

PREFACE.

The intention of this book is to bring before the reader the salient features of England's industrial and commercial progress in the past. Progress is not uniform in all branches at all times; in one period we may find expansion in commerce, in another new developments in agricultural life and methods, in a third a growth of a maritime spirit, in a fourth a succession of mechanical inventions. The facts about these events have been related before, although owing to the preference that is generally bestowed on political and constitutional history, they are apt to be regarded as of secondary importance. I make no claim to originality so far as the matter of this book goes; yet as each historical event is important, not only by itself but also in its bearing on other events, I have tried by a new arrangement to bring out these connections more fully. I have chosen what appears to me to be the chief Landmark of each age, and grouped round it the events which led up to it, and the consequences which came from it.

This has involved the sacrifice of any attempt at a strict adherence to a chronological order, and the omission of much that is in itself important and interesting; but the compensation will be found, I believe, in an increased simplicity of treatment, and a clearer impression of the main outlines of our country's economic development.

As the novelty of my book lies merely in selection and arrangement, I have not thought it necessary to burden the text with numerous foot-notes of reference to authorities. To two books in particular I owe much, and it is right that I should make special mention of them. They are Cunningham's *Growth of English Industry and Commerce* and Ashley's *Economic History*.

It only remains for me to express my thanks to those who have helped me; and especially to the Rev. W. Cunningham, D.D., who has assisted me with numerous suggestions and criticisms.

G. T. W.

HARROW, *November, 1898.*

CONTENTS.

Chap.		Page
	Introduction	1
I.	Before the Norman Conquest	8
II.	The Manorial System. Service and Commutation	26
III.	Towns, and the Beginnings of Town Life	45
IV.	The Exchequer. Money and Accounts	62
V.	England under the Three Edwards. National Unity and Commercial Policy	74
VI.	The Black Death	95
VII.	Later Developments of Towns and Gilds	116
VIII.	Enclosures for Sheep-Farming and the Progress of the Woollen Industry	134
IX.	The Mercantile System—The Policy of Power	150
X.	Elizabeth's Legislation	168
XI.	The Trading Companies and the Beginning of Colonial Expansion	187
XII.	A Survey of English Industries	209
XIII.	The Rise of Banking	227
XIV.	The Growth of Greater Britain—The Trade Wars of the Eighteenth Century	244
XV.	Machinery and Power	262
XVI.	The Agrarian Revolution	281
XVII.	Laissez-Faire and State Charity. Artisan and Pauper	301
XVIII.	Remedies by Legislation	329
XIX.	Modern Conditions: Trade and the Flag	350
	Index	361

LANDMARKS IN INDUSTRIAL HISTORY

INTRODUCTION.

History is opening out so vast a field that by common agreement we have come to recognize certain divisions in it. We speak of Ancient History and Modern History, Political History, Constitutional History, Ecclesiastical History, Military History, Economic or Social History, and so on. But although these divisions are convenient, we must not draw a dividing line too rigidly; we cannot take each fact of history and label it as belonging to one subject or to another, however tempting this may be for the sake of clearness, because there are many events which are important, not only in one, but in several branches of history. With some this multiple importance is evident: no one would dream of assigning Magna Carta to the constitutional historian and forbidding the political historian to mention it; events like the Reformation, or the Model Parliament, or the colonization of Ulster, or the Union with Scotland are plainly many-sided. But there is another class of events which, though they appear to belong very definitely to one division of history, yet on a closer scrutiny reveal influences, at first not suspected, reaching into other divisions. Philip II.'s and Louis XIV.'s persecutions of their subjects seem at first sight events to be classified as political or religious, yet they turned out to be of great economic importance in English history, for the immigration of alien craftsmen into England stimulated our industries at the expense of those of the Netherlands and France. When, as the story goes, an Indian pursuing some deer along a steep mountain side in Peru, slipped, caught hold of a shrub to save himself, dragged it up by the roots and saw revealed a mass of silver—a discovery which led to the working of the Potosi mines and the bringing of immense quantities of silver to Europe—we are tempted to say that this is an event purely economic. Yet it had far-reaching political consequences, not only in Spain, but in our own country, for the rise in prices which the new silver caused had no slight share in making it impossible for the Stuart kings to live on the revenue which had been enough for Elizabeth, and eventually brought Charles I. into violent collision with his parliaments. No doubt there were other and graver reasons, but money difficulties were the beginning of the disagreements between King and Parliament, which led to rebellion. Again, as we shall have occasion to notice more in detail, commercial needs or ideas have often led to prolonged wars, in which, amid the clash of arms and the rejoicings over victories, the original causes are apt to be obscured. For example, we find it easy enough to recognize Clive at Arcot and Wolfe at

Quebec as makers of the empire, but we may not discern at first sight that the British regiments at Minden were doing their share in the same work.

While it is thus necessary to pay attention not only to the immediate results of any event or course of policy, but also to the remote and sometimes unexpected consequences, we must not neglect beginnings, even if they are very small and silent. Anything which acts cumulatively, which, with ever so trifling a beginning, goes on attaining a wider and wider importance as it spreads further and further, is likely to turn out to be of greater consequence than many things which make a great stir and commotion at first, but with the lapse of time become of less account. Compare, for example, the importance of the Great Fire in London in 1666 with the foundation of the Bank of England about thirty years later.[1] The first left the trade of London paralysed, but only for a very short time; the second, intended to be nothing more than a temporary financial expedient, has ended by influencing profoundly the whole commercial system of the country, because its effects have been cumulative. A modern writer on economic history would dismiss the first in a few sentences, and deal fully with the other. Yet to a London merchant who had witnessed both, the immediate impression of the Fire would be far greater, far more dramatic; he would rate the immediate consequences high, and fail to see those which were more remote. Time, however, reveals the two events in their true proportions.

[1] In 1694.

Since events are so intertwined and draw with them such ramifying threads of after-events, and since in this tangle we cannot use a knife to cut one piece apart from the rest, the whole may well seem too vast to deal with satisfactorily. But, after all, the impression that will be gathered must depend upon the point of view. Just as in looking at a jagged mountain from different standpoints we get different pictures, one face looking smooth and steep when seen from the front, yet revealing its actual slope from the side, a tower of rock standing out against the sky from one place, being lost when we move to another, while fresh crests and shoulders come in sight; so it is with history. The political, the constitutional, the economic historian, each looks from his own point of view; the great features of history will be visible alike to all of them, but the minor ones which they pick out will be different; each writer deals with what has an appreciable concern with his part of the subject and omits the rest.

The task of selection, then, is of necessity one of the main difficulties; it is perhaps greater in economic history than in any other branch, for economic history is by its very nature barren of incident and somewhat destitute of great landmarks. The ordinary reader would be able to mention ten political or constitutional events to one economic one. Economic history is the history of causes and tendencies and policies, and most of these act very slowly. The movement is so gradual that it is only when comparison is made over considerable periods that we can be sure that movement is going on at all. Economic history is not often influenced by human personality or character; there are none of the flashes of interest which biography gives; what it has of dramatic interest is not gained from the rapid succession of incident, or from the varying turns of fortune, but from the slow intensity and resistlessness of the causes which it reveals at work. From a mass of events, few of them at first sight standing out as of much greater importance than the rest, selection has to be made. And if by the nature of things we cannot select much that is in itself striking, we must be careful to choose what has far-reaching connections. Isolated facts may be neglected, if we make sure that they are isolated; the links in the long chains of social progress or industrial development or commercial policy are what should be sought out and fitted together. We may omit what leads backward and what leads nowhere; our concern is with the "low beginnings" from which our country's wealth has grown up. Institutions, policies, ideas rise and flourish and fade again, and there are few of them that leave no mark behind them on the history and development of a nation. What England to-day has either to be proud of, or to regret, is the fruit of the past; how this fruit has been ripened or been blighted in the course of the ages is what history alone can teach us. And it is such a continuity in the social and economic development of England that we must endeavour to trace.

It is a newspaper commonplace of our time to marvel at the speed with which we are progressing. Discovery has succeeded discovery with bewildering rapidity, and inventions have become antiquated almost as soon as they are complete. Politics have shared with trade and commerce the same restless activity. But from this attitude of mind there is a danger of condemning the past unheard, or pushing aside with contemptuous tolerance what it has to tell us. With a pitying smile we are tempted to say that such facts are interesting, of course, from an antiquarian point of view, but quite out of date, and that it is best to try and understand modern conditions without wasting time over what is past and gone. Or else, self-contentedly applying modern considerations and modern standards to old motives and old conditions, we are prone to dismiss the past as hopelessly benighted, carelessly wondering how our ancestors could have been so foolish, and thanking Heaven that we manage things better nowadays. Such attitudes of mind are thoroughly wrong-headed; to condemn the past because it is the past is only to invite the condemnation of the future upon ourselves; the amount of commercial and industrial wisdom may indeed vary from age to age, but there is no reason for supposing that the latter part of the nineteenth century possesses a monopoly of it, and we cannot hope to understand the policy of the past if we obstinately refuse to regard it from the point of view of the past. Further, to disregard the past is both unscientific and ungrateful; unscientific, because the whole course of modern scientific progress has of late laid more and more stress upon observation, tabulation, and comparison, upon the importance of tracing things step by step from their origin, instead of beginning with theory and selecting facts to fit the theory; and ungrateful, because England of to-day is what Englishmen of the past have made her. If modern conditions are all that we need attend to, are we then prepared to say that our own is the only epoch in which England has been great? Was not England great in the eighteenth century, and in Elizabeth's day, and under Edward III.? Was not the vigour of the country at home and abroad at least as conspicuous as it is now? Nay, further, England and Englishmen of those days were tried and not found wanting, while our age has been happy in escaping trials and knowing little of enemies in the gate.

We owe our empire to those who have gone before us: they made it for us by the way they fought and worked and ruled themselves, and brought up children to carry on the work on their lines. If we were to draw a contrast between ourselves and other nations, it might well be found in the fact that Englishmen have not in past times rested content at home, but have embarked on wide schemes of expansion, and have spread their dominion over the face of the world; and that then the State and those who stayed at home have stepped in with the resources of arms and an almost unbounded supply of wealth to maintain what the vigour and enterprise of individuals had begun. Other nations have had great colonies; some are still struggling to get them. England stands alone in having in the main retained her colonies, and this she has been able to do principally by her unequalled material resources. The development of these resources, the growth of her industry and commerce, first at home and afterwards abroad, is a subject which ought not to be neglected. The story may seem dull, destitute of the glamour which attaches to the deeds of soldiers and sailors; commissariat work is unromantic when compared with the fighting in the front, but it is on the unromantic commissariat that the army depends. Piece by piece has been raised the stately pile which is called the British Empire; who thinks of the national industry, thrift, enterprise, and material resources which form the foundations of it? Not very many; the majority stare at the pinnacles which crown the whole. But if the pile is to endure it is well to consider these foundations.

CHAPTER I.

BEFORE THE NORMAN CONQUEST.

When in the month of September B.C. 54, Julius Cæsar made his landing on the coast of Kent, the Britons came for the first time into direct contact with a power which was to influence them for a time as profoundly as it did the rest of Western Europe; but with this difference, that while in Western Europe the Roman civilization lasted long and left many traces behind, in Britain it crumbled away under the hands of the Saxons with surprising rapidity. In most respects the history of Roman Britain is an episode in our history, almost complete by itself, and having few threads of connection with what came after.

Neither Cæsar's first expedition, nor the second in the following year, led to much. He crossed the Thames and defeated Cassivellaunus at St. Albans, but no Roman garrison was left, and for nearly one hundred years nothing further was done. The real work of conquest began with Aulus Plautius and Vespasian in A.D. 43. The south of England and the basin of the Thames were subdued. Scapula carried the troops into Lincolnshire and Shropshire, and Suetonius Paullinus pushed into North Wales. The consolidation and pacification of the country began with Agricola (78–89 A.D.). It was in his time that the Britons first copied Roman habits, built temples, houses and baths in the Roman style, assumed Roman clothes, learned the tongue of their conquerors, and settled down into the life of the Roman provincial. Roman roads, elaborately constructed with successive layers of concrete, stones, lime and gravel, took the place of the imperfect British tracks. Villas in the Roman style arose to astonish the Britons, whose dwellings had hitherto been of roughly squared timbers or wattles, with the interstices filled with clay. These villas were solid edifices of stone or brick, or of wood on stone foundations, sometimes extending 200 feet in length, surrounded by an arcade, and paved with marble and mosaic. The development of agriculture was on the same scale. Even before the coming of the Romans, Britain had the reputation of a fertile country in which corn grew well, and there appears to have been some export trade to Gaul and Ireland. But, as a rule, communication being imperfect, enough corn was grown for food and little more. Under the Romans the corn growing was systematized, and the trade enlarged. To get plenty of corn, and get it cheap, was always an object of Roman administration; it was needed for the troops in the island, for the Roman camps on the German frontier, and for the free gifts of corn made to the population of Rome. Accordingly, as the land was allotted on the Roman principle to soldiers and settlers, under whom the old inhabitants were employed to cultivate the soil, which had once been their own, the amount of corn raised increased vastly. Zosimus speaks on one occasion of 800 vessels being sent to fetch corn from Britain for the Roman cities on the Continent, and though the number is probably exaggerated, there is no doubt that Britain was regarded as a land of exceptional fertility. Eumenius speaks of it as "a land wealthy from its heavy crops, its rich pastures, its veins of metals, its revenues, and its many harbours". He says, too, that Nature had dowered it with all the advantages of soil and climate, that it neither suffered under extreme winter cold nor summer heat, while the fertility of the land was sufficient either for corn or vines. This again is a panegyric; experience convinced the settlers that if it was not snowy, it was often rainy and foggy, while the cultivation of the vine never was really successful. But for corn-growing the island was indeed admirably suited; besides what was taken as *annona*, a tribute of a fixed supply of corn for the maintenance of Roman soldiers and officials, enough corn was exported in actual commerce to justify the title bestowed on Britain—"The Granary of the North". The introduction of fowls, geese, and hornless sheep, and some fruit-trees, such as the pear and cherry, are the chief agricultural novelties credited to the Romans.

The same stimulating effect of Roman control is to be observed in industry. Before the invasions we know that the Britons had attained a certain amount of skill in weaving, dyeing, metal-working, pottery, and enamel work. The cloth made was coarse and thick enough to be some protection against a sword. Stripes and chequers in bright colours, of which the favourite was red, were used for coats and cloaks; dyes were obtained from various barks and lichens; rings, circlets, pins, brooches and beads of amber and jet were worn. Though the first iron swords and spears were brought from Gaul, the Britons speedily learnt to make them for themselves, ornamenting the handles and the bronze sheaths with gold and enamelled work. Coins copied from the Greek had been made since the visit of Pytheas (330 B.C.), and before the Roman conquest coins were lettered in the Roman style, *e.g.* "Cunobelinos Rex". Although iron came mostly from abroad, some iron ore was worked in the Severn valley before the Romans came, and the mining of tin and lead in Cornwall is very ancient, dating from the days when Phœnician commerce was prosperous. Posidonius[1], Cicero's tutor, visited Cornwall and describes the method of tin

---
[1] Born B.C. 135, died B.C. 51.

work; the tin was found in earthy veins, ground down, melted, purified, and made into slabs for exportation. It was shipped off by merchants from the Tin Island (generally supposed to be St. Michael's Mount). From his description it appears that the tin was got by "streaming", that is, washing out alluvial tin; in this form it is purest, and needs little refining. Other native arts were the building of chariots, coracles, and ships. The chariots were armed with iron scythe-blades, also of native make; the coracles of basket-work and hides were used on the rivers. The western Britons made frequent voyages to Ireland in ships with flat bottoms, so as to draw little water, but high in bows and stern, built of oak, secured with iron spikes, fitted with anchors with iron chains, and equipped with sails made of hides, painted blue to avoid observation at a distance.

All these rudimentary industries made progress during the Roman occupation. The invaders were not themselves to any great extent planters of new trades, but they understood well enough how to foster existing ones. Mines, for example, were mostly in Roman hands; the output of tin in Cornwall increased; lead from Derby and the Mendips was so abundant that the output was limited by law; iron works existed in the Forest of Dean, Hereford, and Monmouth; copper was mined in Anglesey and Shropshire; the practice of stamping bars of metal with the date was apparently common; coal was dug and burnt in Northumberland. The houses of the new masters called for stone-cutting, slates, and bricks; while their tastes demanded glass and pottery, of which the best was made at Castor, near Peterborough, and rougher kinds in Lincolnshire, Somerset, Worcestershire, Northamptonshire, and Essex. Even at this early date beer was a national product. Care for commerce is shown by a Roman lighthouse in Dover Castle, and it is possible that the Romans began reclaiming and protecting low-lying ground by embankments. Luxuries, such as keys, steelyards, hair-pins, glass bottles, spoons, statues, and bells, were all due to Roman civilization.

The export trade in corn, cattle, hides, metal, British dogs, furs, and slaves, involved some imports. Salt, an article of prime necessity if meat was to keep through the winter, came mostly from abroad, although some was got by evaporation on the sea-coasts. Wine, too, was imported in considerable quantities, as well as some amber and ivory, used for decorative purposes, though the quantity was small. The finer kinds of cloth could not be made in the island, and were imported, as was also the best ironwork. Generally speaking, the exports were raw materials, while the imports were either luxuries or necessities unattainable at home, or manufactured articles. Imports and exports were, as elsewhere throughout the Roman Empire, subject to duties (*portoria*).

Another effect of the Roman occupation may be seen in the growth of towns. The most important of these were London, on which so many roads converged, and York (Eboracum), the military centre of the north. Bath (Aquæ Sulis) was frequented for the sake of the waters. Colchester

(Camulodunum), Wroxeter (Uriconium), Chester, St. Albans (Verulamium), Cirencester, Dorchester, Lincoln, Gloucester, Silchester, and Caerleon, were all places of some size. It is related that 70,000 colonists perished in Boadicea's raid on St. Albans and London. The best houses in these towns were occupied by officials, civil and military, while round them clustered the huts of the poorer classes, generally built of wattles. During the later years of the occupation, churches were built, in towns mostly of stone and brick, in the country of wood. The term *municipia* is applied to some of the towns, and there is evidence of town councils at York, Gloucester, and Lincoln. Presumably they existed in other towns, but in any case it is probable that the office of town councillor became hereditary, and passed from father to son, in spite of every effort to get rid of the troublesome obligations which the office involved. As the government held these municipal bodies responsible for the taxes, and left them to arrange for their levy and collection, the office was most unpopular. Judging from what happened on the Continent, we may infer that trades gathered in corporations (*collegia*), but there is no very certain evidence of this in Britain.

The principal benefit conferred on the country came from the Roman peace. Quarrels hitherto adjusted by violence were settled in the law-courts, roads brought dwellers in different parts of the country into connection and made internal commerce easier, agriculture and industry were protected from wanton destruction. When the country was once subdued, peace, save on the borders, was complete. None of the country houses of the Roman period show any sign of fortification. This security was at the bottom of all the prosperity which spread over the country, yet it cannot be denied that the Britons felt the occupation in some ways as a burden. Besides the natural preference for independence, and the dislike of strangers who spoke a strange tongue, there were specific grounds of grievance. Those who were turned out from their lands by new settlers could not be expected to acquiesce quietly, and if this trouble was confined to the early days of settlement, others were more permanent. Taxation was heavy, and the tax-gatherers rough, peremptory, and unreasonable. In addition to the corn dues and port dues, there was the property tax (*tributum*), and after 212 A.D., when the mass of the people became Roman citizens, legacy duty had to be paid. And even more annoying was the levy for the army, by which a number of young men were annually chosen for the *auxilia* and drafted off abroad, from whence none could be sure of returning.

We may find an analogy to the Roman occupation in our own Indian Empire, but the analogy must not be pressed too far. The Romans made no deliberate efforts to improve the lot of their subjects, to educate or train them. The province was considered frankly as a possession to be administered primarily for the advantage of the conquerors. If violence, crime, and hideous customs, such as human sacrifice, were repressed, it was done in the interest of the Government, not of the people. If agriculture and trade were systematized and encouraged, this was because revenue could be drawn from them. If more comfortable habits and more refined tastes came to prevail, it was because the invaders could not dispense with these habits and tastes. Whether the Britons copied them or not was a matter of little consequence. It is not so in India; there the first object of Government is professedly the good of the governed. In India, too, the peoples to be ruled are divergent, of different races and religions, while Britain was more homogeneous. But in the peace and order maintained by alien rule, the superposition of alien habits of thought and justice, the introduction of an alien civilization with strange methods, appliances, and luxuries, there is a strongly-marked resemblance. And just as in India it is clear that if the British rule were withdrawn, most of the British work would fade away, railways would go to ruin, sanitary improvements be neglected, oppression of the weak take the place of equal justice between all, while the country would lie at the mercy of a powerful invader; so in Britain, the veneer of Roman influence and civilization was quickly broken through and destroyed when the power that had applied it was gone. The Romans taught the Britons much, but they did not teach them to be strong or united; rather they took away what unity and national initiative they possessed. Centuries of peace, alien government, and the copying of masters, left the Britons soft, dependent, anxious for peace, yet unable to make an organized and united resistance to secure it, and consequently they fell victims to the ruder and more vigorous Saxons.

Throughout the fourth century Britain formed the starting-point of many claimants to the empire, and was harassed by raids of Scots, Picts, and Saxons. In 400 A.D. Roman aid was finally withdrawn, and the Britons left to look to their own defence. An imitation of the Roman policy of employing barbarians against barbarians proved fatal. Vortigern enlisted a band of Jutes to war against the Picts and Scots; these they overthrew, but then turned on their employers; their success attracted their fellows, migration followed migration, battles were fought up and down the country, victory inclining now to one side now to the other, but on the whole the Saxons made steady progress. The Britons were driven westward, till by the end of the fifth century all the east, midlands, and south belonged to the invaders; all that remained to the Britons was Devon, Cornwall, Wales, and the strip of England lying west of the Pennine Hills. The invasion was extremely destructive. It was the work of men who were to the Britons everything that was alarming, barbarians untamed by Roman influences, pagans unsoftened by Christianity, warriors of reckless courage and hardihood. The new-comers had indeed none of the civilization of the Britons, nor any desire to make use of it. They saw a well-kept, orderly land, rich in corn and pasture, sheep and cattle, orchards and farms, and these lay before them as spoil. In their old home in Frisia they had held their land by force of arms, each man being warrior at one time and husbandman at another. If they resembled the German tribes pictured by Tacitus. their methods of agriculture were rude, their industrial skill hardly going beyond the weaving of coarse cloth, the construction of ships, waggons, and arms. Indeed the constant reference to the latter shows how large a part warfare filled in their lives. Towns were unknown; they settled, when they settled at all, in isolated groups, generally bound by some tie of kindred. But their migratory habits were very imperfectly abandoned, and it is not certain that they had entirely given up extensive[2] cultivation by the time they began to invade Britain. It is not difficult to picture, from the accounts that have been left, what the work of such invaders must have been, the slaying, burning, and stormings, the devastated crops, the deserted towns, the fierce pursuit, the flight of the Britons to the recesses of the woods and hills. In the general confusion the civilization introduced by the Romans had little chance of surviving.

Whether it is correct to describe the destruction as complete is a question to which the answer cannot be given with certainty. It is important in its bearing on the land-system of England. By the time of *Domesday*, England was covered with manors, and in the manorial system the cultivators are unfree. The Saxon cultivators in their old

---

[2] Extensive cultivation is the method practised among migratory tribes. The land is cultivated for one year only. The first preparation for taking a crop is to burn the brushwood; the ashes are then ploughed in for manure and the crop sown. Next year another piece of land is chosen and treated in the same way. "Intensive" cultivation means that the same land is used over and over again, fertility being restored by manure, repeated ploughing, and an occasional interval of lying fallow. It is obvious that extensive cultivation is possible, even with settled homes, provided the cultivators are few and there is plenty of land for all. It is still practised in parts of Bengal and in Russia, and a similar system existed in parts of Scotland as late as last century.

home were free, but it is doubtful if on settling in England they kept their old free methods, or began cultivating with captured Britons, held as slaves; whether, in fact, the manor grew out of an originally free system of village communities, in which the weaker and less powerful owners lost their freedom by putting themselves under the care of greater land-owners for the sake of protection, or whether the manor is but an extension of the Roman plan of big farms worked with slave labour. It is not possible to do more than state shortly the arguments on either side. Those who argue for the free cultivators point to the completeness of the conquest, the absence of mention of slaves, the fact that the towns fell so entirely into decay during the invasion, that when rebuilt, the rebuilding was done on a new plan, the old Roman roads being so blocked and covered with rubbish as to be indistinguishable or useless. They hold that the Britons left their towns, farms, and houses, and those who escaped the sword fled rather than trust to the mercies of the invaders; and they urge that had the Britons lived on as a subject population, the natural language would have had, if not a Celtic basis, at least a very large admixture of British words. They instance also the habits of the Saxons before the invasion, and the prevalence of the village community system in Germany. On the other hand, evidence that many of the cultivators were unfree from the first is found in the universality of the manorial system by the time of William I., in the difficulty of explaining how free cultivators lost their freedom so completely, in the probability of the Saxons stepping into the places of the departed Roman masters, and carrying on things as they were, and in the strong documentary evidence for the existence of Saxon estates of a manorial type in early times. It has also been urged that the Saxon method of cultivation was a "one-field" system, crops being grown year after year from the same ground, while the system in use in England was the "three-field",[3] and that this was copied from Roman methods. This brief summary may serve to show some of the grounds on which opinions as to the original status of the agricultural labourer are based, but further discussion is beyond the scope of this book.

In any case, the main occupation of the Saxons was agriculture. They neglected the towns, which fell into decay, and settled after their former fashion in small villages, the inhabited part of each "tun" being an enclosure protected with a wall of mud or stone. However the size of a man's holding of land may have varied, it seems that each group of timber buildings, hall, barn, cowshed and rickyard, stood in its own enclosure.[4] If there were bondsmen, they lived in wattled cottages close by. The ordinary operations of tillage went on. Swine, sheep, and cattle were pastured and tended. The villagers would include men with some skill in carpentering, smith's work, and shoemaking. Besides shoes, the shoemaker made gaiters, leather bottles, jugs and drinking-cups, and harness. These men were not

---

[3] See p. 27.

[4] In the east of Scotland the farm buildings are still usually built round three sides of a square, the dwelling-house in the centre, and barns, byres, stables, &c., at the sides, and the enclosure thus formed is called "the farm toun", evidently a survival of old Saxon fashion.

artisans in our sense of the word; like the rest, they worked in the fields in the spring and summer. Rye, oats, wheat, beans, and barley were the principal crops. Fish were in considerable demand, especially after the introduction of Christianity for use on Fridays and in Lent. The village fisherman used nets or line, and by his own account caught eels and pike, minnows and eelpout, trout and lampreys. At times he went sea-fishing, but was of opinion that it was a perilous thing to catch a whale.[5] Honey was used for mead, and beer was brewed. Corn was ground, usually in hand-mills by women, and baked at home, wheaten bread for the rich and for the feast days, barley-meal for the common folk, and a mixture of rye, oats, and beans for the very poor.

Rural industry was indeed almost entirely self-sufficing, that is to say, each group provided for its own wants, and did not traffic with others. Salt had to be bought at the nearest fair, coming partly from the wiches or salt-springs in Worcestershire, and partly from abroad, but, as in Roman times, it was also made by evaporation of salt water in most of the sea-coast shires. Iron for agricultural implements was imported from Spain, and millstones came from France. A travelling pedlar would sometimes come round the country-side with his pack on his shoulders, bringing small articles, mostly from abroad, ornaments, silks, embroidered work, spices and the like, but the course of village life went on in the regularity of isolation, with little change or desire for it.

[5] Ælfric's *Dialogues*.

From this unenterprising existence England was roused by the Danish invasions. The Saxons, at first as daring and confident at sea as any other set of sea rovers, had soon lost their maritime inclinations. The necessity of resisting the Danes led Alfred to build new ships, larger, swifter, and higher than the Danish vessels, and though at first he had to get pirates from Friesland to man them, yet his son, Edward, could collect a hundred ships to hold the Channel, and Edgar sailed round the coasts with an English fleet each year. Hostility to the Danes had called forth a fleet; imitation of them brought commerce. In the eighth century foreign trade was fitful and scanty. The appearance of English merchants at continental fairs, such as those of St. Denys, Rouen, and Troyes, was rare. Charles the Great's letter to Offa of Mercia speaks of the visitors as being rather pilgrims than merchants, though they were not above doing a stroke of business on the journey if the opportunity served them—a worldly, commercial spirit that was held ill-suited to their professedly pious objects. But under the stimulus of the Danish example, these small beginnings developed into a regular trade with Normandy, Ponthieu, France, and Flanders. A settlement of "men of the Emperor" was established in London; they imported wine, fish, cloths, pepper, gloves, and vinegar. Merchants who fared thrice oversea at their own cost were declared thegn-right worthy. Ælfric's *Dialogues* speak of the merchant bringing in his own ship skins, silks which were highly valued, gems, gold cloths, pigments, wine, oil, ivory, brass, copper, silver, glass, and such like. Eastern goods came from Constantinople to Venice, and from there to Flanders. The Danes brought furs, skins, ropes, masts, and tar. Exports were tin and lead, wool and slaves. The centre of the slave-trade was Bristol, but it flourished also in the North German ports in spite of all the efforts made by churchmen to put an end to it.

Another important consequence of the Danish immigration, one, indeed, that was closely connected with the revival of commerce, was the growth of towns. At first the Saxons had shrunk from towns, as if they indeed regarded them, as Tacitus says, as the graves of freedom. Such towns as they had were merely overgrown villages where most of the inhabitants lived by agriculture. But the example of the Danes led to the growth of towns in which trade and industry were more highly developed. Shrines, to visit which men went in pilgrimage and took the opportunity of trading; monasteries, such as St. Edmunds', which employed smiths, carpenters, millers, masons, fishers, hunters, and labourers; fortresses, built to keep off invaders and command important roads; the crossings of these roads; the farthest points inland to which the ships of the day could be brought; all offered advantages for the growth of towns. Thus Glasgow gathered round the shrine of St. Ninian, St. Albans round that of the first British martyr, having the added attraction of a Roman road and an old Roman town to quarry from. Oxford had an excellent position on a natural highway, as had Nottingham; Cambridge, Ely, and Norwich were similarly favoured. York, Exeter, and Ipswich could be reached by the sea-going vessels which drew little water, and so merchants were saved the necessity of breaking bulk. Chester and Bristol traded with Ireland and the Danish settlements there. Sandwich was the centre of a great fishing trade. Winchester, Canterbury, Rochester, Southampton, Lewes, Wareham, Hastings, and Chichester became important. London, almost deserted in 601, the lines of its chief streets lost, had by the time of Alfred grown to be a place of great consequence. Frisians, Easterlings, French, and Picards came there to trade. Many churches were built, not a few of which were dedicated to Danish saints.[6] When danegeld was paid to Canute, London found one-seventh of the total amount, a striking proof of its wealth compared to the rest of the country.

Yet on the whole the industry and commerce of the Saxon period do not show much progress; indeed, compared with the days of the Roman occupation there is retrogression. The mines were little worked; even the scanty quantity of iron required could not be produced at home. The one trade introduced was that of glass-making, when in the seventh century Benedict Biscop obtained workmen from France who made the windows for his church at Monkwearmouth, and taught the inhabitants the lost art of making glass cups, lamps, and drinking vessels. The one purely native art that had a reputation abroad was embroidery, gold thread and gay colours making English work famous in Germany and Italy. During the six hundred

[6] *E.g.* St. Olaf and St. Magnus.

years from the Saxon conquest to the Norman, the conditions in England were indeed altogether adverse to industrial and commercial progress. The Saxon invasion left the country divided and thinly settled; means of communication were bad; disorder and insecurity prevailed. No sooner was the kingdom beginning to be united under the Wessex kings, than fresh invaders came to cause fresh confusion, and for two hundred years the struggle with the Danes absorbed the energies of the country and wasted its resources. Means of exchange and regular markets were also wanting; the amount of money was too small to act as a circulating medium, and barter is always a complicated process. In the general ignorance of writing, transactions were carried out before witnesses, who could testify to their completion on both sides—a cumbrous and dilatory plan. In spite of the heavy tolls which fell on those who used roads or rivers, both means of communication were perilous. Robbers were so common that every stranger was suspected and bidden to give warning of his approach as an honest man should, by the sound of a horn. At sea pirates swarmed, and they often made raids far inland up the rivers. In these circumstances a vigorous inland trade was not to be expected.

CHAPTER II.

THE MANORIAL SYSTEM. SERVICE AND COMMUTATION.

Whether the mass of cultivators in England were at the first free or servile, there is no doubt that for some time before the Norman conquest the general form of land-holding was that of the manor. This was essentially an unfree system, and even if we suppose that the original cultivators were free, it is not so very difficult to account for the loss of freedom. Something of the same kind happened in Italy, where the small land-owners, the men who, like Cincinnatus, came from the plough to serve their country, disappeared and were succeeded by large proprietors with wide farms (*latifundia*) tilled by slave labour. Side by side with the village and its associated cultivators grew up estates in the hands of lords, grants by charter which had passed into permanent ownership. Necessity of protection or the pressure of misfortune may have compelled freemen to bind themselves to a lord; the practice of commendation[1] worked the same way. A dependence once established tended to grow, so that by the time of *Domesday* we find a system of lords with servile tenants so widespread and so settled that it may be termed the rule; the exceptions are

---

[1] A man *commended* himself to some lord or powerful person, doing service at the lord's court and so getting protection. Commendation was at first a relation between man and man; the holding of land was not dependent on condition of performing service.

few, and are confined to a district of England which was under different influences.

It is then important to notice that the English cultivator was not enslaved by the Normans. The manorial system was not introduced by them; they were indeed familiar with it; and though it was hardened and consolidated by the Conquest, yet *The Domesday Book*, by its continual references to "T.R.E."[2] is evidence that the manor was substantially the same institution in the days of Edward the Confessor as of William I. And similarly the plan of cultivation in general use in England at the time of *Domesday*, known as the "three-field system", was not new. The village land consisted of three kinds—arable, meadow, and waste. The arable land was divided into three huge fields, and these further subdivided into acre or half-acre strips, marked off by balks of unploughed turf, each man's holding being made up of a number of these scattered strips. Each field went through a rotation of a crop with autumn sowing (wheat), a crop with spring sowing (barley or oats), and a year fallow. Thus in any particular year two of the three fields would yield a crop of wheat and a crop of barley or oats, while the third was lying fallow. This curious mixture of complexity of tenure and uniformity of method was the outcome of the needs and difficulties of the time. Originally land had been regarded, not as individual property, but as village property common to all the villagers, and the strips annually re-allotted to give each a chance of the most fertile spots in turn. When the

[2] *Tempore Regis Edwardi*—the time of King Edward.

practice of redistribution came to an end, owing to the natural desire of each man to retain the land which he had improved by his work and reap the advantage of the still unexhausted improvements, it was still convenient that a man's holding should be scattered as before. Obviously, if all his holding lay in one field, he would be poorly off for food in the year that field lay fallow. Moreover land varies greatly in quality even in closely adjacent places, and all the more before a good system of drainage has been introduced; if each man held one plot in each of these large fields the difficulty of crops would be met, but the problem of how to give each one equal advantages would remain unsolved. So as a means of avoiding unfairness and jealousy the plan of scattering each man's holding in acre or half-acre strips was a practical one. The uniformity in method was due to the fact that it was necessary to combine to do the ploughing. One villager would rarely possess enough oxen to do it for himself, but when they joined, teams of four, six, or eight oxen could easily be set to work. In addition to his share of strips in these wide fields each villager had rights to a portion of the meadows inclosed for hay, and further rights to pasture cattle or swine upon the village "waste", woodland, or pasture, and to make what use of it he could by gathering wood for fuel or cutting turf. Further, each villager generally owned a small patch of land, the *close* or *toft* round his cottage. The fact that, with the exception of these closes, none of the land was permanently hedged in, cattle being allowed to wander over both arable and meadow land after the corn and hay harvest was gathered, gives the name by which this method of tillage is sometimes distinguished, "open field".

Such farming might have been carried on by agreement among the tenants, but at the time when we find it described land was held in large estates by lords of the manor. The whole of the cultivated land then fell into two species: demesne land, land cultivated entirely for the benefit of the lord, which might consist of a separate enclosed portion, or of holdings scattered among the holdings of the villagers, or both; and land held in *villeinage*, that is land held from the lord by his tenants, who were unfree, and were bound to pay certain services to the lord. The amount of land owned by each tenant, and the services due to the lord, depended on his status. Two main classes can be distinguished: the ordinary holding was a *virgate* or *yardland*, usually thirty acres, held in scattered strips; the holder of a virgate was called a villein (*villanus*). Next came the bordars or cotters (*bordarii* or *cottarii*), the general size of whose holding was one or two acres, though it sometimes rose to five or more. These did not possess either oxen or a plough, and were in a decidedly lower position than the villeins. Both villeins and cotters were unfree, but their position was not that of slaves; a slave is bound to his master; his servitude is personal, he is destitute of rights, he may be called on to do anything. No doubt on the first coming of the Normans the new lords made use of some actual slaves either on their land or in their houses. But the villeins and cotters were territorial serfs, bound to the land to perform certain fixed services, and they were not destitute of rights, in general opinion at any rate; how far these rights could be enforced by law was another matter.

Services were paid in labour on the lord's demesne, and out of the very great variety of them two main classes emerge: "week work," that is labour for certain days a week regularly all the year round, villeins generally giving three days' work and cotters two; and "boon work" (*precariæ*), extra labour in addition to the week work at times of the year when there was special need for it: such boon work would be demanded at harvest, haymaking, and ploughing. In addition to week work and boon work there were often small tributes or payments in kind; fowls and eggs, bushels of oats, and so forth; and the villagers had to do what carting the lord required. These duties discharged, the tenant had the rest of his time to work on his own holding.

It is evident that the principal task in managing an estate was to see that the villeins and other tenants paid their services duly, and to superintend them at their work. Such work when ill looked after would tend to be little, for the labourer had no inducement to work hard, and in the case of the boon work, the villein had every incentive to evade or put off fulfilment of his duty. As the course of three-field cultivation went on its regular round both for demesne and village land, the time that the demesne needed extra labour was naturally just the time that that villager would be anxious to work on his own land. In such times as haymaking and harvest, when delay might mean a change of weather and a lost crop, it was most irksome to be called off to gather the lord's hay or reap his harvest. Consequently there were needed on each manor officials whose chief duty was to exact the villein services.

An account of these officers is given in a thirteenth-century book, the *Seneschaucie*, by an unknown author, which treats fully of the different officials and how they ought to perform their duties. The *Seneschal*, who had to overlook several manors, was to make his rounds two or three times a year to inquire about the rents, services, and customs, to check the yield of corn, the amount used for seed, the land ploughed, and so forth, to see the horses, oxen, sheep, and swine were well kept, to inquire how the bailiff, hayward, and keeper of cattle performed their duties. The *Bailiff* was the head of the estate; it was for him to see that the customary tenants did their proper amount of ploughing, and that it was well done with small furrows, and sown with good seed. He had to keep account of how many acres of meadow they mowed and cut, and to see that nothing was wrongfully sold from the manor. The *Provost* or *Reeve* was elected by the village as the best husbandman among them, and was responsible for the villeins' labour, keeping a tally of the services performed. The *Hayward* was to be over the customary tenants at times of ploughing, harrowing, haymaking, and harvest, and see they did the work they ought to do. The same need of watchfulness and supervision comes out in *The Dite of Hosebondrie*, by Walter of Henley. He advises that the estate should be surveyed and valued, and a record kept as to how much each tenant holds and by what services; "and because customary servants neglect their work, it is necessary to guard against their fraud; further, it is necessary that they be overseen often".

Whether an estate was valuable or not mainly depended on the amount of labour available. Fertility would be undeveloped, size would merely prove cumbrous, if there was a want of labour. There was no class of labourers who could be hired; a lord must depend on the services of his tenants. Thus pains were taken to keep up the labour on an estate. It was, generally speaking, impossible for a man on it to leave it; heavy fines were asked before permission was given. New holdings could easily be bestowed out of the waste, or existing ones divided if more land was required. But above all, when the aim of good management was that each manor should be self-sufficing, that the customary labour should be enough and no money disbursed to hire more, it was important to have an exact account of the labour on each estate. To know this was to know the value of the manor, and hence the attention paid in *Domesday* to the servile tenants.

Before giving an account of the Great Survey, it is well to remark the object of it. It has been of such incomparable value to the historian, it has given so much information that would otherwise have been lost to us, that we are led to regard it chiefly as a historical document, a record of the conditions of agricultural life and status in England at the time of the Conquest. To take such a view is to make a great mistake. Interesting as the Great Survey has proved to our own time as a record, there never was a record of more immediate practical value for its own time. Its object was fiscal. To the king, by whose order it was compiled, the land of the realm was enormously important. From it he drew his wealth, and not he alone, but his Norman followers also. On land fell all taxation. Nay, more, under the feudal system much of the organization of society rested on the possession of land. It was with land that the king rewarded his supporters; and while the security of the throne and the peace of the country depended largely on land being in trusty hands and undisputed in ownership, no greater danger was to be found than in a reckless acquiescence in the formation of great and concentrated territorial estates in the hands of nobles, and a neglect to guard the royal rights against infringement. The nightmare of Stephen's reign offers the best comment upon the wisdom of the Conqueror in insisting upon a settlement of rights and obligations in the matter of land.

The matter for the Great Survey was collected by commissioners sent round the country. These were to inquire on oath from the sheriff, the barons, the hundred, the priest, reeve, and six villeins from each village, the name of the manor, who owned it, and who had owned it in the time of the Confessor, how many hides[3] there were in each manor, how many ploughs on the demesne, how many tenants, and what their status, how much wood, meadow,

---

[3] The hide was 120 acres.

and pasture, what mills and fishponds, whether the manor had altered in size, and what its worth was. These instructions were thoroughly carried out; "so very narrowly he had it inquired into that there was not one single hide nor one yard of land, nor even—it is shame to be telling of, but he did not think it shame to be doing it—one ox, nor one cow, nor one swine was left out that was not set down in his record". With the exceptions of the counties of Cumberland, Westmoreland, Northumberland, and Durham, and the north of Lancashire, the returns for England are complete, though they are not all equally full; some are very short, while others are fuller; but even these seem to have been abridged if we may judge from the original return for the county of Cambridge,[4] which is a copy of the verdicts delivered by the Cambridgeshire jurors, and goes into very full detail. The general result of the Survey was to show that villeins and cotters formed the bulk of the agricultural population, but there was a considerable number of bondsmen or slaves proper, and of free tenants or *socmen*.

The existence of each of these classes seems traceable to special influences. The slaves, whose average percentage among the cultivators is nine, often do not appear at all in eastern and midland shires. In the south-west and on the Welsh border, on the contrary, the percentage rises as high as twenty-four, and it is reasonable to suppose that these were mostly Britons who had been slaves before the coming of the Normans, or had been made slaves by the conquerors. The free tenants

[4] The *Inquisitio Comitatus Cantabrigiæ*.

and socmen are found almost entirely in the eastern counties, where they sometimes number forty-five per cent of the whole. The terms *liberi tenentes*, and *socemanni* seem to have been used more or less interchangeably by the barons who drew up the survey, and no very clear distinction need be drawn between them. They differed from villeins and cotters in not being bound to week work. On the other hand their holdings are reckoned in virgates or portions of virgates, which means that they formed a part of the original village fields as did the villeins' land. These men could neither sell their lands, nor leave the manor without the lord's consent, and they had to do boon work, so that their freedom was not to our ideas complete, but relative; compared to the villeins they were free; the tenure on which they held was technically free, though their liberty was in many ways restricted. The part of England in which these freemen and socmen are most numerous suggests that Danish influence was at work; that these men were the descendants of Danish followers who were willing to do some work for their Danish lord in return for a grant of land, but who were yet kept above the level of the English villeins.

The minuteness and patience with which the mass of information in *Domesday* was collected and recorded is perhaps most appreciated by one who looks over its pages for the first time. If he has no particular object in view he will naturally turn to a piece of country with which he is familiar, to see if by any chance any of the villages or parishes he knows are mentioned, and only half expecting to find them. It is almost a shock as the well-known names, some a little disguised, others clear enough, come one after another under his eyes, with the record of men and stock, mills and dues. No fortuitous extract of some unfamiliar manor brings home the same vivid sense of how the present is linked with the past, how men and methods have come and gone, and the land has remained. Yet in spite of the comparative unreality of an extract taken at random, it is worth while to present one or two as an illustration. The first is of a very ordinary type, the manor of Beauchamp in Essex.

> Terra Canonicorum Sancti Pauli in Exsesse Hundredum de hidingforda Belcham tenuit Sanctus Paulus tempore Regis Edwardi pro manerio et v hidis. Semper II carucae in dominio et XII carucae hominum, XXIIII villani X bordarii V servi. Silva LX porcis, XXX acrae prati, IX animalia II runcini XL porci C oves V caprae. Semper valuit XVI libras.

"The land of the Canons of St. Paul in Essex, and The Hundred of Hinckford. St. Paul held Belchamp in the time of King Edward for a Manor and five hides. There were always two plough-teams in the demesne, and twelve plough-teams of the tenants, 24 villeins, 10 bordars, 5 serfs. There is a wood there for 60 hogs, 30 acres of meadow, 9 animals, 2 load-horses, 40 hogs, 100 sheep, 5 goats. It was always worth £16."

Here we have set down the ploughs in the

demesne and on the land in villeinage, the villeins, bordars, and slaves (these latter rare in Essex), the wood, meadow and land, and the stock: finally, the worth of the estate. The example is selected as being typical rather than interesting. More curious is this one from Worcestershire.

> Rex Wilielmus tenet in dominio Chideminstre . . . Hoc Manerium fuit totum wastum. In dominio est I caruca et XX villani et XXX bordarii cum XVIII carucis et adhuc XX carucae plus ibi possunt esse. Ibi II servi et IIII ancillae et II molini de XVI solidis et II salina de XXX solidis et piscaria de centum denariis. Silva de IIII leuuis . . . Totum Manerium tempore Regis Edwardi reddebat XIIII libra de firma. Modo reddit X libras et IIII solidas ad pensum.

"King William holds in his demesne Chideminstre . . . This Manor was all waste. In the demesne there is one plough-team and twenty villeins and thirty bordars with eighteen plough-teams, and twenty plough-teams more could be there. There are two serfs and four bondwomen, and two mills of the value of sixteen shillings, and two salt-pans of the value of thirty shillings, and a fishpond of the value of one hundred pence. There is a wood of four miles. The whole Manor in the time of King Edward paid fourteen pounds for ferm, now it pays ten pounds four shillings by weight." This furnishes an example of the way in which not only the land was considered, but its capacities for improvement gauged. More ploughs could be set to work if necessary; the slaves, both men and women, were to be expected near the Welsh border; the dues brought in by mills are recorded, because the tenants were compelled to grind at the lord's mill; salt-pans show how old the industry of salt-making is in the country, and the high dues show how valuable the industry was; fish were necessary for days of fasting, and consequently a well-stocked fishpond was a part of each well-regulated estate. The fall in the total "ferm" since the Confessor's days may be explained by the entry that the manor had been devastated.

As by the time when we again take up the story of the land we shall find a great increase in the number of free tenants, and a diminution of dues paid in labour, even by tenants who were not reckoned to be free, it is necessary to trace how these things came about; and there is some evidence for doing so after *Domesday*, in the *Extenta*, or Surveys of manors, which give an account on the same lines as *Domesday*, though with more detail, especially about conditions of tenure,[5] the manorial accounts (*compotus*), the Court Rolls, records of proceedings in manorial courts, relating changes in holding, new-comers, those who left, or committed offences, and so forth. It is from these that the process of changes between *Domesday* and the middle of the fourteenth century can be illustrated.

First, as to the growth of free tenants. In 1086 Beauchamp had no free tenants.[6] There were

[5] *The Hundred Rolls*, Edward I.'s survey of the royal demesne, consist largely of embodiments of *Extenta*.

[6] The changes amongst the tenants on the Beauchamp Manor are given in detail in Ashley's *Economic History*. Vol. i. part i. page 23.

thirty-four servile tenants and five slaves. But in 1181, in a record of the same manor, in addition to thirty-five servile tenants with very small holdings, there are eighteen free tenants, and in 1222 there are thirty-four of them, and there are also a number of holders of work-lands. These "free tenants" paid annually sums of money for their lands, which were holdings of virgates or fractions of virgates, and were also bound to boon work, so they may perhaps be regarded as descendants of the villeins of 1086,[7] but it is impossible to be sure of this. Some cases are found where free tenants commuted their boon work for a payment, and gained a more complete freedom, holding their land by "charter" granted by the lord. Other free tenants had holdings, not in the common fields, but reclaimed from the waste which lay contiguous to each village. These generally paid money and not services. Others again had portions of demesne land let to them for a money payment; where a lord had plenty of land and insufficient services to till it, this would be a convenient arrangement, and thus in a third way the number of free tenants was swelled.

What constituted freedom is hard to say precisely. A man might be free or servile by status, and although nowadays we are not very clear what the distinction was, it is reasonable to suppose that it was well enough understood in its own day; that the confusion, where it exists, is rather of modern than mediæval manufacture. For whatever this "freedom" was, we are apt to confuse it with another notion, that of economic freedom, and

---

[7] Professor Ashley takes this view.

think of a man as free or unfree according to whether he worked for himself or paid services to a lord. It is obvious, however, that these two kinds of freedom are not necessarily connected. A man might be a serf by status, and yet hold a piece of land on condition of paying a rent, while another, free by status, might, for his own convenience, take a holding to which payment of services was attached. From the point of view of the time the first was a serf and the second a free tenant, but according to ideas of economic freedom the case would be exactly reversed. We should naturally turn for exact definition to the lawyers, but we meet the same difficulty of correctly interpreting the decisions that were given. They may have been consistent according to some rule with which we are not fully acquainted, or they may have been contradictory; certainly they sometimes seem to be of the latter character. Thus, for instance, the most generally accepted mark of servile tenure was the inability to marry a daughter or sell an ox without the lord's consent; and a case in John's reign was decided in favour of a tenant's freedom, on the ground that he was not bound in this way, although it was admitted that he had to pay boon work. But, on the other hand, tenants by charter, who were undoubtedly free, were sometimes tied in selling cattle and giving in marriage. Molmen, men who paid a rent or mol in place of service, were sometimes reckoned as free and sometimes not. The plan of succession by Borough English, instead of primogeniture, was also regarded as a mark of servile status, although here again free tenants sometimes succeeded by it. And finally it must be remembered that as the law came to be more and more based on Roman ideas and Roman maxims, it would tend to take a harsher view of servile position, for in the eye of Roman law a slave was not a person at all, but a chattel. Thus the lawyers of the thirteenth and fourteenth centuries were much less favourable to persons claiming to possess some degree of freedom than their predecessors.

Confused as the question of free tenancy is, there is no doubt that in the course of the two centuries and a half which followed *Domesday*, many who had originally been servile became free. But there was a still larger class who commuted their services without thereby gaining freedom. The custumals of the manor recorded the money value of the services, at first, no doubt, for the sake of the fine to which a defaulting villein was liable. But if the fine was an adequate compensation for the loss of the day's labour, the lord might prefer to accept it. No distinction in principle would arise between payments for week work or boon work. In any year when it was convenient for the lord to permit commutation he would permit it, provided the tenant was able to pay. It might be that the boon work would be retained longer than the week work, as labour enough might be hired for ordinary seasons, while in harvest or seed-time every one would be busy, and labour scarce; thus the task of carting seems to have been rarely commuted. But the whole question was one to be decided on principles of advantage or disadvantage; there was no sentimental desire on the part of the lords to keep their tenants in a condition of servility, though they would naturally prefer to get as much as possible from them, either in the shape of work or money. Further, there was very little that could be described under the term "rights". The lord had a right to a certain amount of labour, and could inflict punishment—generally a fine—if the labour was not paid. But it is not clear that he had any right to claim the fine in place of the labour; nor, on the other hand, could the tenant demand the acceptance of payment instead of his services. When commutation had been in steady use for a long time, it was natural that a custom so well established should come to be regarded as binding, and attempts to break it be resented as illegal; but lords were under no legal obligation to permit commutation unless they had made some definite agreement, and cases of this kind were rare.

As, however, the practice of at least occasional commutation spread over the country, it is clear that there must have been labourers ready to undertake agricultural work for hire. These may have been men who had a small quantity of land, not enough to take up the whole of their time, or more rarely landless men, entirely dependent upon wages. Where commutation was tardy, the probable reason was that these men were scarce. But the practice of commutation, begun in some cases before *Domesday*, was the general rule by the middle of the fourteenth century, and in some cases the tenants had a right to pay in money.

If we compare the village of these times with the

village as we know it, several striking differences emerge. In the first place, villages were then as far as possible self-sufficing. Difficulties of carriage were great, and little produce was raised for sale. Though in cases where the lord was habitually an absentee, some selling must have been done, and though the mere fact of villeins being able to pay dues in money instead of services, and bailiffs being able to hire extra labour, points to a certain circulation of money, yet, as a rule, the manor was a unit by itself, the lord living on the produce of his demesne, or if he owned many estates, travelling round with his household to eat up the substance of each in turn, as did the King and Court to the royal manors. At first village artisans, blacksmiths, and wheelwrights, were paid for their services by a holding of village land, and not by each person for what he wanted done. Rough cloth was woven, and shoes made in the village; there was no shop, and no goods made except to order. It is unnecessary to indicate how widely different are modern conditions. The village then was isolated; this isolation has now practically vanished.

Further, there was a permanence in village life which is no longer the case. It was difficult to come, and harder still to go; holdings passed naturally from father to son. His services rendered, or the commutation paid, the villein had security of tenure. It remained for the lawyers of a later century to assert that villeins had no rights against their lords, in cases where they were dispossessed. And just as the labour was permanent, so the system of cultivation was unchanging. There was no exercise of individual judgment; the rotation of crops was mechanical for lord as for villein. In the three-field course there was no room for originality or experiment. The results were poor, but improvement was hardly possible.

Thirdly, instead of the three classes of to-day—landlord, farmer, labourer—there were only two; the farmer did not exist. And where rent was paid for land, it was not the rent of to-day, a competitive rent. Rent is now paid according to the amount of advantages, fertility, position, and the like, possessed by one piece of land compared with others. But rent then was a quit-rent, that is, it represented the value, not of land, but of commuted services. Although it was usual that those with the heaviest services held the most or the best land, this was by no means invariable, and so it is clear that quit-rents might be high where competitive rents would be low, or *vice versa*. For example, the descendants of the slaves of William I.'s time seem gradually to have obtained grants of land; but these were always very small and generally of poor quality, and the services heavy. If they subsequently managed to commute these services it would be for a considerable sum, and they would hold land at a very high quit-rent, although it would fetch a low competitive rent under modern conditions. But to understand the agricultural conditions of the time, modern ideas, such as competition, individual liberty, mobility of labour, and capital, in the sense of "a store of wealth that can be turned into new and more profitable channels as occasion arises ",[8] must be put on one side, and the forces of custom and status put in their place.

CHAPTER III.

TOWNS, AND THE BEGINNINGS OF TOWN LIFE.

Domesday mentions eighty towns as existing in England, but these cannot all be classified under the same heading. To our ideas very few of them were towns proper; London, York, Winchester, Bristol, Norwich, and Lincoln had long passed beyond the village state, but the rest were in the main large villages, surrounded by a wall and protected by some fortification, yet still essentially villages in that the principal occupation of the inhabitants was not trade or commerce, but agriculture; a small association of cultivators made the village, while a larger association would be called a town. The difference was one of size and not of character. The inhabitants of these towns, dwelling on either the King's lands or that of some manorial lord, were under the control of a superior. The land they cultivated was probably held on conditions of servile tenure, and carried the obligation of payment of service, just as was the case with the villeins; the manorial officer looked after his lord's rights and enforced their payment just as elsewhere; the affairs of the town came before the Manorial Court Leet, where suits were heard,

[8] Cunningham's *Industry and Commerce.*

nuisances amended, fairs and markets granted, trade regulated, and fraudulent traders who sold goods of bad quality or short weight, and persons who committed misdemeanours, punished, all privileges being made occasion for payment which went to the lord of the manor. In short, the town had no corporate existence at all. It will be the task of this chapter to trace the removal of these disabilities, and see the substitution of a system in which the towns gained the corporate existence which they were at first without, and were thus enabled to manage their own affairs, both financial and industrial.

Roughly speaking, the control of the manorial lord showed itself in two ways; the first, the exaction of service on condition of holding land, was common to all cultivators, while the second, the payment of dues in return for "liberties" of trading, concerned only the inhabitants of the towns. And in the towns, as in the villages, commutation would supersede services. Thus there is mention at Leicester of "the pennies which were accustomed to be taken yearly from my burgesses of Leicester on account of reaping my corn at Leicester".[1] But this freedom was a matter, at first at any rate, of individual arrangement between lord and townsman. What we are concerned with are the liberties gained by the towns as units.

The towns were under a twofold authority, that of the lord of the manor—of which examples have already been mentioned—and also that of the King. In the case where the town was on the royal

[1] Thompson, *English Municipal History*, 40.

demesne, both authorities were in the hand of the same person, for then the King was himself lord of the manor. But the rights were distinct, some being special to the town and imposed by its own lord, and others general to the realm and imposed on all alike by the King. Whether the payments were collected for the lord of the manor by his bailiff, or for the King by his sheriff, the townsmen had no share in determining the manner of the assessment. The exactions of the sheriff were always unpopular, and seem sometimes to have been unfair and excessive. By The Inquest of Sheriffs[2] in Henry II.'s reign a very strict inquiry was ordered into the conduct of these officials, and a hint is given that some of them had been offering hush-money to those whom they had defrauded; no report of the commission exists, but the fact that most of the sheriffs were removed from their offices and replaced by others more closely connected with the Exchequer shows that their honesty was not above question, even to their master, while those beneath them had probably more cause to complain. An example from so late a date as Edward I.'s reign illustrates the way in which sheriffs could oppress a town: Roger of Estra, at Cambridge, took a total tax of 2s. 6d. per hide, nominally to pay for the building of a stone bridge, but in the end he built a wooden one, and in the meantime charged exorbitant sums for the barge which he provided as a ferry while the bridge was building.

Whether the townsmen were hardly treated or not, the desire to get free from the incubus of the sheriff's

[2] 1170.

or bailiff's control would be great; and just as in the case of commutation of service, the lord would make no objection to granting this freedom, provided it was certain that he would be no loser. It was a question of security and money, and particularly during the time when the barons were much in need of ready money, either for castle-building, or fitting out an expedition to the Holy Land, if security and money could be found they would be readily accepted. Thus from the Conquest onwards there is a process of emancipation at work in the towns; if the townsmen were rich, a charter might be bought outright; if this could not be done, privileges might be secured from King or lord on condition of an annual payment. In either case the town became free, a *liber burgus*, though obviously the degrees of freedom were different. But in either case the responsibility for payment would often be too heavy to fall on any individual. It fell on the townsmen as a body, and thus grew up the notion of corporate responsibility, and with it corporate power. If the citizens undertook to pay a sum instead of the annual impositions, then it was for them to collect the sum. A house rate was levied, and those who paid it were said to be at *scot* and *lot* in the borough. To reward them, they had the advantage of being burgesses of a free borough. These advantages were real. In the charter granted by King John to Ipswich, it is specified that in return for the usual ferm being paid into the Exchequer each year, together with an increment of 100*s.*, the burgesses were to be free from various tolls, stallage, lastage, passage, pontage, and other customs throughout the land; they were not to be compelled to plead out of the borough, and justice was to be done according to their ancient customs; they were to have their lands as before; no one was to be billeted there, nor was anything to be taken by force; and they were to have a merchant gild. In addition to this, freedom generally implied the right of holding markets and fairs, of regulating and restricting trade, and of electing their own town officials. Thus at Ipswich the burgesses chose two bailiffs to be responsible for the provostship of the borough and make the payments to the Exchequer, four coroners to take charge of the pleas of the Crown, and twelve portmen to govern the borough and maintain its liberties.

This maintenance of liberties was no empty phrase. Towns while under the control of a lord had yielded a considerable revenue. In any case, whether freedom was gained by handing over a lump sum once and for all, or by a fixed yearly payment, money had to be raised somehow; and townsmen would naturally look to the same source of revenue as that by which the lord had profited. This was mainly the regulation of trade, and during the century following the Conquest trade grew fast. The connection with the Continent became closer: merchants from Normandy, Poitou, Gascony, Cologne, Flanders, Italy, and the Hanse towns, came with their merchandise to the principal towns, bringing wine, spices, Eastern goods, and the finer sorts of cloth, and buying lead and tin, fish, meat, fat cattle, wool, and jet; alien craftsmen, especially weavers, settled in the kingdom, at first scattered here and there, afterwards mainly concentrated by Henry I. in South Wales; castles and cathedrals found employment for masons, carpenters, and glass-makers; smiths and iron-workers were busy with arms and armour of more elaborate kinds; the strong hand of the Norman and Angevin kings on each side of the Channel did something to suppress piracy, and the good order they kept in the realm made communication easier. The statement that in William I.'s reign "any man might travel over the kingdom with his bosom full of gold" may be somewhat in the way of a picturesque exaggeration, but it expresses an important truth, namely, that the Norman rule, exacting as it often was, gave by its security far more opportunity for trade and intercourse than England had known since the Roman occupation.

To manage this growing trade to the advantage of each town was the policy of the burgesses. It was an exclusive policy; they did not regard trade for its own sake; they did not aim merely at a great volume of it; but they wished to keep it in their own hands, to prevent "foreigners", whether from abroad or from another town, from getting a share. It was iniquitous in the eyes of a burgess that if he paid his share towards the freedom of the town, an interloper, who paid nothing, should interfere with profits that might have been his, buy and sell in his market, and rob him of his customers. To maintain the liberties of the borough meant to maintain the privileges of the burgess who paid scot and lot against the rivalry of the outsider.

The body into whose hands this regulation of trade and maintenance of burgess liberties fell was the Merchant Gild, which sprang up in most of the towns during the twelfth and thirteenth centuries. As these Gilds are known to have existed in 102 towns in England,[3] 30 in Wales, and 38 in Ireland, it may be inferred that few towns of consequence[4] were without them. The commonest clauses in the charters founding merchant gilds are to this effect:—" We grant a gild merchant with a hanse and other customs belonging to the gild, so that no one who is not of the gild may merchandise in the said town except with the consent of the burgesses"; and also, " We likewise grant them and their heirs that if any person's villein remain in the town, and hold land in it, and be in the said gild and hanse and scot and lot a year and a day without being claimed, then he cannot be reclaimed by his lord, but may remain free in the said town".[5] This latter clause secured the burgesses, even if villeins in origin, from attempts to revive old servile claims, while the former gave them protection against outside rivalry. The regulations of the merchant gild at Southampton, which was granted by Henry II., afford an excellent illustration of the way in which such a gild worked. The officers, at whose head was the alderman, were to be elected in the gild, and were paid by receiving dues from each one who entered the gild. Money was to be given in charity,

---

[3] Out of the 102 English towns, 82 had acquired them by the end of the thirteenth century. The Irish Gilds are mostly later, if the first recorded mention is to be taken as approaching the date of their foundation. This, however, is doubtful. [4] With the important exception of London.
[5] Gross, *Gild Merchant*, vol. i., p. 8.

and sick members helped and visited; when a gildsman died, the brethren in the town were to attend his funeral, and if a member was imprisoned in England, the alderman was, if possible, to purchase his deliverance; peace was to be kept, and there were penalties for slander, or violence committed on gildsmen. Further, the exclusiveness of the gild was to be maintained. No stranger might be brought to a meeting; no one but a member was to buy in order to sell again in the town; nor could he buy honey, salt herring, oil, millstones, leather or hides, nor sell wine, save on days of fair or market, or hold more than five quarters of corn to sell by retail; there were to be no partnerships between gildsman and stranger, nor could strangers buy any merchandise which a gildsman wished to buy; one gildsman could demand a share from another brother in any bargain that he made. Regulations were in force against any system of fraud among strangers whereby the people of the town were to "lose their gain". The fish and meat markets were to be supervised by officials; butchers were not to sell bad meat, nor to cast offal into the streets, nor to smoke pork before their houses or in the street; fish brought in a ship was not to be unloaded or sold without leave of the bailiff; only he who had caught the fish could offer fresh fish for sale in the street, nor was fish to be bought save between sunrise and sunset. Regrating (buying in order to sell again in the same market) of kids, lambs, birds, ewes, capons, fowls, fresh cheese, butter and eggs, was forbidden until a certain hour, and until the townsmen had had time to buy their food. All these rules, and many others, were enforced by fines, or, in some cases, imprisonment and the "loss of the Gild" when it was a gildsman who was at fault, a heavy penalty, for it reduced the offender to the rank of a stranger.

The rules of various merchant gilds vary a good deal, but we may notice a few main divisions into which they fall. There are rules of charity and neighbourliness among gildsmen; there are rules for the conduct of gild business and gild meetings, election of officials and the like; there are rules for maintaining the jurisdiction of gild officials, not only over their own members, but also over all coming to trade in the town; finally, and this is the largest class, there are rules to secure advantages for the gildsman against the outsider. Some goods are not to be dealt in by strangers at all, and retail trade is generally forbidden to them; other articles they may traffic in after the gildsman has had his choice, or after they have paid a toll; good quality was to be assured by having transactions in open market, dealers in each article having their appointed place. Strangers were to give surety that they could pay, and were generally hampered and placed at a disadvantage. Victuals alone were free to anyone to deal in, though any attempt at buying to hold stocks, and thus raise the price, was forbidden. In fact, the greater the disadvantage which a stranger was under the better, for then he would be induced to join the gild and share the burdens of gildsmen, while the larger the membership, the smaller became the individual share in the payment to the Exchequer.

Two further considerations about the merchant gilds remain to be noticed. In the first place, though it is impossible to lay down any general rule about the exact origin of them, for the creation of each gild differed in different towns, it is clear that the merchant gild was not necessarily the same as the governing body of the borough. Thus at Ipswich the town was given its charter and leave to form a merchant gild, but the two were distinct. Here the grant of a *liber burgus* preceded the formation of a merchant gild, but not infrequently it is the other way; merchant gilds flourish in towns which were not technically free, towns where the lord's bailiff presided in the courts, or towns where the lord himself claimed the right of deciding who might enter the gild. Further, foreigners and persons not resident in the towns could become gildsmen by election and payment of fees; cases occur where women and members of religious houses belonged to a merchant gild, but these could not be burgesses. Again, a man could be of the franchise yet not of the gild, and in the statutes of the merchant gild a distinction was often drawn between them; while finally a person could be an inhabitant of the town without either having burgess rights, or being in the merchant gild. To this class belonged all the Jews. But though these distinctions are clear at first, yet there was a strong tendency drawing the burgess-ship and the membership of the merchant gild into one. The same man would hold office in town and gild, the duties to be performed were something the same, there was a close union of interests. Thus, as trade grew, the two often merged into one, and when in the fourteenth and fifteenth centuries formal grants of incorporation were made, they would often be made to the merchant gild, which thus became in name and in fact the governing corporate body of the town. Consequently though the merchant gild was not necessarily the origin of corporate powers and feelings in towns, it had a great influence upon their growth.

Secondly, the merchant gild, though an exclusive body, was not a narrow body within the town. It did not consist of a small aristocratic body of merchants who prevented the poorer craftsmen from joining; on the contrary, in its origin the merchant gild was open to all who were able to pay the fees. This is important to remember, for a widely different account is sometimes given. It is asserted that, to resist the oppression of the merchants, the craftsmen, being refused admission to the exclusive and aristocratic merchant gild, formed gilds of artisans called Craft Gilds, and that between merchant gilds and craft gilds there was a natural opposition. This view is the result partly of generalization from what happened in Germany, where there was such an opposition; partly of misinterpreting the term "merchant" to mean a large dealer. But circumstances differed widely in Germany and England; while in the latter there was an effective royal power, in the former there was none, and in consequence the town government had more opportunity of becoming oppressive. Further, the term "merchant" was not confined to the rich, but included all who traded. Everyone who bought materials and worked them up for sale was a merchant; coopers, glovers, butchers, bakers, tanners, weavers, fullers, dyers, were all equally merchants, and the term is even applied to one "bearing his merchandise on his back, and called a hawker".[6] And, finally, in London, Beverley, Oxford, Marlborough, and Winchester, where indeed there is evidence of some antagonism between craftsmen and the town authorities, it is only weavers and fullers who are concerned, and these men were largely aliens who had brought a new trade with them, and were relying on royal protection and patronage. But even if occasional quarrels did occur and some alien artisans were excluded, the evidence for this is so scanty that it is fair to say that opposition between merchant and craft gilds was the exception; that as trades became more diverse the task of regulating each grew too complex for the merchant gild, and so was naturally assigned to the master craftsmen of each craft. Craft gilds in each town included, or strove to include, all the workers at each particular industry in that town, cordwainers, weavers, lorimers, smiths, and so forth, each in their own gild, all being as well members of the general wider body, the merchant gild.

The powers of these craft gilds, which began to spring up throughout England during the thirteenth century,[7] were in the main economic and not political. At the bottom of their regulations lies the same exclusiveness that existed in the merchant gild. The right of working at a particular industry, and

---

[6] Gross, *Gild Merchant*, vol. i. p. 107, n. 2.
[7] There are some earlier examples.

selling the product, is reserved to the craftsmen in the gild; the outsider is not permitted to interfere. But this monopoly was not used against the town. The craft gild restricted work to its own members, for only by so doing could it guarantee good work. It could thus insist on a proper apprenticeship, on the use of good materials, on work being done at proper times, not, for example, at night when the craftsmen could not be overlooked. Each gild had its wardens, who inspected the goods and exposed false work and all fraudulent tricks, such as stretching cloth, adulterating groceries, and other means whereby the customer might be defrauded. The wardens of each legally constituted gild had powers of punishment by fine in cases where their rules were broken, and all matters belonging to their own trade.

Thus, by the end of the thirteenth century, urban life in England was developed with some degree of complexity. The normal town had got free from the exactions of its manorial lord, and had the privilege of self-assessment, self-government, and jurisdiction within its walls. Its merchant gild, more or less closely connected with the actual governing body, superintended the trade of the town, regulated the general conditions under which goods were brought in, bought and sold, or taken out, maintained the privileges of the gildsmen, and appointed days for markets and fairs. The task of more minutely inspecting the conditions of industry lay in the hands of the craft gilds, who laid down how and by whom goods should be made and sold. Under this system towns had grown and trade had expanded, but rather through the benefits of order and certainty than by any removal of restrictions. Towns as units had gained freedom, but they had not extended it to individuals. Indeed, the idea of leaving each person free to trade as he liked was undreamed of. Trade was not left to flow as best it could; on the contrary, the best channels were to be found for it, the channels from which the town as a whole could derive the most advantage. Men traded, not as individuals, but as members of an association. It was the fact of being in the gilds that put them in a position of privilege. Restricted as even the gildsman appears in modern eyes, yet the amount of his actual freedom must be measured, not by modern individualistic standards, but by the disabilities of the stranger who was hampered by prohibitions, customs, checks and tolls of all kinds, because, not being a member of the town gilds, he was practically without status as a trader at all. The country had not yet begun to recognize itself as an economic whole. A fellow-townsman was a "brother", but a man from another town was a "stranger" or a "foreigner", whether that town was but ten miles distant or a hundred, whether he came from another county or another country, whether he spoke English or a foreign tongue. There was a protective system, and it was a protective system for each town. The question was not whether a trader was an Englishman, but whether he was a gildsman. Commerce had not become national; it was intermunicipal.

How general this treatment of trade was, comes out even more clearly in the examination of two things which seem at first sight to make against it, the existence of the great fairs, and the practice by which debts could be reclaimed from the merchant gild of the debtor. Such fairs as those of Winchester, Stourbridge, Boston, St. Ives, St. Edmundsbury, and others, seem to be national, and even international, in character. The Winchester fair was thronged with merchants from Flanders, Normandy, Gascony, as well as from London, Southampton, Bristol, and other English towns. Traffic went on in wine, cloth, salt fish, spices, meat and wool. There was a court of "Pie Powder" (dusty feet), in which disputes were settled by Law Merchant. But there was no real freedom for trade at these fairs. Leave had to be obtained to hold them; they were not to be continued beyond the proper time; dues had to be paid on bargains; the members of the merchant gild of the town near which the fair was held had privileges and exemptions which strangers had not. Each craft was grouped in its own place; the craftsmen from the neighbouring town were generally forced to go to the fair while it lasted, and trade in the town itself was suspended. Everywhere there was the same regulation for some local object; there was an unusual volume of trade, and forms of restriction differing from the ordinary town rules, but there is no more idea of individual freedom in the fair than in the town.

The practice by which debts were recovered from a "foreigner" shows equally clearly how slight were the rights of the individual in commerce, and how powerful the idea of membership of some corporate body. English traders might naturally have difficulty in recovering money from traders of another country, and there is nothing strange that recourse should then be had to the defaulter's merchant gild, though even this shows how closely the interests of gildsmen and gild were twined. But if commerce had been really national in character it would not have been necessary to call in the merchant gild when dealing with another Englishman. This, however, was frequently done. For example, a gildsman, or even a burgess of, let us say, Southampton, who was owed money by a merchant of York, could claim against, or, if necessary, sue the merchant gild of York for the debt. Often the matter would be taken up by the sufferer's own town. Thus, the mayor and corporation of London would write, insisting on the payment of debts due to London merchants from, it might be, either merchants of Bristol, Florence, Yarmouth, Bruges, Ghent, or Oxford, to almost the same effect, namely, that the town authorities should cause justice to be done, as they would wish it done to their own townsmen, under threats of distraint on property belonging to merchants of the defaulting town then in London. The necessity and frequency of such action give a striking example of the powers and responsibilities of the towns as units in all commercial relations of the time.

In comparing the conditions of trade and industry inside the towns with those of the present day, very wide differences appear. Commonplaces of this century, such as capital, labour, employer, competition, have very little meaning as applied to the thirteenth century. Employer and labourer are one; the craftsman works at his craft assisted by apprentices who will, in their turn, become craftsmen; the retail shop is practically unknown, for each craftsman sells the goods he makes; there is little change in fashion, and demand is steady; large stocks are not made or held; there is no underselling or cutting out of rivals by improved process or specious goods; there are no wealthy employers struggling to become still wealthier. On the contrary, townsmen live much the same lives, and aim rather at standing well with their gild than exciting envy by their individual prosperity. Craftsmen work year after year on the same method with the same materials. It is not competition which determines price, but usage and regulation. The price of any ware is to be a fair price, fair to the producer and fair to the buyer, and this was far more easy to estimate then than it is now. Under the diverse conditions of modern production, the idea of justice as a determining factor of price has gone; we do not trouble over what is the right price, we accept the price under usual conditions as being right. But when craftsmen lived similar lives, and produced on a similar scale with similar advantages of situation and market, and with similar costs of production, a just price was not so difficult to determine. Thus the trade of the time is pervaded with a morality that is unfamiliar to our day. Now, trade is not immoral, but it is unmoral; price is left to competition, to the conditions of the market. But in the thirteenth century, current opinion, if not perhaps on so high a level as St. Thomas Aquinas would have had it, when he urged the wickedness of selling defective articles without indicating the defects to the buyer, or of asking a high price when there was a temporary scarcity, yet made strongly against deceit, fraud, and concealment. Neither buyer nor seller was to take advantage of the other's necessities, but payment was to be a fair return for the labour expended upon honest work.

CHAPTER IV.

THE EXCHEQUER. MONEY AND ACCOUNTS.

In very early states of society money is not used at all. Men live by the produce of their own labour; what they want for themselves they make, or if they cannot make it, they obtain it from those who can, by an exchange of goods which is called "barter". But, save in the most simple cases, the process of barter is extremely inconvenient. In making a purchase it is only required to find someone who is willing to part with the thing which you want; he is sure to be ready to accept money for it, if enough is offered. But in the case of barter, the man you deal with must not only have what you want, but also be willing to take what you have to offer. Thus barter is only suitable where men have very simple wants, and in small areas. A man who is at a distance from home with portable goods to dispose of, will not be willing to take bulky articles in exchange, even if they would be useful to him, because he cannot carry them with him.

Thus there is a clear distinction between countries where buying and selling is carried on by means of barter, and those in which money is used. The latter have taken a great step in advance of the former. But although this transition from a "natural economy" to a "money economy" is very important in its results upon the trade of a country, yet it may be very gradual. Traders, who travel from place to place, may use money—indeed it may well be impossible for them to carry on their trade without money; the King and the Court may use money, and it may further be common in the towns. Yet the country districts may remain still in a condition of natural economy. There, payments may be made in services or in kind; the labourer may live on the food he raises from the land which he pays for by service; simple wants, such as clothes, boots, or the repair of implements, can be satisfied in the village by payments in kind, even though coins may be used as units by which the value of things is measured, and thus one of the functions of money be fulfilled, without money actually passing from hand to hand.

This condition, where a country is partly under a money economy, and partly under a natural economy, existed in England at the time of the Norman Conquest. From the earliest days the country had never been without some coinage. The silver *sceattas* of the seventh century, coined in Kent, Essex, and Mercia, were followed in the eighth century by silver pennies, bearing the name of the king who issued them. The numerous regulations about fines and wergilds, so common in Saxon laws, show that money was familiar, and the impositions of Danegeld in 991 and in later years afford sufficient proof that money was, on occasions, to be found all over the country before the end of the tenth century. But its common use was confined to the merchants and traders, and the dwellers in London, Winchester, and the greater towns. On the manor, money at first played no part; payments in service and payments in kind, corn, wood, fowls, eggs, were what had to be reckoned. Lords who held many manors, and especially the King, the largest landowner of all, went from one estate to another, eating up the produce. This was their revenue on which they lived. When, however, commutation became general, a new impulse was given towards establishing a money economy in rural districts. It is true that although the commuted services were valued in money, they were not always paid in it; they were still sometimes paid in kind. But the necessity of paying the labourers, hired to replace the servile tenants' labour, compelled the lord, or his bailiff who managed the estate, to have a certain amount of money at hand, and accordingly it became usual to take money payments instead of service. The fact that a money economy was taking the place of the old natural economy is marked by the practice of keeping manorial accounts. These begin to be common in England in the early years of the thirteenth century. Until that time there had been in rural districts little or no money to account for.

If the merchants were the first and the land-owners and labourers the last to adopt a money economy, the Crown comes between the two. Where the Crown held land a natural economy lasted almost as late as it did on other manors. But the King was not solely a land-owner. He drew revenue from other sources as well. He had tolls on goods entering or leaving the kingdom, fines for breaches of the law, payments from towns who had bought freedom, occasional taxation, Danegeld, tallage, carucage as the time might be. Besides this, it was part of the royal duty to possess a hoard and to add to it, if possible. All this necessitated the keeping of accounts before it was required on the ordinary manor, and royal revenue was dealt with at the Exchequer.

The Exchequer was an offshoot from the Curia Regis, the King's Council with the King himself at the head of it, which had to do indiscriminately with justice and finance. But it was impossible for one body to transact all that had to be done, and consequently as time went on and business increased, the Council was subdivided. The first distinction which emerged was between the judicial side and the financial side, and this financial side developed into the Court of the Exchequer. It is unnecessary to dwell upon the early history of it, but let us take a view of the Court itself and its methods of work at a time when its organization was complete. This is the easier to do, as the *Dialogus de Scaccario*, the work of Richard FitzNigel, Bishop of London, gives a full account of the Exchequer and its officials.

During the reign of Henry II. the Exchequer was permanently established at Westminster; it was inconvenient for it to follow the King in his wanderings on account of the bulky nature of the rolls, chests, table, tallies, and writs required for its business. At the head of it was the Justiciar, who represented the King in financial, as in judicial matters, but beyond a nominal control he had few duties; not infrequently he was absent, and the real superintendence fell to the Treasurer, whose clerk kept the great Roll which recorded all the incomings and outgoings. The Chancellor was in charge of the King's Seal, and his clerk kept a duplicate Roll, whereby the accuracy of the Treasurer's accounts might be checked. Besides these, the Constable paid stipends from the Exchequer to royal officers, and the Marshal had charge of the writs and tallies. These were the chief officials, and they belonged to the Upper Exchequer, or Exchequer of Account. The Lower Exchequer, or Exchequer of Receipt, had a permanent staff of less important officials, the Chancellor's scribe, the Assayer, the Cutter of the Tallies, the Ushers, Deputy Chamberlains, and others.

Before proceeding to explain the proceedings by which money was paid in, allowed for, and dealt with at the Exchequer, it may be well to notice difficulties which had to be surmounted, difficulties indeed which no longer exist. Nowadays the arts of reading, writing, adding, and subtracting are so familiar that it is hard to realize how money and accounts could be managed without a knowledge of them; further, a written receipt is understood and accepted as satisfactory; and finally, our coinage has its face-value. But in the thirteenth century it was different. The officials of the Exchequer of course could read and write, add, and subtract well enough. But this could not be assumed of the Sheriffs and of all the King's debtors who came there to pay money. Consequently figures were not satisfactory, nor were written receipts acceptable; and the coinage was often deficient both in weight and fineness. These things called for a manner of treatment widely different from what is used now. Two problems had to be solved: how to make accounts ocularly plain without employing figures, and how to ensure that out of a miscellaneous mass of coins of various fineness and weights the King received a proper amount.

Two great sessions were held at the Exchequer each year, at Easter and at Michaelmas. At Easter the sheriffs attended and paid in an estimated half of what they expected to have to pay, namely, the ferm of the shire, made up of profits from Crown lands, and lands temporarily in the hands of the Crown, by forfeiture or escheat, the ferms of such towns as were under royal control and had not bought charters, revenue from tolls and markets, treasure trove, goods of felons and outlaws, fines for breaches of the law, the regular feudal aids and other feudal dues, tallages, carucage, scutage, according to the time; at Michaelmas they gave an account of the whole, and paid up the balance of what was still owing. The rendering of the account was done in the upper Exchequer, the payment made in the lower. Accordingly at Michaelmas all the officials took their places round the Exchequer table, the Justiciar presiding if he was there, the Treasurer and his clerk, the Chancellor and his clerk, and other subordinate officials, including the Calculator, and at the foot of the table the Sheriffs and those who had to pay in money. The table itself, ten feet by five, was covered with dark cloth, and divided across its width by chalk lines or wands. These formed columns of account, being pence, shillings, pounds, scores, hundreds and thousands of pounds, as taken from the right of the Calculator, who sat on the left side of the table from the president. Without going into the details of how the counters were set out, it is obvious that a counter in each of the five spaces would represent £1121, 1s. 1d.[1] In the top row what was owed by the debtor was thus laid out by the Calculator. The sheriff, or whoever was rendering his account, was then called on to make his statement, and in the rows below was figured out what he had paid on account at Easter, what he had received under one heading and another, and what he had disbursed by order of the King. When the whole was set out by the Calculator under the eyes of the Exchequer officials on the one hand, and the sheriff on the other, the whole financial position was clear; it only remained for the Calculator to take off the counters in pairs—pence, shillings, pounds, hundreds, or whatever it might be—one from the sheriff's counters and one from the King's. No subtraction beyond this was required; if nothing remained upon the table, the sheriff was quit, his accounts balanced; if the King's counters had gone, and the sheriff had still

---

[1] Perhaps it is worth while to point out that the figure 2 in the above sum is owing to the fact that the column between hundreds and units was not tens, as we might have expected, but scores.

some left, he would be credited with the amount; or if, as was generally the case, the sheriff's counters were all gone, while some still remained to the King, then they represented the amount the sheriff had still to pay. No mistake was possible; there were no calculations and no figures to trouble the illiterate; all that was required was to be able to reckon up counters on a table. Thus it was from these counters or dummy coins[2] that the name Exchequer is derived.

Before we go on to see how the money was paid which the "counter game", the *ludus scaccorum*, as played on the Exchequer table, showed to be still owing from the sheriff, something must be said about the form of receipt used. We have seen that it was customary for the sheriff to pay in an estimated half at Easter, and that this was allowed for in the Michaelmas reckoning. The form of receipt or voucher used was called a tally. It was a rod of willow or hazel some eight inches long, and the sum paid was recorded upon it by cutting notches with a knife, the principal sum being put on one side, and the lesser items on the other. Thus, supposing the tally was for £1261, 4s. 5d.,[3] the thousand would be marked by a notch the width of a man's palm on one side. Then on the other would be two notches, each of a thumb's breadth (two hundreds), three notches the breadth of a little finger (three twenties), one notch the breadth of a barleycorn (one pound), four small jags (four shillings), and

---

[2] German *schach*, a dummy.
[3] A large sum is taken for the purposes of illustration. It must not be supposed that a sheriff's usual payment in any way approached this amount.

five strokes with ink (five pence). The tally was then split, so that the line of the split went through the notches on each side, and the sheriff took one half, and the Exchequer kept the other. It was an absolutely perfect form of receipt, for neither party could falsify it; the notches could not be got rid of, and if it was attempted to add a notch the fraud would be instantly revealed, when the two halves were put together. Thus the sheriff paid his sum at Easter, and received a tally for it; on his producing the tally at Michaelmas, it would be compared with the duplicate in the Exchequer, and if they corresponded the sheriff would be allowed the amount marked on it.[4]

The account dealt with, it remained to proceed with the payment, and for that we must pass from the Upper Exchequer to the Lower. Though we have been speaking of pounds and shillings, it must be remembered that these were terms of account. The only English coin in circulation was the silver penny; round (*i.e.* coined) silver half-pennies and farthings were not issued before the thirteenth century; until that time they were made by breaking the silver penny in pieces. Henry III. issued a gold coin, but it was very rare indeed, and it was not till Edward III.'s reign that a gold coin (the noble) came into use at all, and even then it was not common. Shillings and pounds were first issued by Henry VII. Silver pennies then were what the sheriff had to pay with.

---

[4] Tallies were used in the Exchequer as lately as the beginning of this century. They are still in use among bakers in the country districts of France, *e.g.* in Touraine, each loaf delivered being marked by a notch on the two halves put together, and one half being kept by the customer.

As a race the English kings have been singularly free from the stain of debasing the coinage, or of issuing light coin. The standard of fineness, namely, eleven ounces two pennyweights of silver to eighteen pennyweights of alloy, was maintained till Henry VIII.'s reign, and the standard of weight, though slightly lowered by Edward III., was not greatly altered till Henry VIII. sacrificed it together with the standard of fineness. This uniformity, however, only holds true of the king's money. The disorderly reign of Stephen had seen a good deal of irregular minting by the barons, and although Henry II. had put a stop to that, he could not get in the bad pennies which were in circulation. The coinage was further tampered with by clipping and sweating; having no milled edge, and not being always of the same size, it was possible to pare silver from the coin without danger of detection, while sweaters rubbed the coins and shook them together so that they became light. While coins were so roughly made as they were, being placed in one wooden die and another die hammered down on them, false coin was easy and profitable to make; and if we may judge from Henry I.'s action in striking off the right hand of every moneyer in England for fraudulent dealings, it would seem that even the royal coinage was in danger of being debased in spite of the King. Indeed, so long as coining went on in so many places in England, it was very difficult to supervise the coinage adequately. And yet it was necessary to have a number of mints, as otherwise money would not be sufficiently distributed through the country, and the King might find great difficulty in collecting his taxes and dues in money. Thus at the commencement of the thirteenth century money was struck in London, Canterbury, Carlisle, Chichester, Durham, St. Edmundsbury, Exeter, Ipswich, Lincoln, Lynn, Northampton, Norwich, Oxford, Rochester, and Winchester,[5] and although efforts were made to secure that each mint should use similar dies, yet the imperfect nature of the dies themselves prevented complete uniformity. When in addition we remember that silver coinage wears very fast if it remains long in use, it is obvious that there was always much light coin, and generally a good deal of debased coin, in circulation.

Thus it became necessary to take precautions against the King being paid in this light or debased coinage, and thereby being a loser. To allow payment by "tale", that is by the number of pennies owing, would be to invite this bad coin, while to inspect every penny was clearly impossible; hence the first precaution was to exact from the debtors an extra sixpence with each pound to make good a presumed shortness of weight. This was payment *ad scalam*. This was not found to be enough, and the next step was to weigh each counted pound and call on the debtors to make up the deficiency, or to accept from them one shilling per pound as vantage money or compensation. This was payment *aa pensum*. This precaution was effective against lightness of the coinage, but it was of course no safeguard against debased money, and accordingly in Henry I.'s reign, Roger of Salisbury introduced

[5] Ashley, *Economic History*, vol. i. part i. page 163.

a new plan of "blanching" money, that is, testing the fineness (or whiteness) of it. When any payment was made, forty-four shillings' worth of coin was selected at random out of the heap, weighed and handed to the Master of the Assays, who carried off a pound's weight of it, and, accompanied by the sheriff and his own subordinates, proceeded to the furnace to make the assay. The coins were melted and the dross skimmed off until pure silver alone remained. So long as the surface of the melted mass was clouded there was still dross to be removed, but when the surface was bright and mirror-like, the impurity was gone, and nothing but silver remained. Both sides watched the operation, the sheriff anxious to prevent any waste of silver, the Exchequer officials careful to see that all dross was removed. The assayer had an interest in being accurate, for if either side challenged the assay, he had to make a second, for which he received no fee. When the operation was complete the mass was weighed, and if it was short of its proper weight the sheriff had to cast in enough pence to turn the scale. These pence were counted, and the sheriff had to pay that number on each pound of his total "ferm" as a quittance.

It was in this way that the King's revenue was collected from the sheriffs and accountants, and in Edward I.'s reign from the customers, who paid it in. Having been reckoned up on the Exchequer table, and the money tested by this "Trial of the Pyx", as it was called, it was stored in the royal treasury, and an account of it kept in the Great or Pipe Roll of the Exchequer drawn up by the Treasurer's scribe. When this system was once in force, it is obvious that a money economy would soon replace a natural economy all over the country. The transition between the times of Henry I. and Henry II. is strongly marked. Richard FitzNigel, writing in the latter reign, records what he had heard from old men, of herds of cattle and the numbers of loaded wagons that crowded the roads wherever the Court was, and of the days when wheat, flesh, and provender were actually paid in and placed to the royal account, their value being reduced to money—wheat for a hundred men, one shilling; a ram or sheep, fourpence; provender for twenty horses, fourpence. But in his own time the necessity of paying soldiers for distant expeditions, and the increased convenience of payments in money had led to a complete alteration. The sheriffs' accounts were not only reckoned in money but paid in money also.

CHAPTER V.

ENGLAND UNDER THE THREE EDWARDS. NATIONAL UNITY AND COMMERCIAL POLICY.

Hitherto we have seen commerce in the inter-municipal stage. If a townsman of the early thirteenth century had been asked to describe an ideal condition of commerce, he would have laid down that the dues owing by his town to the Exchequer should be reasonably small; that the town itself should be well governed, and its liberties maintained; that those who wished to trade there should be members of the merchant gild, and the craftsmen further enrolled in craft gilds, each under such regulations as were for the good of the town; that strangers and aliens should bring abundance of goods, which should be sold to townsmen, and townsmen only; that no foreigner[1] should sell to another foreigner save on fair days, nor should he, on any pretence, engage in retail trade; while in the town he was to reside with a townsman, so that an eye could be kept on his proceedings; he was to sell his goods speedily, not holding them back in the hope of getting a better price; he was expected to buy goods from the townsmen with the money he had received, and this done, to be off again. The townsman would further admit that easy and safe communication by land and sea was a good thing, and that trade might be forwarded by a good currency and by a uniformity of weights and measures, and hampered by an excess of tolls. But these things were not, he would say, the concern of the town. If the town was prosperous, then all was well; that other towns were less prosperous was rather the occasion for self-congratulation than for sympathy. In his eyes the town was everything and the nation nothing.

Now, however, the time was come to take a wider view. Local tolls were no inconvenience to those who were exempt from them; local customs did not appear strange to those who were familiar with

---

[1] In this chapter "alien" is used to denote a stranger from abroad. Any man was a "stranger" or a "foreigner" in a town who was not a burgess or gildsman of that town.

them; national concerns were not visible to those who did not look beyond their own town walls. But the King could not content himself with this narrow habit of mind. Under the Normans, when the King lived more or less "of his own", that is, like any other great lord, on the produce of his estates, it had been possible to leave the towns to enjoy their exclusiveness, so long as they paid for it. But by the time of Edward I. the kingdom had grown consolidated; the memories of the hostility between Saxon and Norman had passed away; commerce from outside had grown; wider plans were coming forward, and with them the need for a revenue. The King would approve and support town regulations which contributed to order, security, and good government, but he could not approve town jealousies and town rivalries. And hence we see the Crown step in to smooth away local inequalities, to treat the kingdom as a whole, to look to national interests and not town interests, to adopt a commercial policy which should be uniform, applied as far as possible to all alike.

In dating the commencement of a national system of trade, as distinguished from a municipal system, from the accession of Edward I., it must not be assumed that prior to this there had been no such national treatment. The merchant gilds and some of the craft gilds themselves were held under charter from the Crown, and such gilds as were not licensed were called "adulterine", and liable to be broken up. Further, it was through the gilds that such general regulation as existed was put in force. Thus the merchant gild at Southampton provided for the holding, twice a year, of the Assizes of Bread and Ale. The first Assize of Bread (1202) established a scale according to which the weight of the farthing loaf was to vary with the price of a quarter of wheat. The same principle was followed in subsequent re-issues, and in 1266 more elaborate rules were added, providing for all prices of wheat varying from twelve pence to twelve shillings, and also setting forth what the baker might gain. Ale was included in this assize, and the number of gallons to be sold for a penny made dependent on the price of barley. Wine had been placed under Government regulation in 1199, though it was dealt with differently, a maximum price being fixed, and if more was demanded the town authorities were empowered to close the offender's shop pending the King's pleasure. Richard I. had issued an Assize of Weights and Measures, commanding uniformity throughout the realm, and this was repeated in Magna Carta. The currency, as has been seen, was admittedly a royal matter. So far, as well as in the imposition of taxes and in the administration of justice in more serious offences, the kingdom had been treated as a whole. But the commercial side of these regulations does not amount to very much; such as they were, they were mostly enforced by being embodied in the regulations of the towns; and some of them, such as the Assize of Weights and Measures, and the stipulation of Magna Carta that all merchants should "have liberty to enter, dwell, and travel in England for the purposes of commerce without being subjected to any evil tolls, but only to the ancient and allowed customs", must have been very generally disregarded. Local differences of weights and measures have survived, in some cases, to our own day, and the amount of "liberty" left to the foreigner after the "ancient and allowed customs" had been put in force was very little.

In the matter of national regulation the reign of Edward I. marks a new epoch. There is, first of all, a great mass of legislation on all subjects, mainly attributable to the King himself; and then there are the results which flow from the King's greatest exploit, the establishing of a Parliament which adequately represented England. Edward did much himself, and in making an assembly in which local ideas and jealousies could not be dominant, he gave the nation an opportunity of doing still more. It is impossible to separate rigidly what the King did alone from what was done with the advice and approbation of those whom he called upon to aid him, nor did Parliament do much of its own initiative; but the co-operation of King and Parliament was a new force in English history, and acted on commerce as well as on politics.

Three of Edward's great statutes, Mortmain (1279), De Donis (1285), and Quia Emptores (1290), are concerned with land tenure, whether by religious bodies or by feudal tenants, and are not of special importance for our present purpose. If, however, these are left on one side, there yet remain many in which commerce was directly concerned. From his Parliament of 1275 came the first statute of Westminster, laying down regulations on the question of wreck, which make it easier for the owner of the wrecked cargo to save it from being claimed as wreckage by some lord or the Crown. In the same year the royal customs were established on a fixed plan. Hitherto royal rights had been ill defined; "prisage", the power of "taking" what tolls on merchandise the King saw fit to take for the use of his ports, had been fitful and uncertain in amount and incidence. But now the old right was given up in exchange for a definite scale, called the "Ancient Custom", half a mark on each sack of wool, and one mark on each last of hides, and the "*recta prisa*" on wine of one tun from before and abaft the mast on each cargo. Aliens paid the New or Petty Custom, which appears in the Carta Mercatoria of 1303, an increase of 50 per cent in the amount paid on wool and leather, and a "butlerage" of 2*s.* a tun on wine and a poundage on other exports and imports. These customs were collected by royal officials—"customers"—who acted also as a check upon smuggling: for the better management of trade pains were taken to force it to the chief ports of the kingdom, and Edward interested himself in founding commercial towns; Yarmouth, for example, owes its beginning to him. The advantages of this uniform regulation were great. The conditions of harbours and ports improved; and traders were attracted by the knowledge that they would not have to pay excessive and unexpected tolls. Similar benefits of order and security were aimed at in the Statute of Winchester (1285), which issued rules for the better discovery of robberies and murders on pain of making the district liable in case the offender escaped; towns were to be walled, gates closed at sundown, and no persons to live outside unless under surety; highways were to be enlarged and cleared from underwood that might shelter robbers. A special ordinance [2] provided for the keeping of the streets of London. A further benefit to traders was the establishment of a better system of enforcing the payment of mercantile debts. The old plan of proceeding against the defaulter's merchant gild had been cumbrous and tardy, and the practice of seizing goods from a fellow-townsman of the defaulter had been harsh, and in many cases had worked unjustly. By the Statute of Acton Burnel (1283) a creditor could bring his debtor before the mayor, and if the debt was proved the debtor had to affix his seal to a bond binding him to pay by a certain date. If he failed to pay by that time, his movables in the district could be distrained, or if he had none, a writ obtained for distraint upon movable property in his possession elsewhere. In 1285 this statute was made general to all merchants throughout the kingdom. That alien merchants might be assured of fair treatment, it was provided in the Carta Mercatoria that where there was a dispute between a native and an alien, the jury should be half aliens. In all these respects there is an evident care for national trade.

Edward I.'s most striking act for the good of England, namely, the expulsion of the Jews, is often blamed as a sign of racial jealousy or religious intolerance. The Jews certainly were unpopular; they stood in a peculiar position, partly owing to

[2] Statuta Civitatis Londonie.

the fact that English law did not apply to them, and still more because they were naturally disinclined to mix in any way with Englishmen. Even when English-born and of English speech, they remained aliens. And further, they did not readily engage in any handicraft or industry. What they did do for a living was money-lending at usury, and to mediæval ideas the taking of usury was hateful. It will be necessary to return to this subject in a later chapter,[3] but we may notice shortly the grounds on which the mediæval opinion was based. Nowadays we draw a distinction between interest and usury. Usury, we say, is oppressive or iniquitous interest. But in the Middle Ages gain accruing from the lending of money, when the lender was secured against all risks, was condemned by Christian teaching. Gain which came from work was justifiable, because something was produced by work; but gain from the lending of money was wrong, because no work was done for it; it was, as Shakespeare describes it, "a breed of barren metal". It was also generally true that if a man was obliged to borrow, it was to relieve a temporary necessity, not to make more money with what he borrowed; provided there was security that the money would be returned, it was thought that the lender should lend without expecting payment for his loan, for in lending money he was doing an act of kindness, not of business. While the money was on loan he lost nothing; had he kept it, he did not contemplate making anything by it, and supposing that it was restored, he was none

[3] See chapter xiii.

the worse off. The usury which the Jews demanded was very high, and those who borrowed often found themselves reduced to ruin; and since usury was forbidden to Christians, it was particularly obnoxious that Jews should take it.

Nor were the Jews always a cringing race, as historical novels are apt to picture them, reviled and bullied by feudal lords, unable to obtain redress for their wrongs, merely allowed to live miserable lives that they might be plundered at pleasure. On the contrary, they had hitherto been under the very direct care of the Crown; they were, in fact, King's chattels. Against him they had no rights; what they possessed, land or movables, was at the King's mercy; debts due to them might be regarded as debts due to the King; and consequently, though the Crown often plundered the Jews, it would not approve of other persons doing so. The Jew would demand his debt with the knowledge that he had the royal power behind him. Their bonds were registered and preserved under the King's care, and a special court, the Exchequer of the Jews, looked after their affairs. They were a source of much revenue, doubly valuable in that there was little difficulty in collecting it. This being so, the King's natural policy was to foster the Jews. He could tax them; he could borrow from them without being obliged to pay his loans; in fact, they were most useful and convenient.

Edward I., however, looked not to his own convenience, but to the good of the country as a whole. From that point of view, the Jews were a burden, their presence distasteful, their habits unpopular;

they did not work, they took no part in town life. What they did was to lend money at usury, and they were further suspected of tampering with the coinage. Parliament and the Church alike called for their expulsion, and in 1290 Edward agreed to this. Care was taken that they should suffer as little as possible in going. For example, their debtors had the choice of paying half the sum they owed to the Jews, or being held liable for the whole amount by the Crown; the Jews were not to be molested or ill-treated on their journey. The King got rid of them, not as hated aliens, but as persons who broke up and disturbed the national commerce that he was fostering. Subsequent events showed that the measure did not produce all the good results that the King had hoped. Money-lending, as we shall see, passed into the hands of the Caursines and Lombards; ingenious justifications for taking usury in fact, though not in name, were set up, and by degrees, as with a widening commerce the field for employing money widened, the hostility to what we now call interest passed away. This does not affect the fact that Edward's action was a deliberate and disinterested attempt to improve the condition of commerce, although as King he might be the loser.

Edward I. had done much towards giving England a commercial unity, and, as the representative of it, a Parliament in which large and small land-owners, clergy and burgesses, found a place. Edward III. went further, and was the first to employ a commercial policy. Commercial policy has done much to influence the history of

England, far more, indeed, than is generally recognized. Edward III.'s commercial policy did not lead to such striking results as that which successively involved us in a series of wars with the Dutch, lost for us our American colonies, and led to a prolonged duel with France, although indeed it had much to do with the beginning of the Hundred Years' War. It was indeed somewhat of a tentative nature. The means he used to attain his ends were various and not always consistent. Nothing at that time was very settled; his legislation is largely experimental. But he set before him three objects: to develop foreign commerce, to plant new industries, and to check extravagance by sumptuary legislation.[4]

In all early times the connection between the Crown and aliens was necessarily close. The position of one class of aliens, the Jews, has been already mentioned. But all aliens owed what position they had to royal favour. Save by goodwill of the King, it was impossible for them to come to the kingdom at all. Licenses were at first given to individual merchants and then to associations. The position of alien merchants was made the subject of treaties and defined by charters, privileges of trading in each other's dominions were reciprocally granted by kings, and such aliens as came would have to obey royal regulations. As early as the time of Ethelred the "Men of the Emperor" had an establishment and regular privileges in London. The Hanse of London, associated merchants from towns in the Netherlands

---

[4] Cunningham, *English Industry and Commerce*, i. 276.

and the north of France, lived in the Steelyard, somewhat in the fashion of a garrison in an enemy's country. Within the walls of their fortress, which embraced dwellings, wharves, and warehouses, the members led a common life, dining together according to their degree, ruled by officers of their own election, yet trading within these walls each for himself. Privileges given by Richard I. to Cologne merchants to buy and sell at fairs throughout the land, free from toll, led other German traders to join the Cologne hanse. By degrees the new-comers outnumbered the old, and the association, under the name of the Teutonic Hanse, passed from the control of Cologne to that of Lubeck and the Hanse towns of the Baltic. Merchants from Florence, Lucca, Piacenza, and Gascony also held privileges from the King of somewhat the same nature.

To a certain extent both King and native merchants were at one over these aliens. In the twelfth and thirteenth centuries, England was commercially far behind the Continent. If the aliens did not bring imports of fine cloth, wine, spices, and other things not to be had in England, it did not appear how they were to be brought at all; and further, as the export trade was chiefly in the hands of these same aliens, to exclude them would have meant robbing exporters of their market. So far then, as importers and buyers, they commended themselves alike to King and burgesses; but there unanimity ended. The burgesses wished them to bring goods, sell them, spend the money in buying English goods and depart again, and the sooner the better. But the King did not take the same view; he saw that if aliens were given larger privileges, more would come, and commerce would grow to larger proportions. Hence for the first part of the fourteenth century, there was a struggle between the towns trying to keep up their exclusive privileges against aliens, and the King trying to break them down. At the end of the thirteenth century Edward I. quarrelled with the city of London, and under his government of the city, aliens were first allowed to exceed the forty days' limit of residence hitherto granted them. When the London merchants regained their privileges, aliens were again restricted, but by the *Carta Mercatoria* of 1303, the King, in return for additional customs, gave liberty to aliens to stay as long as they pleased and live where they pleased. They were not to engage in retail trade except in spice or merceries, but otherwise they could sell to whom they pleased. In the days of Edward II.'s weakness the burgesses again obtained the imposition of the old restrictions, but when the King recovered his power in 1322, he gave back to the aliens their liberties. In 1327, when Edward III. was newly come to the throne and the government was still weak, the forty days' limit was prescribed afresh, and residence with English hosts enforced. But in 1335 the King seems to have made up his mind for the policy of freedom, and complete liberty of buying and selling was granted to all strangers despite all local charters. In spite of some concessions to the city of London, this policy of freedom continued to the end of the reign of

Edward III. Alien merchants might live with whom they pleased, and stay as long as they pleased, provided they paid the ordinary taxation, and they might sell and buy as they liked. The date at which the extension of privileges to aliens began is worth special notice. It is just before Edward began his great war against France, and as he was meditating the war at the time, and Parliament was in anticipation voting him supplies for it, it is reasonable to suppose that his concessions were intended to bind together the allies, principally on the north-eastern frontiers of France, whom he brought into line against the enemy. Flemings would be particularly interested in liberties of trading in England. And though at the beginning of the war Edward had but few alien subjects,[5] yet his claim to the throne of France carried with it an assertion that all Frenchmen and Flemings were his alien subjects; and even though this claim was dropped in the Treaty of Bretigny, yet when the war revived, it was easy to rake up old titles to Anjou, Maine, and Brittany. So that Edward had, in the possession of an unusually large number of alien subjects, a special inducement to do something for them.

Whatever reasons Edward had, his action was a heavy blow at the exclusiveness of the towns, and it was naturally not at all popular with the townsmen. The King, however, was looking beyond the towns. He was treating the nation as

---

[5] He was lord of Gascony and Ponthieu, for which he had done homage in 1331. After the Treaty of Bretigny he owned in full sovereignty the whole of the duchy of Aquitaine, and Ponthieu, and the town of Calais.

a whole. He was anxious to increase the volume of foreign trade, and to have imported goods plenty and cheap, without caring into whose hands the trade fell. Somewhat the same spirit influenced his dealings with the Staple, although, as this concerned exports, the object was to have plenty of buyers, so that the price should be good for English sellers, again regardless of whether the carrying was done by natives or aliens.

The chief exports, wool, hides, leather, and tin, were the staple commodities; of these wool was so much the most important, that it by itself is often called the staple commodity of the realm. Until the reign of Henry III. the export trade had been almost entirely in the hands of aliens, but either in that reign, or in that of Edward I., arose the Staplers, or merchants of the Staple, native merchants who exported and sold wool. As the export of Spanish wool had scarcely begun, England was almost without a rival, but in the backward state of the weaving industry it was impossible for all or indeed any large part of the English wool to be worked up at home. The home of weaving at the time was the Low Countries, and thither the English wool went. For more than one reason it was advantageous that the export trade should run in a regular channel to a regular place. There would be less risk of loss by piracy, or by non-payment of debts; the king's customs could be more easily collected; better prices would be obtained where there was sure to be a large number of buyers; and thus the practice was to appoint a regular staple town to which the wool should go, and where buyers and sellers could meet conveniently. In 1313 Edward II. declared for "one certain staple", and though different towns were chosen at different times, the staple was generally in Flanders. Just as with the aliens, Edward III. tried a number of experiments with the staple. In 1328 all staples were abolished, so that merchants might go whither they thought best. This complete freedom did not work well, and in 1341 Bruges was made the staple town. But Bruges did not give satisfaction either; the citizens tried to exclude Lombard buyers in order that they themselves should get the wool cheap, while the growing disorder in Flanders made the conditions of trade there uncertain and dangerous, and accordingly, in 1353, Edward transferred the staple to England, setting up Newcastle, York, Lincoln, Norwich, Westminster, Canterbury, Chichester, Winchester, Exeter, and Bristol as staple towns. Alien merchants were encouraged to come, and the trade was to be under the management of Mayors of the staple. It was thought that there would be plenty of buyers, since none would be excluded, and thus the price would be good; and it seems further to have been hoped that the cost of carriage and the risks of the sea would be transferred to the alien. The fact that the carrying trade was also transferred to him was not regarded. This experiment was not continued long, in spite of the fact that the volume of wool exported was greater than it had ever been before, for in 1363 the staple was again placed at Calais, where it remained for the rest of the reign.

The whole course of proceedings is curious; Edward tried everything in turn; first the staple abroad; then no staple; then the staple in England; and finally returned to the old plan, making choice of a foreign town, yet one in English possession. The wisdom of the alterations is not, perhaps, conspicuous; such constant changes must have been distracting. But they indicate a desire on the King's part to put trade on the best footing possible. There is a real commercial policy at work, though its methods are fickle and experimental.

Similar signs of Edward's interest in commerce may be found in his assertion of the sovereignty of the sea. Holding a more or less complete control on each side of the Channel, he was able to do something towards putting down the pirates who swarmed in many of the French ports. Convoys were arranged for English fleets and letters of protection given to native subjects. The King's war with France also took the form of gaining power in districts which were seats of important trade. From Guienne came most of the wine imported into England, and there was a considerable salt trade, and by the Treaty of Bretigny (1360) Guienne was secured as an English possession. Flanders, the seat of the weaving industry, sided with Edward against Philip, and in the first campaigns Flanders was Edward's base of operation. It is possible, of course, to make too much of these facts, to find a connected commercial policy in actions which may have been dictated by military or political considerations. Edward had family claims on Guienne and family connections with Flanders; the Flemish towns were at odds with the French King, and so was Edward; what could be more natural than to make an alliance? Still, though the motives are difficult to estimate correctly, the result was simple enough. The wine trade passed into English control, and the connection between England and Flanders became much closer.

The fact that in the subsequent Treaty of Bretigny Edward secured Guienne, but gave up his claim on Flanders, is capable of the very commonplace explanation that he took the best terms he could get, and could get no more. But why Guienne was preferred to Flanders, if indeed a choice lay between them, was probably that wine could not be produced satisfactorily in England, whereas by 1360 the King was in a fair way to get control of a weaving industry without meddling in Flanders at all, and that by establishing it at home. From the earliest days there had been weaving of a sort in England, but the cloth had been very rough, acceptable only to the poor. Those who wanted fine cloth, properly fulled and dyed in bright colours, had to get it from the Netherlands. As has been mentioned, a certain number of foreign artisans had come over with William I., but they were quite unable to supply all that was wanted. The import of cloth was considerable, and this was noted with disapproval by those who wished the realm to be self-sufficing. Thus, in 1258, among the baronial recommendations of reform, had been one advising the use of English cloth, rough though it was, in preference to foreign cloth. In 1271, as a political means of putting pressure on Flanders, both the export of wool and the import of cloth was forbidden for a time. But troubles in Flanders gave Edward III. an opportunity. In 1328 the Flemish artisans were defeated at Cassel by their count, aided by the French King, and many of them banished from Ghent, Ypres, and Bruges. Three years later Edward granted his protection to a Flemish weaver, John Kempe, who came to England with servants and apprentices, and promised like advantages to other weavers, fullers, and dyers who were willing to work in England and teach their craft. Two Brabanters and fifteen Zeelanders received similar protection in 1336 and 1337, and in the latter year the offer was made general to all immigrant weavers: the import of foreign cloth and the export of wool was prohibited. These last clauses were again a political stroke at the Flemish towns and were soon given up, but the influx of alien artisans continued all the more when England and Flanders fought side by side against the French King, and Edward urged the kindly reception of the immigrants because they had been banished "owing to their adhesion to our cause".

Yet with all the protection the King could give, aliens were regarded with great jealousy by the existing weavers' gilds, especially in London. They petitioned that the aliens did not pay the gild fees, and meddled with their industry by making all sorts of novelties in cloth, but the King stood by the aliens and exempted them from all liability to join existing gilds. Riots and attacks seem to have been frequent, for stringent orders were given that none should molest the aliens, nor were they, on the other hand, to carry arms. Supported in this way, the aliens prospered; they formed an association of their own, and for the time at any rate, defied the English gilds, and to a great extent cut them out in the English market.

Whilst the woollen industry was spreading in England, another branch, that of worsted goods, was growing in the eastern counties, around Norwich and the town from which the goods take their name. We hear of these workers owing to their quarrels with the aulnager, the official appointed to see that the cloth was woven the right length and of proper quality. At first the worsted industry was unregulated, and complaint was made that cloths were fraudulently sold as of greater length than they actually were. An aulnager was appointed, but he went beyond the mere repression of fraud, by compelling all weavers to make cloth of certain specified lengths; to this and to the aulnager's fees the weavers objected, and eventually they gained their point about lengths. This was in accord with general policy, for in 1353 the government gave up trying to secure a uniform practice, and merely provided that the aulnager should certify the length and quality, so that none should be deceived.

The century which is covered by the reigns of the Three Edwards is, indeed, no less important in commercial history than it is in political or constitutional history. The events belonging to the latter classes are more resplendent, more striking. We are apt to have our minds filled with the conquest of Wales, the great legislative achievements, the struggle against Scotland, the growth of Parliament, the Confirmation of the Charters, the rivalry between the barons and Edward II., the national glory of Cressy and Poictiers, to the exclusion of what looks commonplace beside these great matters, namely, the growth of a national industry and prosperity. But the achievements in this line too are great. England is consolidated. The realm is set above the town. Traders, whether alien or merely coming from another part of the country, are encouraged by the removal of harassing local restriction, and the volume of trade increased. Export and customs are made the King's special care. The weaving industry, destined to be for long the industrial mainstay of the kingdom, is fostered by the statesman-like policy of affording a refuge to alien craftsmen who were ill-treated at home; England was to gain much by the same policy in later days. The privileges of the towns are not destroyed, save as regarded the foreigners, but they are superseded; merchant gilds are restricted to the needs of municipal and intermunicipal trade; the guidance of King and Parliament is bestowed on national commerce. The general freedom of trade in the days of Edward III. is the more remarkable as it was short-lived. The next period will see the reversal of much that had been done, towns recovering many of their exclusive privileges, aliens again hampered with conditions about residence and sale. What had been done, indeed, was the work of the King; with the industrial classes, as a rule, it was not popular.

Yet, though the freedom granted to trade was soon revoked, all that the two great Edwards had done did not perish with them. An example had been given of national unity and forethought in directing commerce, and this example remained for future rulers of England to imitate.

CHAPTER VI.

THE BLACK DEATH.

Economic history differs from political or constitutional history in that it is less rapid in its movements, and less distinct in its steps. It has few great events and hardly any great dates. There is little to compare with the momentous changes which are called up in our minds by such dates as 1215 or 1689, little to set beside Simon de Montfort's Parliament, or the Armada, or Waterloo, or the Reform Bill. Instead we have to deal with changes which only reach greatness by a cumulative process, by spreading slowly all over the country, with tendencies that begin by being exceptional and only gradually become general. For example, we know nothing certain about the earliest case of commutation of service, or the first grant of freedom to a town; such things would certainly command an interest, though not the same interest as that devoted to the first appearance of the representative principle in Parliament, or the beginnings of the jury system. But although the movement of economic history is generally slow, now and then it quickens its pace, and we are no longer content with the term change; we employ a stronger word—we speak of "revolution". And such a revolution was brought about by one of the salient events of economic history, one of the few that possesses a date by which it is at once conjured up to the mind, namely the Black Death.

The catastrophe was all the more striking in that it was unexpected. The gradual course of action by which labour was freeing itself, the commutation of services for payment, the increase in the numbers of tenants who had gained a certain amount of freedom, seemed to indicate that villeinage was waning, and would perish by degrees, quietly, and without any interference. But things were destined otherwise. When in the autumn of 1347 Edward III. landed in England fresh from the triumph of Cressy and the capture of Calais, he was welcomed as a great conqueror. But a still greater conqueror was at hand, none the less formidable for the fact that few remarked his coming.

When we read that the Black Death swept away one-third, or as some estimates put it, one-half of the population of England, the mortality seems appalling, but even so we may find it difficult to realize fully what such a calamity meant. General statements of this kind fail to convince through their very magnitude. Thanks partly to Defoe, and to the name, the "Great Plague", the visitation of 1665 seems to be regarded as the worst of all English epidemics. But this is not really the case, and it is worth while to see a little more in detail what the Black Death in England actually meant. Beginning at Melcombe Regis in August, 1348, it quickly spread to Bristol and Gloucester. By the end of the year it had travelled eastwards to London and westwards to Bodmin. The meeting of Parliament was prorogued from January 19th till April 27th on account of the pestilence at Westminster. Even yet the gravity of the visitation was not recognized, but early in March Parliament was again prorogued, this time indefinitely. Alarm was becoming serious, but the worst was not over, nor in fact reached. The disease spread northwards and eastwards. East Anglia was ravaged: then the Midlands and the north. The turn of Ireland and Wales came next, and Scotland last, the worst year there being 1350. By the autumn of 1349, indeed, the plague in England had abated: fourteen months had been sufficient time for it to run its course over the kingdom; six months or so was the limit of its stay in any one district. As even when the virulence of the disease was abating, about half those who took it died, it is scarcely an exaggeration to say that when the Black Death quitted a district, it did so because there was little left for it to prey upon.

Lest anyone should be tempted to think that fourteenth-century estimates are not to be trusted, and that the numbers of those who perished by the Black Death are just as likely to be exaggerated as the chroniclers' accounts of the numbers engaged in battles of the time, it may be well to point out the grounds for the belief that from one-third to one-half of the population died. This is not a contemporary estimate. They are much less moderate, Walsingham,[1] for example, quoting the general

---

[1] Walsingham is not quite contemporary. He wrote in Richard II.'s reign.

belief that the mortality was nine-tenths of the population. The modern estimate is based upon records and not guesses, upon the Institution Books, which registered the appointment of clergy to livings, upon the records of gilds and corporate bodies, and, most important of all, upon the Court Rolls of the manors. As it was the business of these courts to record all the changes among the lords' tenants, and as fines were paid on such changes, the Court Rolls are scrupulous in chronicling deaths; and it is from evidence of this kind that particulars of the Black Death can be gathered. Thus we learn that two-thirds of the parish clergy in the diocese of Norwich perished. In July, 1349, 209 clergy were instituted; that is to say, for that one month the number was about three times that of an ordinary year. In the monasteries the mortality was equally great. We are told[2] that in the house of Augustinian canons at Heveringland, prior and canons died to a man, that at Hickley only one canon survived. Of the sixty monks at St. Albans, forty-seven fell victims to the disease. At Heacham, in April, 1349, a case came up in the manorial court between husband and wife about a question of dower. It was postponed for two months, but when the day came round the husband was dead, and all the wife's witnesses. Eight months of the plague in Hunstanton, a small parish, saw 172 tenants of the manor dead, 74 of them without male heirs, and 19 without any heir at all. Though the plague was most fatal to men, yet women and children fell

[2] A. Jessopp, *The Coming of the Friars*, from which most of the examples here given are quoted.

victims too; in many cases whole families perished one after the other. The court rolls bear witness of the wide-spread destruction as much by what they omit as by what they record. In some rolls the year is a blank. From the death of the steward, or general panic, no courts were held, and when the entries begin again they are often in a scrawling illegible hand, and informal in style and language; the former scribe had gone, like the rest, to the grave, and was succeeded by one who was an unskilful penman, and new to the business. Severely as the Black Death fell on the diocese of Norwich, it is difficult to say that its severity was exceptional there. In London four new wardens of the Goldsmith's Company were appointed in the year; a third of the burgesses of Colchester died, and half of the population of Bodmin and Leicester; in the diocese of Bath and Wells it was difficult to find priests to perform the last offices for the victims; in Bristol the living could scarcely bury the dead. High and lowly, rich and poor, town and country fell before the pestilence. By the autumn of 1349 the first violence of the storm had passed; and though for the next twenty years the country was never free from renewed outbreaks, none approached the severity of the first. The storm had indeed passed, but the wreck remained behind.

Putting aside for the present the case of the towns, it is easy to see two main effects of the Black Death upon the country districts. Labour became scarce, and owing to disorganization the harvest was insufficient, even for the diminished population. Hedges were broken down, and cattle wandered at will over the corn-fields; even where the crop had ripened there were often no hands to reap it, and it rotted where it stood. Ploughing and sowing were neglected, and there was prospect of further scarcity. From the short supply of labour and of corn, modern ideas would expect two things: a rise in the wages of labour, and a rise in the price of agricultural products of all kinds. But in the fourteenth century men were not prepared to receive either of these things as necessary, and if not necessary, they were clearly undesirable. Consequently Parliament set to work to restrain them.

As Parliament principally consisted of men who were land-owners, and as at the head of Parliament stood the King, who was the greatest land-owner of all, it is important to see how the land-owner was affected by the mortality among his tenants. Had the death been only a little above the average number, the land-owner would not have been injured; rather in some cases he would have profited, for the heir of the dead tenant would take his father's land, pay his services or commutation as before, and the fines taken by the lord on land changing hands would have been an additional source of revenue. This, however, depended on the existence of an heir; but in many cases whole families were swept off, and no heir left to pay either services, rents, or fines. In this case the land escheated to the lord. This again was not necessarily a disadvantage if he could hire labourers to cultivate it at the old rate. From a mortality that was above the average, but not excessive, the lords had little to fear; some services might be lost where men died without heirs, but the increased number of fines, and the land which came back to the owner, would make up for this. But the extreme mortality of the Black Death upset all ordinary calculations. On all estates all over the country there was the same difficulty. Labourers died in such numbers that estates were left impoverished. Demesnes could no longer be properly tilled by the few who remained; and as for the escheated land, what use was that when no labour could be hired? Whatever the practice of the estate had been, whether services had been commuted on it or not, the lord was embarrassed by having too much land and too few labourers, and since the value of an estate lay mainly in being well supplied with labour, the loss was a heavy one. To a certain extent the cases might differ. Those who had retained payment in services still had the services of the survivors, and these services were each worth what they had been before; but where services had been commuted for payment, the money would only hire the same amount of labour as before, provided wages remained the same; if wages should rise[3] the lord would be the sufferer in two ways: his money revenues would be actually less in amount; and further, what he did receive would be less in value, for he would have to pay a larger wage to each labourer.

If we shift our point of view for one moment

[3] The rise in wages of course occurred in the towns, as it did in the country; but it is convenient for the moment to confine our attention to the country, because there the social effects were much greater. Those who hired labour in the towns had to acquiesce in the rise after the Government had failed to check it; no other course was open to them but to pay at the higher rate. In the country there was, as will be seen, an alternative which proved disastrous.

from that of the lord to the labourer, the case is exactly reversed. The lord might have profited, or at any rate have been no loser, had the mortality been moderate, but the very completeness of the disaster held out possible advantages to the labourer. That anyone perceived these in the misery of 1349, when his companions were dying round him like flies, is improbable; but when the plague abated, there was hope in the increased demand for labour. If the villein had commuted his services, he would continue to pay the same amount, while as far as he worked for wages, he might profit by the rise that was spreading over the country. Thus the interest of lord and villein was diametrically opposite. One feared, the other hoped for, a rise in wages; the lord wished to retain payment in services, the villein strove more than ever to be free from them. We are in fact upon the threshold of the first great struggle in the history of England between rich and poor, between capital and labour.

The Black Death was still at its height when the first collision occurred. The rise in wages, especially as harvest-time approached, became more and more pronounced. Labourers were, for the time, masters of the situation; everywhere they were in demand, and they were few. Consequently wages rose sharply. Instead of the one-twelfth of a quarter of wheat paid for harvesting, one-eighth was demanded; the rate for threshing rose thirty per cent; women who had worked for 1*d.* a day now asked 2*d.* and even 3*d.* And the rise was not merely proportionate to the rise in prices; it went further, for labourers lived better, eating flesh and fish where before they had but bacon. The rising wage brought with it a spirit of restlessness, men leaving their villages to search if better pay could be had elsewhere. Throughout England there were men rambling up and down, refusing to work at the old rate, living sometimes by charity and not infrequently by robbery. The whole agricultural system had in fact broken down.

Meantime the lords were nearly at their wits' end. Many of their tenants were dead, dead without heirs, and death quits all scores; nothing could be had from them. The survivors who owed services were anxious to be off to work for wages, slipping away, escaping no man knew whither; those who paid quit-rents paid an equivalent for their labour at the old rates, when wages had been low and labourers many. Ruin stared the land-owner in the face when he had to hire "as many work-folk as amounted to 1144 days' work" at the old rates to gather his harvest, or when he looked back upon the days when his tenants owed him 2000 days' service in winter and 580 in autumn, which now unfortunately were commuted at the rate of a halfpenny and a penny each.[4] Since the Black Death even a woman's day would cost him twopence. The difficulties of the time were great; it was doubtful if there were labourers enough left to carry on agriculture on the old plan at all, and it was clearly impossible to do so, if the labourers were to get double and triple their former wage.

[4] This was the case on the manors of Ham and Great Tew respectively. Denton, *Fifteenth Century.*

To compel the acceptance of the old rate of wages was the first remedy proposed. In June, 1349, while Parliament was still prorogued, the King issued a proclamation, which was afterwards embodied in the Statute of Labourers of 1351. This sets forth the scarcity of labour owing to the pestilence and the demand for excessive wages, and the fact that many preferred to beg than to work; and provided that every man or woman, able-bodied, and not having land of his own to live upon, nor being already engaged, was to accept work when offered at the old rate of wages, that is to say, the rate of the days before the Black Death. Refusal was punishable by imprisonment; labourers demanding or accepting higher wages, or lords offering them, were to be fined; workmen leaving their employment were to be imprisoned, as were those who gave alms to valiant (*i.e.* able-bodied) beggars. The statute applied not only to reapers, threshers, ploughmen, and those engaged in agricultural operations strictly so called, but to carpenters, tilers, masons, plasterers, and other craftsmen whose labour was only distantly connected with agriculture. It, however, went further, and tried to restrain the rise in prices as well as in wages, stipulating that meat, beer, bread, and fish were not to be sold for "excessive" gain. Before proceeding to criticise this legislation, it is as well to follow it to its end. In 1357 the fines were given to the lords to encourage them to be active in imposing them, while in 1360 the penalties were made far more stringent. Imprisonment was substituted for fines, and those who left their employment were declared outlaws, and if caught were to be branded with F. "for their falsity", while towns who sheltered them were fined ten pounds.

It is this last statute that has called forth denunciations of the brutality and selfishness of a Parliament of land-owners, and no doubt it is revolting in the punishment it lays down for acts which we now regard as lawful, or at any rate as not very serious breaches of the law.[5] But it is not fair to judge Parliament by this act alone, for it was the result of exasperation at the disregard of the earlier and milder regulations. By 1360 the quarrel had developed into a bitter struggle between "we cannot" on one hand and "we will make you" on the other. But, as we have seen, the Statute of Labourers of 1351 was not framed in so coercive a spirit. There was nothing strange to the time in regulation of wages or prices; it was no more than an extension to agricultural labourers of what had been done by the craft gilds for the craftsmen. Provided that Parliament had been successful in keeping down prices, there would have been no need for a rise in wages. For a labourer to claim higher wages because he was placed in a position of relative advantage by a national calamity, was to violate mediæval ideas of fairness. He was "extorting" just as much as the usurer who asked for usury on money which, had he not lent it, would have brought in nothing, or as the engrosser who bought up corn to create an artificial scarcity by which he might benefit.

[5] Such an act, for example, as leaving an employer without giving due notice.

But though it is easy to find a theoretic justification of Parliament's policy at first—and there is no reason for thinking that the motives were anything but honest—yet, practically, Parliament and the land-owners were the same. A policy was adopted which would help the land-owners, without at first any intention of pressing hardly on the labourer, but without sufficient reflection as to what the effects would be; and when it was found that the labourer did suffer, the class interest of Parliament stood revealed, by the persistence with which penalty was added to penalty to support a policy that was an obvious failure. Parliament could not do over the realm what the craft gilds had done in their own crafts; the sphere was too wide; the law, ferocious as it became, was not sufficiently effective; the temptation to break it was too strong. The rise in prices continued in spite of all that legislation could do; and if prices rose, then the labourer could not work at the old wage. And further, there was an unrecognized cause at work raising prices. Since the French war there had been much gold and silver brought into the country, and the coinage, too, had been made of somewhat less weight. This increase in the quantity of money caused by itself a rise in prices, slow but steady, and thereby further helped to bring to nothing Parliament's regulation. The policy of the Statute of Labourers was indeed doomed to failure from the beginning, but the oppressiveness of it lay not in what it aimed at bringing about, but in the severity employed to enforce its futile provisions.

The plan of trying to put back the clock, to restore things to their old condition by legislation, having resulted in nothing but mutual exasperation, the land-owners had to think what should be the next step. Since labourers were scarce, expensive, and intractable, the best thing was to try to do without them, or at any rate to employ as few as possible. Two plans offered a prospect of success; sheep-farming, and letting the land on a new system, which is generally called the "stock-and-land" lease. Of sheep-farming it will be necessary to say more in a later chapter; we are only concerned here with the beginning of it. English wool-growing had always been profitable; the success with which Edward III. had fostered woollen manufactures in England offered an increased market; and sheep-farming required much less labour than arable farming. At this time to turn arable into pasture land seemed a satisfactory expedient. But in order to carry it out it was necessary to enclose large amounts of land, and enclosures led to troubles of their own. For the present these may be put aside, and the increase of sheep-farming at the expense of corn-growing noted as one of the main results of the Black Death.

The other plan met the difficulty in a different way. The lord who started sheep-farming continued to farm the land himself, or through his representatives, but only in a way which enabled him to do with much less labour than before. Letting land on lease meant that the land-owner shifted the burden of dealing with labour to an intermediary, his tenant. This tenant's position was a new one;

we have heard of tenants paying rents before, but, generally speaking, these were quit-rents, rents for some services which had been commuted, or signifying some sort of dependence. But to the new tenants their rent represented a payment for the advantages they were to gain from the use of the land; it was based on the land, not on services or dependence, and thus these tenants who took the new leases are the forerunners of the modern intermediary between landlord and labourer, namely, the farmer. But although the general character of the tenant who took a stock-and-land lease and the modern farmer is the same, there are wide differences. Nowadays a farmer has to stock his farm himself, all he gets from the landlord being the land and buildings. It is the farmer's business to find seed, stock, implements, and labour. But the tenant of 1349 found only the last. Labour was his concern, and the landlord was only too glad to be quit of the tiresome matter. But as the new tenants were generally poor and unable to stock the farm for themselves, the landlords provided everything needful to set the tenant up; in return the tenant paid a yearly rent on his "stock" (as well as his rent for the land), and at the end of his tenure was bound to restore to the lord an equivalent of what he had received, seed, corn, horses, sheep, cattle, implements either in actual stock or the value in money. Thus, in a lease of 1360, the tenant took 2 horses and 7 affri,[6] each valued at 10s., a bull at 10s., 10 cows, each at 11s., 4 oxen, each at 18s. 5d., 24 quarters of wheat at 6s. 8d. the quarter, and so on with

[6] Horses for the plough.

barley, peas, vetch, and oats; when he left the farm he would be bound to restore these, or an equivalent in stock or money. A curious arrangement was sometimes made under which the tenant was only bound to replace the stock if the mortality was moderate. In a lease it was provided that if a murrain came, and "if sheep die of disease in a year to the number of 29 or under, and ewes to the number of 16 or under", the farmer was to pay, but if the number rose above this limit the lord was to bear the loss. As the farm was stocked with 294 sheep and 160 ewes (valued respectively at 1*s.* 6*d.* and 1*s.* 3*d.* each) the farmer was liable if the rate did not exceed 10 per cent of the stock. But it must often have been risen above this, and losses of stock ran away with a good deal of the lord's profits. For example, in 1507, Magdalen College, Oxford, had to make allowance to their tenants, who held stock-and-land leases, for 607 sheep.

Stock-and-land leases were not indeed unknown before the Black Death, but the agricultural crisis which ensued from it gave a great impulse to their adoption, for they held out real advantages to both sides. Lords were enabled to let some of the land which they had lately been unable to farm for want of labour, and the tenants preferred terms which made them independent of the lord's bailiff, and allowed them to share the advantage of the rise in prices. The difficulty, insuperable to the lords, of getting labour did not affect the tenant so acutely; most of the labour required would be provided by himself and his family, and if he hired, he would hire at the new rate, without grumbling and looking back regretfully to the old days of lower wages, for he had never paid them. But the amount of hired labour employed by these tenants was at first small; they did most of the work which was needed themselves. The compromise was a happy one, for it enabled men to work for themselves with all the incentive to diligence which that brings. It was not that men were unwilling after the Black Death to work at all; they had been anxious to work, but they could not take the old wages with the new prices.

Unfortunately this plan, to which England owed the class of yeoman farmers who were for so long the backbone of the country, was not adopted sufficiently widely or speedily to be a complete remedy for the troubles of the time. It was a palliative, and no more. While some land-owners had sufficient foresight to adopt it, others, and apparently the larger part, were determined to fight the battle with the labourers to the bitter end. Having failed in their first policy of keeping down wages, they took another step backwards and tried to abolish wages. As we have seen, there had been a time when no hired labour had been used in agriculture at all, when all labourers had been serfs and estates had been cultivated by their services. To re-exact these services would not indeed re-people the depleted manors, but it would put a stop to the ruinous process of receiving dues now worth perhaps one-half of the labour they had represented originally. Not only did the extension of commutation cease, but wherever there was a doubt whether the tenant owed dues or service, service was exacted. How far tenants were disturbed who held land on which the services had been formally commuted is not clear. It was, of course, far more easy for the lords to prove servile tenure, than for tenants to show they were quit of one of its incidents. Documents were all in the keeping of the lords or their stewards, and the old services were registered in them. Where accounts showed commutation it was easy to argue that these were cases of occasional remission at the lord's will, and that he could resume his old rights if he pleased. Stewards were set busily to work to find omissions or informalities, which could be instanced to show that the villein had broken the agreement under which he claimed to be quit. The tenants were in fact at a disadvantage all round; they were uneducated, and had to oppose legal technicalities; their cases were tried in manorial courts, for the royal courts would not interfere between villein and lord. Even under so strong a king as Edward I., with all his desire to restrict manorial powers, this had been clear. In 1280 the abbot of Burton had evicted all his tenants because they had taken action against him in the royal courts. The judges declared the villeins "to be at the abbot's mercy on account of their false claim" of owing him no service, and eventually, in spite of obtaining a royal writ, the villeins were forced to submit and declare that they were serfs at the will of their lord. And behind the courts, with their prejudice against all villeins owing to the influence of Roman law, lay Parliament, and Parliament was the land-owners under another name. All this made it hopeless for the villeins to make good in law their claim to be exempt from service.

To drive a mass of men into an intolerable position, from which there is no escape but by violence, was no more wise on the part of the land-owners than their first attempt to disregard the effects of the Black Death by statute. Where services were exacted they were given grudgingly; we may be sure that the work done was of the smallest quantity and the poorest quality possible. But far worse than the economic wastefulness was the spirit of hatred that sprang up. Lord took a new name; he became oppressor. Discontent spread all over the country, muttering, threatening; the teaching of Wyclif's followers, and the preaching of John Ball, helped to undermine respect for authority. The country was further disorganized and upset by the return of soldiers who had served in France, and who, while acquiring a taste for an easy life without working, were ready enough to vapour about using arms. The immediate cause of the outbreak was the necessity of increased taxation to support the war. In the course of four years three poll-taxes were levied, the first (1377) at the rate of a groat a head, the second (1379) graduated from the £6, 13s. 4d., paid by the Duke of Lancaster, to the 4d. from the labourer; even so the tax was oppressively hard on the poor, but when in 1380 a fresh tax of three groats[7] was laid on every person in the kingdom over the age of fifteen, patience was exhausted, and the Peasant Revolt began.

The worst outbreak was in the home counties,

---

[7] A tax of 12s. or 15s. per head would represent about the same burden now; although no definite attempt was made to graduate the tax, the rich were expected to contribute more than their share to alleviate the burden on the poor.

where the peasants of Kent, Essex, and Hertfordshire all moved upon London; but the rioting was by no means confined to these; the Eastern counties, Yorkshire and Devonshire, were also affected. Proceedings were of the same character, the peasants demanding the abolition of villeinage and services, and land to rent at a reasonable rate. That the attack was mainly against the lords was shown by the burnings of manor houses, and especially of all muniment rooms, where lay the evidence of the hated serfdom; lords' mills were destroyed, for the serfs had been compelled to grind their corn there; some lawyers were hanged; the peasants had come to regard them as hand in glove with their oppressors. Although the number of rioters was not generally great, the resistance was at first feeble. A band of seventeen, detached from the main body of Suffolk rioters under John Wrawe, attacked Thetford, summoned the mayor and burgesses, and, by the terror of their leader's name, compelled them to ransom the town by a payment of forty marks in gold. A night attack of 400 men, led by the Abbot's carter, upon the Abbey of Benedict de Hulm, was beaten off by the monks, who rose from matins to repel the rioters, but many unpopular landowners and justices were murdered. John de Cavendish, flying from a hot pursuit, was brought up by a river; he called to a woman to ferry him across, but when she learned his name, she pushed off the boat from the land, and left him to the vengeance of his pursuers, who beheaded him. The townsmen of Cambridge looked on at the sack of Corpus Christi, where the beldam, Margaret Starre, as she flung to the winds the ashes of priceless documents cried: "Away with the learning of clerks, away with it!" Panic spread in the capital as the rioters approached, and Richard had to pacify the men of Essex by promises of emancipation and pardon. But the peasants ruined their own cause by their senseless violence. Perhaps they may have felt that the King's promises would not be kept, for, indeed these went beyond his power. Pardon he could grant, but he could not release them from their obligations to their lords; further, when called on to present their grievances, they could not formulate much that was definite, save a demand for land to be let at a reasonable rent, and as they followed this up by murdering the Archbishop of Canterbury, the Treasurer, and the official who had charge of the poll-tax, the bulk of the nation speedily saw that they must be put down. Thus supported, Richard was soon able to gain the upper hand. The rioters were treated with severity, Spenser, Bishop of Norwich, especially taking vigorous action with the rioters of the Eastern Counties. "The pious pastor therefore left London, and came, as he was bound, to succour his people. And first finding certain of this wicked mob at Cambridge, he slew some, imprisoned others, and others he sent back to their homes, after taking their oaths that they would never thenceforward turn out for a like purpose."[8] The King refused to admit the validity of his first concessions, and Parliament backed him up by declaring that all releases made during the revolt were to be cancelled, and

[8] E. Powell, *Rising in East Anglia*.

that those who complained about losses due to burnings of charters and deeds should be allowed to enforce their rights there recorded, just as if the charters still existed. It was made illegal for any who served at husbandry till the age of twelve to leave it for any other occupation, or for anyone to educate children of the poor so that they might escape serfdom by entering the Church.

Thus the Peasant Revolt was at the time unsuccessful. The labourers did not terrify the lords into granting freedom; their freedom was completed, not then, but gradually in the course of the next two centuries; and even so freedom came not through violence, but through the steady action of natural causes which made servile labour less valuable, so that in the end the lords yielded easily what had come to be not worth keeping. A certain picturesqueness attends the idea that after the Black Death, lords oppressed labourers till the latter arose in their might, and struck off the chain which bound them. But the facts are less simple and the results less decisive than this theory suggests, and the far-reaching consequences of the troubles of the time have to be traced, as we shall find them in the later history of England, before we can fairly estimate the outcome of the struggle of the fourteenth century.

CHAPTER VII.

LATER DEVELOPMENTS OF TOWNS AND GILDS.

The effects of the Black Death in the rural districts were so violent and so far-reaching as to deserve the epithet "revolutionary"; revolutionary, that is, in the policy pursued both by landlord and labourer, one striving by the aid of legislation to put things back and prevent all further change, the other struggling for an actual freedom of contract which was in the main quite new. Neither party, indeed, attained its object completely; territorial serfdom was not revived wholesale, nor, on the other hand, did it perish in the Peasant Revolt. From the shock of the conflict emerged a new antagonism between the rich and the poor, each thinking it saw in the other an enemy who unreasoningly desired its injury. But the quarrel did not develop on these lines; the hostility passed from its acute stage, and was gradually absorbed or diverted by the new methods of farming, leasing land or sheep-farming. But they in their turn were new, and profoundly changed the history of English agricultural life. It would be, of course, going absurdly too far to say that had it not been for the Black Death, England would never have had a mass of yeoman farmers or have become a great wool-growing country; the point is that these changes were made rapidly during the latter part of the fourteenth century, and continued through the fifteenth and sixteenth centuries, and it was the wide-spread destruction of the Black Death that set them agoing.

The Black Death was not one whit less destructive in the towns than in the country. Whether one reads of London, where Parliament was afraid to sit, or of Norwich, where the churchyards were so crowded that the level of the soil was raised, and even then corpses lay unburied, or of Colchester, where one of every three burgesses died, the tale of mortality is the same. Indeed, one is prepared to think the country more healthy, to regard towns as more exposed to pestilence through difficulties of sanitation in narrow streets and crowded dwellings, and this presumption of the greater unhealthiness of towns is fully justified by the continual outbreaks of plague or sweating sickness which were frequent in the fifteenth century. Thus in 1406, 1438, and in 1449 London was ravaged, in 1476 Hull became almost desolate owing to deaths and flight of the survivors, and in 1477 Norwich was again devastated, and these outbreaks seem to have been confined to the towns. But while in 1349 and 1350 town and country suffered alike, the consequences in the towns were in no sense momentous or revolutionary. There were indeed consequences. There are traces in the Statutes of Labourers that the dislocation of prices affected artisans, as it did labourers, but wages and prices in towns had always been fixed by gild and municipal regulation on the basis of what was actually reasonable; if what had happened was accepted in a reasonable way there was no need for any serious trouble to occur. The serious troubles in the country arose because the land-owners had not followed what was reasonable, but what was customary, and custom no longer applied when conditions were widely different. Beyond the temporary scarcity of food, the results in the towns came from outside—came, indeed, from the agricultural disturbances. To the labourers the towns offered attractions. If they were anxious to escape from taking the wages which were not enough to maintain them, their natural resource was to learn a handicraft in a town; were they unfree, then unclaimed residence in a borough for a year offered a chance of freedom. Hence there was a flow of labour from the country to the towns, a flow which brought troubles of its own, for the new-comers often were too poor to pay the entrance fees to the gilds, or tried to evade the gild regulations, and so excited the jealousy of the gildsmen. But this, though traceable in a way to the Black Death, was not a direct consequence of it; the direct consequences in the towns beyond the actual mortality were small.

Attention has already been called to the efforts made by Edward I. and Edward III. to treat England as an economic whole, by limiting local privileges, or in any case bringing them under royal control, or by allowing foreigners to come and go, buy and sell, as they pleased. This course of policy had not met with the general approval of English traders, but the King had forced them to give way, so that for the last twenty-five years of Edward III.'s reign aliens had enjoyed almost complete freedom. But this freedom, which would seem to the eyes of a modern free-trader to be abnormally enlightened for the fourteenth century, was premature, like the development of Parliament that marks this reign and that of the Lancastrian kings. Just as the interests of the Commons came to nothing among the struggles of the great baronial families, so the wants of the consumer passed unheard among the clamour which merchant and craftsman raised against the foreigner. In fact, with the death of Edward III. began a new period—a period of reaction, during which the towns recovered many of their old exclusive privileges. Richard II.'s policy was at first fluctuating. On the one hand, there was the tradition of his grandfather's days to influence him, while the land-owners, who were supreme in Parliament, did not dislike the aliens, and indeed believed that by encouraging them a better price could be got for English wool. On the other hand, the townsmen raised the cry that their bread was being taken from them by foreigners engaging in English trade, and they pointed with some force to the fact that while aliens in England could do much as they liked, English merchants in foreign countries had no such liberties to reside or engage in retail trade, but were strictly limited in their dealings. It might have been expected that the King would have sided with the land-owners, and had they taken a strong line it is probable that he would have done so. But with the growth of the English weaving industry more of the English wool was being worked up at home, and the wool-grower became less dependent on foreign buyers. Hence the land-owners were apathetic in the matter. The townsmen, especially in London, grew more and more determined. The King, residing in London, was bound to hear a great deal of the London view; and more than that, Richard II. borrowed largely from London merchants, and in order to get money was further disposed to do what the merchants wished. Accordingly, in 1392 Parliament enacted that, as London and other towns were much damaged by the statutes granting liberty to aliens, for the future no merchant stranger was to buy or sell to another alien, nor to engage in any retail trade, save in victuals, nor to export any spicery that had once been brought into the realm.

This was a triumph for the English merchant as against the alien, and it was an enduring triumph. Centuries were to pass before the alien regained the freedom he had enjoyed under Edward III. It is true that the townsmen would have wished prohibition to go further; they strove to prevent aliens not only from dealing with each other, or selling by retail, but even wholesale, except with those who were free of the town, and they wished further to drive the alien to go to "host", that is, to live with a burgess, so that a rigid watch might be kept on him. They were only partially successful in these aims. A statute of 1406 expressly permitted aliens to deal wholesale with any of the King's subjects. Yet popular opinion continued to be strongly opposed to alien trade, as was shown by the great riot against the Steelyard in 1493. Neither did aliens escape from vexatious tolls and imposts; complaint was made that 3*d.* had to be paid at Calais and 3*d.* more at Dover; 6*d.* for a bond pledging them to buy

English commodities to the value of the goods imported and a similar fee to the superintendent of packages, whose task it was to prevent fraud, and so on, mounting up in all to six or seven shillings on each pack. A statute of 1439 provided that all aliens were to report themselves, within three days of their arrival, to the proper authority, who was to assign them to "hosts". These were bound to send in a formal return to the Exchequer, and to keep a register of their lodger's transactions, receiving a percentage on the value of all merchandise bought and sold by him. Such a system of prohibition and espionage reflects the narrow view of the time.

Although the Government did not carry out to the full the wishes of the native merchants, and though the driving of aliens to "host" fell into disuse in the latter part of the fifteenth century, yet in one matter the exclusive policy triumphed: aliens were prevented from engaging in retail trade, or from trading with each other. This was indeed only one feature in the beginnings of a new commercial policy which it will be necessary to set out more fully hereafter. It meant in the main the restoration of the exclusive privileges of towns which had been partially lost, though the privileges were not quite on the same footing as before. It would be an exaggeration to say that in the earlier stage the gilds had done their work independent of the Crown, or with no more than a tacit consent on its part, while in the later stage they were very definitely under its rule; royal charters indeed had been the source of their authority from the beginning. But the difference is somewhat of this nature. As the power of Parliament increased, its sphere widened, and less and less was left to the initiative of the gilds. They carried out much regulation, even in their later days, but they did so at the command of Parliament; they were the agents through which it worked. And by degrees even this dwindled, and direct legislation came to play a more and more important part.

In attempting to sketch the condition and progress of the towns during the fifteenth century we encounter again the difficulty that has met us before. If we confine ourselves to generalizations, there is a danger that these will be only approximately true. The towns did not all pass through the same stages; nor even where the method of development was the same, did it go on at the same time. Each town, indeed, has its own history. But if we try to follow individual peculiarities, the main course of the movement is apt to be obscured and lost among a number of details. And therefore, inaccurate as generalization is liable to be, it is necessary to draw what general conclusions we can, illustrating them from what happened in London and one or two other of the large towns, being at the same time careful not to think that what is true of one town is necessarily true of another.

The main feature in town life during the thirteenth century had been the rise of merchant gilds, bodies which aimed at including the whole body of those who wished to trade in a town, and issuing regulations for trade and industries as a whole; in the fourteenth century the industries came under a set of more specialized bodies, the craft gilds, each of which, under the general control of the merchant gild or the town authorities, made rules for the members of its own craft. During the fourteenth century the merchant gilds declined in practical importance. The name survives, and here and there the powers, but as a general rule there is but a shadow. The breaking down of town exclusiveness, worked by Edward III., was indeed only for a time, yet when in Richard II.'s reign the towns recovered most of their privileges, the power did not return to the merchant gilds. It was either exercised by the mayor and the town officials, or it passed into the hands of richer members of the craft gilds. Thus it is to the later history of the craft gilds that attention must first be directed.

The spread of the gild system, whether we use the term gild, or craft, or mistery, or company, to denote the organization binding men of similar trades together, was, with one exception, general all over England. The one industry excepted is very important, for it is the woollen industry, which was by this time the first industry in the kingdom. To its peculiar development it will be necessary to recur.[1] But the rest may be taken together. Beginning in the association of workers at any particular craft in a town, bound together in a fellowship under subordination to the merchant gild, or the municipal authorities, these bodies at first did not aim at more than regulating their trade according to what was right in the ideas of the time. A sound article was to be provided at a fair price. Hence it

[1] See chapter viii.

was necessary that work should be supervised to guard against fraud, that persons learning the trade should serve an apprenticeship, that all who practised the industry should belong to the craft, and so forth. But as the merchant gild decayed, or the body of the craft gilds took its place, we have to notice new developments.

(1) The craft gilds became exclusive. In one sense indeed they had always been so, for they had always resented the competition of those who practised their industry without being in the gild. But while at first they had objected to outside competitors, they had not made it difficult for them to enter the gild. There was an entrance fee, but not an excessive or prohibitive one; and once in the gild the new member was in the same position as any one else free of the gild. But in the fifteenth century there is quite a different form of exclusiveness. Gilds not only put down outside competition, but they also hindered new members from entering. The craft was to be kept for members and sons of members. Entrance fees became heavier; the newcomer was to get sureties of men already in the craft; none might set up in the craft unless he was free of the city, or unless the wardens of the craft admitted him, or again unless he had been previously proved a good workman. In some cases the craft obtained letters patent excluding strangers, or, in other cases, the municipal authorities granted a similar privilege. In 1437 the tendency towards exclusiveness was so well marked as to call forth a statute against the "unlawful and unreasonable ordinances" made by masters, wardens, and people

of gilds, fraternities, and other companies " for their own singular profit and to the common hurt and damage of the people ". It was laid down that new ordinances were to be submitted to the justices of the peace, but as the Yorkists, relying largely on the towns and the trading classes, supported the gilds, Henry VI.'s statute came to little. Through the fifteenth and the following century the gilds displayed a selfish character, no longer making their regulations for what was fair and reasonable, but for what turned to their own advantage. Of course they did not admit this, indeed were often loud in the protestations that they were only looking to the public welfare, but their eyes were mainly on their own pockets in spite of their expressions of disinterestedness.

(2) Class differences became more marked. Originally, as we have seen, industry was but a supplement of agriculture; the rise of the craft gilds was a step forward, in that it implied the existence of a body of men who were artisans and nothing else, who made industry their means of livelihood. But the master craftsman, though distinct from the agricultural labourer, yet combined functions which we are now accustomed to see kept separate; he worked himself, and so far was an artisan, but he also sold his goods to the public, and so far was a retailer; he kept an apprentice or two, and so to a certain extent was an employer, and a capitalist, as he provided the shop, the tools, and the materials. Differentiation, indeed, was not complete, and in using terms such as manufacturer, tradesman, capitalist, employer, artisan, we are looking

with the eyes of the present, and describing in modern phrases what was only the germ of the modern distinctions with which we are familiar. None the less from Richard II.'s reign and onward during the fifteenth century there is a defining between class and class, and a hardening of social limits which mark the beginning of modern industrial conditions. Just as on the land there arose a new hostility between landlord and labourer, so in the craft gilds the position of the richer masters rises, and a class of poorer masters and journeymen and apprentices comes more clearly into view below. The gilds in London acquired an oligarchic character. The wearing of a special livery was not originally intended to be exclusive, but it became so. The liveries were expensive, and they were only required for show, to be worn at civic ceremonies; many of the poorer freemen neglected to obtain them; but then as they did not possess liveries, they could not be present on formal occasions when business was transacted, and so the government of the gild fell to the richer "liverymen". Thus, in 1493, of the Drapers' Company in London, only 114 out of 229 were "of the craft in the clothing".[2] Where this was the case, power of election and government fell to the "liverymen", who were the aristocracy of the gild. Somewhat similar were the Courts of Assistants, who were chosen from the liverymen, and managed the affairs of the brotherhood.

While thus a division was opening among the master craftsmen themselves, the position of ap-

---

[2] Ashley, *Ec. Hist.* vol. i. part ii. p. 131.

prentices and journeymen was being more rigorously defined. Practice became more uniform; apprenticeship was enforced, in London for seven years, though other periods are not unknown; apprentices were not to be taken unless their parents were in a position to spend twenty shillings the year, nor were any to be taken who were not free.[3] Further, the number was to be limited. At first it had been laid down that no master might take more than he could maintain. Apprentices being rarely paid anything till the last year or so of their indentures, there was a temptation to take a good many; accordingly, to avert the danger that the trade might be overstocked, the liberty of engaging apprentices was restricted. The slaters at Newcastle only allowed a second apprentice when the first was in the last year of his indentures; a more common rule was to provide that two or three journeymen[4] were to be kept for each apprentice. But not content with restricting the admission of apprentices, the masters placed further difficulties in the way of those who were admitted. At first an apprentice who had served his indentures had looked forward to becoming in due course a master-craftsman, if not immediately, in any case after a few years as a journeyman; but now the masters tried to keep the full freedom of the craft to those born in the gild, and to prevent the journeyman from setting up for himself. Journeymen were to remain journeymen, and work for wages under the

[3] This was aimed at those who were coming to the towns to escape manorial control.
[4] An apprentice who had served his indentures and had not become a master, was called a journeyman. He worked under a master for wages.

masters. This caused much discontent. In some cases the journeymen formed gilds of their own, which were disliked by the master-craftsmen, and tried to obtain leave to become masters, or in any case to get better wages. There is not evidence that these "Yeomen's Gilds", as they are sometimes called, were common, or that they were able to do much for their members, but their existence is evidence of a new line of separation between master and workmen; they were, as trades-unions are, workmen's associations, and in their efforts to get better terms from the masters, and act as friendly societies for their members, they followed the same lines.

(3) There grew up powerful associations of dealers or merchants, as distinct from craftsmen or handworkers. In the time of Edward III. the Grocers Company in London had attained great powers, having sixteen of its members aldermen of the city. But it is only a type of other great associations, or merchant companies as they are generally called. Eventually a distinction[5] emerged between the twelve "greater" companies from whom alone the mayor could be chosen, and the remainder, some fifty or so, who formed the lesser companies. Of these twelve, three were employed in foreign trade, six were dealers in home productions, one engaged in import trade, and only two are truly industrial, these being the cloth-workers, the chief industry of the time, and the goldsmiths, who, working in valuable material, handled more wealth than other

---

[5] The distinction is clear in the sixteenth century. But it no doubt existed earlier.

craftsmen. The mercantile character of these companies is clear. They are, in the main, dealers and not artisans. It is sometimes said that this separation was due to the growth of the idea that working with the hands at a craft was derogatory to the dignity of members of these companies, but there is no very clear evidence of it. On the other hand, the position of a man who was both an artisan and a dealer was difficult to regulate. He may have been tempted to take advantage of his position to undersell others, either contenting himself with less than the ordinary profits, or rewarding himself with less than the usual rate of wage. We shall find the small masters who worked themselves doing this in the time of the Industrial Revolution[6] with disastrous results; and it may have been that gildsmen of the fifteenth century suffered under similar "cutting" of wages and profits, and wished to check it. But whatever the motive that led to the distinction, these companies are distinct from craft gilds; it is true that they were associations of men under common rules, as were the craft gilds, but they were not on a level with the crafts; their members did not combine the business of production and distribution as the craftsmen had done. On the contrary, they dealt in goods that others had made; they were wealthy merchants, far removed in status from the ranks of the poorer craftsmen and gild brethren. It should be remembered that this line of difference is most marked in London. But somewhat the same process took place in many of the other towns, and by the end

[6] See p. 318.

of the fifteenth century the separation between producer and dealer was fairly definite.

This growing spirit of exclusiveness and class definition pressed hardly upon those who wished to leave agriculture and take to handicraft. Even to become an apprentice was not easy; it was forbidden by law to the villein and impossible for the very poor. When once apprenticed, the new-comer had seven lean years to pass through, while the position of a journeyman at the end of it was not a great prize. Hence there grew up a tendency which becomes strongly marked in the sixteenth century, to solve all difficulties by setting up outside the towns, where gild and municipal regulations did not exist, and where a craftsman might work unhampered. There is evidence both in statutes and in the rise of such towns as Manchester, Birmingham, and Sheffield, which, while still under manorial government, became centres of the textile, hardware, and cutlery trades, that many persons were working in hamlets and thorpes scattered over the country in order to escape the control of the gilds. Wherever there was a movement of this kind it is certain that the older corporate towns must have suffered. They were injured by the competition of the outsiders, and by the loss of journeymen who preferred to migrate and set up for themselves, and further by the increased share of taxation which fell on the diminished number who remained. It is probable that the greater security which came with Henry VII. encouraged the migration; while England was disturbed by the Wars of the Roses, men might well prefer the protection of town walls, but when the disturbances were passed they would be readier to dwell outside. In any case the end of the fifteenth century and the first part of the sixteenth century are marked by repeated complaints of decay in the older towns. Many were declared to be partly ruinous, others so poor that they could not pay their assessment to the King. Thus in 1487 York paid £18, 5s. instead of £160, while £12,000 was remitted to the towns in 1496. But although there may have been a decay of some of the corporate towns, this did not imply a decay of industry or town activity over the kingdom as a whole. There was a migration of industry. Some towns declined, but others sprang up in their places: those who suffered would naturally complain to Parliament to be released from their burdens, while those that were prosperous would be interested in preserving a judicious silence. And, finally, the evidence of the growing wealth and importance of the merchant class is enough to show that the decline was not general over the country.

To complete this sketch of the later history of the gilds something must be said of the way in which they were affected by the confiscation of the property of religious bodies which went on under Henry VIII. and Edward VI. The religious side of the gilds has not so far come into much prominence, but most of them had this side to their activities, and indeed, with some, religious and social duties had formed the nucleus round which the other powers had gathered. Pageants and processions on certain saints' days, and formal attendance at worship, were part of most medieval associations, and more common still were alms and charities and prayers and masses for the souls of dead brethren. These were generally paid for by a bequest to the gild from the dead man or his family. In this way the gilds came to be holders of a good deal of land and property devoted to religious or charitable purposes. When, after the dissolution of the monasteries, Henry VIII.'s attention was turned to the chantries, charities, and fraternities, and he determined to look into the way their property was held and used, the gilds, in their religious side at any rate, fell into the same class. In 1545 Henry VIII. empowered commissioners to seize such property according as the King should appoint. Two years later a fresh act, this time alleging that masses for the dead led the people into superstition, repeated the act of 1545; it forfeited the property of the chantries, but provided that where a fraternity held property partly for religious and partly for other purposes, only that part which was devoted to religious purposes was to go to the King, while the remainder was to be left untouched. The gilds were, of course, included among these fraternities. Had the confiscation been carried out strictly in accordance with the letter of the law, no great harm would have befallen them; they would have lost but the part of their property held in trust for religious purposes. But there is good reason for thinking that the line of distinction drawn by the Government was not followed, that a very wide view of property devoted to religious purposes was taken, and a great deal confiscated which should legally have been spared. The measure may not have been intended to reduce the gilds to impotence, but none the less such was the practical effect of it.

At a time when from either mistaken actions of their own, or the progress of events which were rendering them less useful, the gilds were beginning to decline in power, the confiscation of even a part of their revenue must have done something to help their decline. One bond of union among their members was removed; they were robbed of some stateliness and some sentimental power over men's minds. The blow was a severe one, but it was not immediately fatal; in town records, in statutes, in the subsidy acts which enumerated taxable property, the gilds are mentioned after 1545 as before it. But they were growing less and less important; and though there is a temporary revival of similar institutions at the close of the sixteenth and during the seventeenth century, they were overshadowed by the royal power, their rules superseded by the authority of Parliament, and their ideas put into the background by the national developments which marked the end of the sixteenth century. They were on the way to becoming what they are now, picturesque survivals of an older time, adding dignity to their cities, remarkable for benevolence and not infrequently for conviviality, but no longer arbiters of trade or centres of independent authority.

CHAPTER VIII.

ENCLOSURES FOR SHEEP-FARMING AND THE PROGRESS OF THE WOOLLEN INDUSTRY.

The change in agricultural conditions caused by the Black Death had set landlord and labourer at enmity. The landlords had recklessly set out on a policy which was from the beginning hopeless; they had tried to make old arrangements fit new conditions. When this policy broke down, when it was realized that enough labour could not be obtained at the old rates, and that no statutes, however severe, could alter the facts of the case, landlords began to try something new. One new plan, that of letting land on stock-and-land leases, has been already described; but the leaseholders could not afford to pay high rents; bad debts and the cost of repairs and renewing stock ran away with much of the profit there was; and further, it was often difficult to find tenants even on the easiest terms. If, however, the land could be farmed on a different plan, a plan in which less labour was required, the difficulty would be at an end. When it was perceived that this could be done by substituting pasture for tillage, and keeping large flocks of sheep which could conveniently be tended by a few shepherds, it was only natural that sheep-farming should spread rapidly. It was doubly profitable; it enabled the landlord to do without the cultivator who was so hard to get, who, if he was a villein, required constant watch to prevent his escape, or if free, demanded wages which seemed exorbitantly high; while, secondly, the increased demand for English wool, caused by the growing prosperity of the native cloth manufacture, raised the price, and rendered sheep-farming more profitable than agriculture even under favourable conditions.

Before sheep-farming could be practised on a large scale, it was found necessary to enclose. The old open-field system of husbandry had left England almost hedgeless. The meadow land in hay time, and the corn-fields when the crops were standing, had indeed to be fenced to keep out the cattle; but the fences were not of a permanent character, and, moreover, they did not divide off one man's land from another; they separated land in crop from land lying fallow, or land not cultivated at all. Within the enclosure, such as it was, the land might belong to one or to many owners; to the lord if it was on the demesne, to the lord's tenants if it was land in villeinage, or even to both lord and villeins where the demesne land was mixed with the villagers' strips. Such a state of things was clearly incompatible with sheep-farming.[1] When a man's land was marked off from that of his neighbour, it would be simple for him to do what he pleased with it. But so long as land remained unenclosed, any departure from the old routine was impossible, unless everyone agreed to it.

In speaking of the enclosures of the latter half of the fifteenth and the whole of the sixteenth century,

---

[1] Enclosing is more obviously requisite when the land belonged to more than one owner and was not depopulated, than where it was all in one hand. But it was found to be profitable in all cases.

it is necessary to guard against confusion. Many different kinds of land were enclosed, and when land was enclosed it was not always enclosed for sheep-farming. In some cases where the open fields were broken up, the old tenant received an equivalent of his scattered thirty acres in contiguous land concentrated in a few fields. He could farm this as he pleased, and as we shall see later, the result of such enclosure was uniformly good. But enclosure for sheep-farming, properly speaking, was the work of lords who wished to turn their arable land into wide tracts on which sheep could be kept in large numbers. It was this process of depopulation that, coming as an after-effect of the Black Death, again caused great suffering among the rural population, and called forth much legislation from Parliament.

Fixing our attention then on enclosure for the purpose of sheep-farming only, it is clear that the results differed according to the kind of land that was enclosed. We may distinguish three main classes: (1) Demesne land, and land held in freehold; (2) common or waste land (the "commons" of our own day); and (3) the land cultivated by villeins or customary tenants.

The case of demesne land is the simplest. If the demesne land was not intermixed with the common fields of the tenants, as appears to have been sometimes the case, the process of change from arable to pasture farming on the demesne could be carried out without disturbing any existing rights. No one suffered damage in the eye of the law by the owner of land doing what he pleased with his own.

But although no legal injury was done, yet great hardship might follow. The lord was encouraged to take to sheep-farming because of the dearness and scarcity of labour. But the labourers looked on it from quite another point of view. They had been accustomed to work on the demesne for wages, in some cases all the year round, in others during the busy seasons of hay-making, harvest, and sowing; but in any case the wages they obtained were a great help towards their livelihood. When the demesne became a sheep-run, the saving in labour which gave so much satisfaction to the lord meant the pinch of poverty to the labourer. A few might get work as shepherds, but the majority lost their occupation. And further, lords were less inclined to live in their country houses. While there was much produce, it was more convenient for them to live in their manor-houses, at any rate for a part of the year, to come to the produce and devour it, rather than have the produce sent to them. But when sheep-farming took the place of arable farming, the lord lived away and spent his money at court, the household was reduced, and the manor-house shut up. This again meant the loss of employment. It is little wonder that one of the most repeated complaints against sheep-farming is of the decay of "good and substantial houses". Somewhat the same process went on recently in the Highlands, where crofters were ejected, and an outcry was raised against the policy which fostered "instead of men, the grey-faced sheep".

But enclosure was not confined to demesnes. The waste land of the manor, used since time out of mind for pasturing sheep and cattle alike of lord and tenant, seemed intended by nature for sheep-farming, and it was greedily enclosed. This, however, was on different footing to the enclosing of demesne land. The privilege of grazing over commons was shared by the lord with the tenants of the demesne. By the Statute of Merton (1235) the lord was empowered "to make his profit" of the waste and pasture, so long as the tenants had sufficient pasture left them. Though this refers only to free tenants, yet it was a general idea that all tenants in demesne had a claim to some pasture and the use of the waste for cutting turf and gathering wood for fuel. While the lord mainly depended on arable farming, the waste was ample pasture for such cattle, sheep, and pigs as he had, as well as for those of the villagers and small tenants. But when the lord turned sheep-farmer, his temptation was to take a very narrow view of what was enough for the villagers, who, in turn, finding themselves stinted in pasture and hay, complained bitterly of the new methods. In some cases they had more serious grounds for thinking themselves hardly used when the lords took the whole of the waste for their own; the remedy at law was too difficult and too expensive to be of much use to the injured tenants, many of whom would in despair leave their tenements altogether.

The case of Stretton Baskerville in Warwickshire aptly illustrates the process of depopulation. "Thomas Twyford having begun the depopulation thereof in 4 Henry VII., decaying four messuages and three cottages", and later in the reign of

Henry VII. the estate passed into the hands of Henry Smith, "which Henry . . . enclosed 640 acres of land more whereby twelve messuages and four cottages fell to ruine and 80 persons there inhabiting, being employed about tillage and husbandry were constrained to depart thence and live miserably."[2]

It is possible that the land enclosed in this case was not common waste, but common field. It was the common fields, the lands cultivated by the customary tenants, that offered the strongest temptation, and that when enclosed caused the deepest misery. The hostility between lord and tenant which dated from the Statute of Labourers, and had manifested itself in the Peasant Revolt, lasted long. The acute stage of the struggle had not led to a complete victory for either party. The lords had not forced the labourers back to the old wage or to the old service; the labourers had not gained the complete freedom they desired. Many still held land on terms of commuted service, which had once been adequate, but which, owing to the rise in prices, were so no longer. Great was the inducement to the lords to make an end of unwilling services or inadequate payments in lieu of service, to get rid of all the customary tenants, and turn the common fields into pasture.

This, of course, might be done either oppressively or fairly. The ousted tenants might be given small holdings of land instead of the scattered acres, while the lord would only take such land as had escheated to him through failure of heirs, or

[2] Dugdale's *Antiquities of Warwickshire*.

land really belonging to the demesne, though scattered among the strips of the tenants. But in this case he would gain little, and if he was oppressive he would gain much. The temptation was the stronger because, in the fifteenth century at any rate, it was not clear that the ousted tenants would be helped by the law. At first after the Black Death the lords had had no wish to get rid of their tenants; their struggle had been to keep them; but when the desire to evict came, the law was in favour of the lords. Even so late as 1530 the question as to whether the villein had any rights was unsettled, though by that time the continued evictions had raised a strong popular sentiment in favour of the tenants. Although in Elizabeth's reign when enclosures of common fields took place, it was often done with the consent of all the landholders, and the land redistributed among all, not seized by one, yet in the earlier stages of the movement, from 1470 to 1550, the general course of events shows that the customary tenants were evicted. The Commission of 1517 records wholesale depopulation, the houses lying waste, and the inhabitants departed, even the churches falling into ruin, by reason of the break-up of the villages and the spread of sheep-farming. Even without having recourse to wholesale depopulation, it was easy for a lord in many cases to get rid of his tenants. Often they held for a life, and a new grant could be refused; or when the term was for three lives, it was possible to demand so large a fine from the next tenant that he could not pay it, in which case the land escheated to the lord.

Where tenants still clung to their fields, the loss of rights of pasture, owing to the enclosure of the wastes, so pinched them that they had little interest or hope in remaining. And so far as the enclosing of open fields went, it was a case of all or none; one or two men could not retain their scattered acres when the rest had departed.

It would be natural to expect with such an increase in pasture at the expense of arable land, that there would be a scarcity of corn and complaint of rise in price. That this was not markedly so may be attributed to two causes. First, the enclosures for sheep-farming were not universal over England. Suffolk, Essex, Hertford, and Kent were mainly enclosed, as was Worcester in the west, and there was some enclosure in Shropshire, Leicestershire, Northamptonshire, and Norfolk; but York, Derby, and Lincolnshire were not affected, nor were the group of counties in the West and Midlands, Hereford, Gloucester, Oxford, Berkshire, Buckinghamshire, Bedfordshire. This left a considerable corn-growing area. And, secondly, where there was enclosure but not depopulation, where tenants got a concentrated holding instead of scattered strips, the farming was better, and a greater quantity of corn was raised. A man could do as he pleased with his land instead of being bound to the common rotation; when he used any of his fields for grazing they were improved by the manure of his cattle; the hedges would protect weakly beasts; above all, what he had was his own, and there was no fear that the lord's large flocks would eat up all the pasture. "Several" was thought so superior to "Champion"[3] for arable purposes that Fitzherbert in his *Boke of Surveying*, written in 1539, says that a township worth 20 marks a year under the old plan would be made worth £20 when divided into "several".

Owing, perhaps, to these causes, the enclosures for sheep-farming did not produce a grave falling-off in the supply of corn, yet none the less they had disastrous consequences. Numbers of small tenants lost their land and suffered all the miseries attendant on finding fresh employment. Some went to the towns, where they helped to swell the numbers of poor men who struggled against the exclusiveness of the gilds in order to get a living. Others became beggars, dependent on charity; more will have to be said of these hereafter. Discontent spread widely through the land. Ket's rebellion in Norfolk was mainly directed against the enclosures of commons. Nor was the Government blind to the evils that were going on, although it interfered not so much on grounds of sympathy as with the idea that the decay of the rural population meant a national danger. More's *Utopia* denounces the sheep-farmers as "covetous and insatiable cormorantes" by whose action honest folks were ruined. In 1489 Parliament attempted to check enclosures in the Isle of Wight; in 1514 a proclamation forbade the holding of more farms than one, and ordered the restoration of houses decayed since the beginning of the reign; but the legislation was not apparently

---

[3] "Several" is separate or enclosed land, "Champion" or champaigne is open field.

successful, for in 1534 a fresh statute complains of the engrossing of land for pasture whereby "a marvellous number of the people of the realm be not able to provide for themselves, their wives and children, but be so discouraged with misery and poverty, that they fall daily to thefts and robbery, or pitifully die for hunger or cold", and goes on to enact that no one should keep more than two thousand sheep. Two years later, the King was to take one-half of land on which houses of husbandry had recently decayed, until the owners restored these houses. When the monasteries were broken up, the new owners were bound to keep up good and continual houses, and to plough as much land as of old in the demesnes. These statutes are severe enough, and no doubt they did something, for when at the end of the sixteenth century they were removed, it was speedily found advisable to reimpose them. But they were less effective than might have been expected. The justices of the peace, who had to enforce them, were often the persons most interested in ignoring them. If a field had one furrow drawn across it, it was held to be ploughed; 2000 sheep might be all a farmer had, but if his children had another 1000 apiece the law was not broken. Evasion, in fact, was easy, and, on the whole, Parliament failed. For a hundred and fifty years the enclosures went on.[4]

[4] Contemporary opinion about the effects of sheep-farming is illustrated by the twentieth epigram in the Fourth Book of *Chrestoleros*, by Thomas Bastard, printed in 1598:—

"Sheep have eat up our meadows and our downes
Our corn, our wood, whole villages and townes

When they slackened at the end of the sixteenth century it was not because sheep-farmers had become convinced that enclosing was unjust, but because it was no longer as profitable as it had been.

In reviewing the long chain of events that the Black Death drew after it, it is not a little curious to note that the same party, the landlords, who at first strove so obstinately to hold their tenants in serfdom on their estates, themselves ended by driving them off whether they wished to go or no. Enclosures and the evictions which came with them put an end to the manorial system, and with it to payment of service and serfdom. The whole plan had passed out of date; there were serfs on royal demesne in Elizabeth's reign, but she ordered them to be set free. Without any change in the law serfdom gradually ceased to exist, not directly owing to any revolt in popular feeling against it, but because under the new conditions of rural economy the serf was not needed. By the end of the sixteenth century the institution was extinct.

The time of the enclosures, like all times of rapid displacement of labour, implied much distress, but this distress was mitigated by the ease with which the labourers, whose land had been taken from them, found occupation in the woollen industries. From the reign of Edward III. the progress of these

> Yea, they have eat up many wealthy men
> Besides widowes and orphan childeren
> Besides our statutes and our iron lawes
> Which they have swallowed doun into their maws
> Till now I thought the proverb did but jeste
> Which said a black sheep was a biting beast".

had been rapid. Not only did the trade increase in volume, but it increased on a new system. We have seen the exclusiveness of the gilds, and the dislike which they showed to new-comers into their trades. But the weavers were the first to break free from the control of gilds, and a new system grew up. Under this there were still small masters who worked at home, took apprentices, and employed a journeyman or two, but these were no longer members of a gild; they did not work under gild regulations or sell at gild prices. In fact, they no longer sold to the public at all, but to a middleman, a clothier, who put out the wool to be broken and combed, received it again, and sent it on to the carders and spinners, receiving the yarn from them, passing it on to the weaver, and then to the fuller and dyer in turn. Thus the clothier was the central figure of the new system; he employed combers, carders, spinners, weavers, fullers, dyers, and paid them for their work; the product was his, and he undertook the task of selling the finished goods; on him fell the risks of the market. The artisans had no longer to judge what they would make, nor had they to trouble to find a market for their wares; but they worked at what the clothier sent them, and were paid by the piece at a regular rate which would be common over the district.

Under this more complete organization, which became general from 1450 onwards in East Anglia and the west of England, spreading from these districts over the rest of the kingdom, the woollen industry developed fast, and new varieties of cloth were made: rayed or coloured cloths round Bristol, cogware in Kendal, frieze at Coventry, Guildford cloths in Surrey. More striking than the new varieties was the increase in export of cloth. In 1307 the Hansards had paid duty on but six cloths, and they were then the principal exporters. By 1422 they exported 4464 cloths, and in 1500 21,389, though by that time they were no longer the chief dealers in cloth. The total export of cloths, believed in 1354 to be less than 5000 pieces, had risen by 1509 to 80,000 pieces, and by 1547 to 120,000 pieces. And as the export of cloth increased, the export of wool diminished; £68,000 was the yield of the wool duty in Edward III.'s reign, but by 1448 it was but £12,000. It is clear that the wool was mainly made up at home. The same progress is revealed by the growth of the Drapers' Company, dealers in cloth only; its first charter is dated 1364, and it soon rose to great power, having a monopoly of the retail trade in London, and a control over all drapers, who were bound to bring their goods to the Drapers' Hall, where all sales were to take place. The new vigour of English woollen industry called into existence another powerful corporate body, the Merchants Adventurers, native merchants who exported English cloth to the Continent. These at first traded to Bruges, but afterwards were driven by the jealousy of the Flemish cloth makers to Antwerp. When the alliance between England and Burgundy broke down in 1434, the import of English cloths into Flanders was forbidden altogether. In revenge England prohibited English wool going to Flanders, and as England was the chief wool-growing country, the Flemish trade was much injured. When by the "Great Intercourse" in 1496 Henry VII. gained leave to send English cloths again to Flanders, the Flemish trade began that course of decay, which was hastened by Alva, and ended by leaving England without a rival.

The increase in the cloth manufacture was on the whole regarded with favour by the Government. The restrictive regulations which attempted to lay down that all cloths should be of the same size were gradually relaxed. Exceptions were first made in favour of new varieties; then, as these increased in number, Parliament[5] provided that they should be "duly and perfectly made according to the nature and making of every one of said cloths"; and finally, in Edward VI.'s reign, by the advice of clothiers, drapers, and others engaged in the cloth trade who were called as witnesses before the Commons, rules were drawn up for twenty-three different kinds of cloth, based upon local customs, and allowing a good deal of latitude in the sizes prescribed. The Government was here going on the old lines of preventing the trade being injured by fraudulent or faulty work. More direct encouragement was given in 1463 by stopping the import of woollen cloths from abroad, and by making the export duty on cloth low, and that upon wool very high. And from the first a check was placed upon the gild exclusiveness, which wished to keep the new cloth trade as a monopoly for the Drapers' Company. In 1405 it was laid down that sellers of cloth, like other merchants, might sell wholesale to any of the King's subjects.

[5] In 1483.

With one new development of the woollen industry the Government did interfere, and that was the tendency to collect weavers in what we should now call factories. The classic example of an employer of this kind is John Winchcombe, "Jack of Newbury", who is said to have had a hundred looms at work in his own house. Whether this is true or not, the Winchcombe goods were well known on the Continent, the English envoy at Antwerp advising Somerset in 1549 to send a thousand of Winchcombe kersies in payment of a loan. Stump, another rich clothier, bought Malmesbury Abbey from Henry VIII., and fitted part of it up with looms, while a clothing mill was set up about the same time in Cirencester. But this development of large workshops under capitalist industry was checked by the Weavers' Act of 1555, which, on the complaint of the weavers that they were oppressed by the rich clothiers, prevented clothiers dwelling outside cities or corporate towns from keeping more than one loom in their houses, or profiting by letting looms. Country weavers might have two looms in their houses and no more, nor might they employ more than two apprentices. Under this enactment it was no longer possible to collect weavers in numbers under one roof, and the industry remained in the domestic stage.

Thus by its various branches and new developments the woollen industry was able to absorb much of the labour turned away by the conversion of arable land into pasture; many of the dispossessed tenants became weavers, fullers, dyers, and drew their whole sustenance from manufacture. In other cases the loom came in as an aid to farming; it gave employment when through stormy weather, or in the long winter evenings, the labourer could not work outdoors. But still more valuable than weaving as a subsidiary or by-industry was spinning; a weaver could use up yarn faster than a spinner could spin it, and spinning could be easily done by the women of the household, who thus were able to bring in a good deal of money. Though in this way some remedy was found for the misery caused by the increased demand for wool and the consequent enclosures, it is well to remember that it was not the English demand for wool that gave the first impulse to enclosures. The impulse came from the new conditions, higher prices which brought higher wages, which made grazing more profitable than arable farming, even before the English demand had become large. It happened that England took to making up the wool herself; the labourers displaced by the sheep found a fresh occupation in working up the wool. But it might not have been so; the woollen industry might have expanded in its old home in Flanders instead of in England. In this case the demand for English wool would have been as great, the temptation to enclose the same, but the effect would have been widely different. Those who were dispossessed would have found no new occupation offering them means of gaining a living. Starvation would indeed have stared them in the face. Great as was the injury and the discontent caused by the enclosures, it would have been immeasurably greater if the wool had been exported instead of giving employment at home; and we may say that whatever Parliament did to encourage the home industry by stopping the import of foreign cloths, and laying high duties on the export of wool, was wisely done. If we describe the policy as " protective " we use an epithet which is now often held to imply economic condemnation, but it is difficult to say that it is blamable in this case on any grounds; indeed it is just one of those occasions where a protective policy seems to have been admirably suited to the needs of the time.

CHAPTER IX.

THE MERCANTILE SYSTEM—THE POLICY OF POWER.

If we compare the policy of England in respect of trade as it is now with what it was in the days of the Tudors, we become aware at once of a great difference. Now, trade is "free"; that is to say the Government no longer considers the regulation of trade, as a whole, to be within its province. Trade, save in some respects, goes unregulated; where it is interfered with and limited, it is in order to raise a revenue by indirect taxation, or else the interference is justified on moral grounds; it is held right to insist on proper precautions in what are called dangerous trades; checks are placed upon adulteration, and control is kept over certain things, like alcoholic liquors, because it is believed that freedom of trade in them would not be to the advantage of the community. But beyond this, Government does not go. It does not concern itself with what a merchant buys or sells, whether he exports raw material or finished goods, whether he employs English or foreign ships to carry his goods, or how he pays for his purchases. An employer may make what he pleases, where he pleases. These are all questions for the individual. But in the times of the Tudors this was not so. Government took a very active part in the regulation of trade; it interfered continually with what was bought and sold, exported or imported, and this with a very distinct object. It held that some trades were good, and others bad; and accordingly it set itself to foster the good trades and put a stop to what it regarded as the bad ones. As the Government makes no such classification nowadays, and as the individual's view of good or bad trades is based on whether they are more or less profitable to himself, it is necessary to see more fully on what grounds the old distinction rested.

Put shortly, the difference is this. In the sixteenth century the Government considered the nation as a whole, and aimed at making it strong, even if this was done at the expense of the individual; while nowadays we are content that there should be plenty, and the individual is allowed to go his own way, even if by doing so he may weaken the power of the realm. An example may bring out the difference more clearly. A merchant may now ship his goods in either English or foreign ships as he pleases, and no restriction is placed on him. If foreign ships were excluded from bringing goods to England, or carrying English goods, there would be a danger that the cost of carriage would be greater, owing to English shippers being freed from competition; the object here is "plenty". But a Tudor statesman took quite another view. To employ foreign vessels was to help the foreigner at the expense of the Englishman, and worse than that, it was to weaken England in a department where it was most essential for her safety that she should be strong. That the merchant and the consumer might suffer by the exclusion of foreign ships was possible, but felt to be unimportant. No sane man would ever weigh the trivial loss or gain of an individual against the power of the nation as a whole. And hence the Navigation Acts, which forbade foreign ships from carrying English goods or bringing to England anything but the raw produce of their own countries.

This idea of national power was what influenced the Government throughout the sixteenth and seventeenth centuries, and it is the set of measures by which this national power was to be fostered and maintained which is called the Mercantile system. The measures employed were not always the same; they varied with considerations of policy, and the views of the age, but for two centuries the dominant idea never varied. The aim was so to regulate trade that England should be strong.

As is often the case with policies which take a deep hold upon a nation, the growth of the Policy of Power was slow, and when decay began, the process of decay was slow also. Roughly speaking, the sixteenth and seventeenth centuries were the heyday of the Mercantile system, when all commercial questions were decided on the lines of national power, and individual interest was hardly taken into consideration at all. The eighteenth century saw the Mercantile system decaying; the idea of national power was no longer dominant; instead there was a policy of protecting the native farmer and the native artisan against outside competition. This, it is true, was part of the Mercantile system, but it was not the whole of it. The protection was piecemeal compared to the broad principle formerly followed, and the whole policy dwindled away till its final overthrow in the nineteenth century. And just as there was a long period of decay, there had been through the fifteenth century a long period of consolidation, when the policy was taking shape, when experiments were being tried, when one measure was being added to another, all tending in the same direction, though the central idea of national power was not expressed, nor clearly grasped. An examination of the chief measures of the Mercantile system, and of the times when they were first enforced, will show how gradual the growth actually was.

The aims of the Mercantile system have been classified under four main heads: (1) the policy of encouraging native shipping by Navigation Acts, in order that the realm might have plenty of ships and sailors from which an efficient navy could be formed; (2) the policy of protecting and helping the native corn growers, in order that England should be independent of food from outside, and should always be able to feed the population from her own land; (3) the policy of protecting home industries, and planting new ones to give employment to native artisans; and finally (4) the policy of amassing and keeping in the country a large amount of money. Of these the last is the most important, for in a sense it embraces the others, which were so managed that they might help in the task of making England strong by providing plenty of money. Measures with these objects were all in force under the Tudors. Most of them were, in their origin, older. But in looking back to find these origins, it will not be necessary to look back beyond the days of Richard II. Edward III. was, as we have seen, in a sense a free-trader; his object was plenty, and he did not regard power. He may have thought that with plenty and prosperity, power would follow; but he certainly did not directly aim at the power of the realm, or he would not have moved the wool staple into England, thereby throwing the carrying trade deliberately into the hands of foreigners. Richard II., however, was much in the hands of the mercantile class; the recovery of town privileges against the alien that marked his reign has already been detailed,[1] and the overthrow of the Edwardian tradition in this one respect was soon followed by its downfall in others.

First as to the policy of encouraging English shipping. The familiar example of a Navigation Act is that of 1651, repeated and made more severe in 1660. But save that this act was an intentional blow at our commercial rivals, the Dutch, and drawn with exceptional rigidity to exclude them

[1] See Chap. VII.

from any share in our colonial trade, it involved no new principle. The same idea of preventing the exportation of English goods, or the importation of goods into England, except in English ships, was enforced under Charles I., who complained about its non-observance in the Baltic trade; under James I., who inquired into the working of the laws; under Elizabeth, who, though somewhat less strict, had forbidden the use of foreign ships in the wine trade; and it goes back to Henry VIII.'s reign, when, in 1540, an act for the maintenance of the navy laid down that, as the navy had been very profitable and necessary, a great defence and surety of the realm, and a maintenance of mariners, English ships were to be used for the foreign trade, and aliens encouraged to employ them. But we can go further yet—to the reign of Richard II. After the measures of Edward III. it was found that the navy was so diminished that in 1381 it was necessary to pass a Navigation Act—the first of the long series—which enacted that no Englishman was to ship merchandise, either as export or import, except in ships of the king's allegiance. This was the beginning of the policy. As was natural, it was not at first very consistently maintained. English ships were sometimes not to be had, and in this case the rule was modified. Still the act was repeated in 1463, and Henry VII. also compelled the wine exporters from Gascony to use English ships when such could be had. The ground of these acts is always, as stated in the preamble of the act of 1540, to encourage the navy as a valuable portion of English power.

But Navigation Acts were not the only way in which this idea shows itself. Henry IV. did something towards organizing a navy, and Henry V. built larger and better vessels. Private owners were also encouraged to do the same. In Henry VI.'s reign a merchant, William Canynges, owned 2853 tons of shipping, one ship being of 900 tons. Efforts were made, somewhat unsuccessfully, to "keep the seas" from pirates. Henry VIII. granted a charter to the pilots on the Thames, and thereby established the Trinity House, under the rule of a governor and wardens who were to make rules for mariners, while Elizabeth gave them power to erect beacons, buoys, and sea marks. Henry VIII. also did something towards restoring decayed ports by building piers; he began to fortify the Thames, and he established a naval arsenal at Deptford. Elizabeth's reign saw measures for providing a good supply of materials for shipbuilding, by enacting that hemp and flax were to be grown, and that oaks were to be planted and existing oak coppices not grubbed up. The fishing trade, important as a nursery for the navy, was encouraged by an act (1548) to enforce the eating of fish on the old fast-days, under penalty of fines. As by 1548 the religious views of the Government did not approve the practice of fasting, the object of the act was political: the preamble states that it was "in order that the Fishers may be set on work". This act was practically repeated by Elizabeth, who further permitted native fishermen to export fish without a duty, and tried to secure a share in the salt-fish trade by discouraging alien importation.

She was not very successful, and the Navigation Act of 1660 shows that the Dutch had at that time more of the trade than English fishermen.

These regulations may seem somewhat trivial, but they did not bear that aspect in their own time; they were all intended to make England strong by keeping up an effective navy. The same policy stands out in the dealings with corn. The motive was twofold. Not only was it thought wise to have a sufficient supply of corn for food grown in the kingdom, in order that in time of war we might not be dependent on precarious supplies from abroad, but further, the agricultural population was considered to be the backbone of the country. Just as the fishermen made the best sailors, so it was the labourers and small farmers who made the best soldiers. If they dwindled in numbers it might be difficult to collect an effective army, and there seemed to be a real danger that the agricultural population would so dwindle, owing to the enclosures and the consequent depopulation. It would have been possible for Parliament to interfere by declaring that the tenants had a legal right to their holdings and could not be evicted. As we have seen, it did not do that, but attempted by numerous acts against enclosures to prevent the amount of arable land being diminished in such a wholesale fashion. But Parliament went further, and tried to encourage corn-growers by preventing the import of corn and permitting its export; these measures were designed to raise the price and render corn-growing more profitable.

The first act of Richard II. which allowed

export was a direct reversal of Edward III.'s policy. He had tried to keep corn at home, so that it should be cheap and plenty, but the new plan gave farmers a market abroad when the price at home fell low, regardless of the fact that the individual at home had to pay more. In 1436 a definite price was fixed; exportation was to be allowed when the price in England fell to 6s. 8d. a quarter, or less. The next step was taken in 1463 when, owing to complaints of the importing of corn by the Hanse merchants and the consequent injury to English tillage, import was forbidden when the price was under 6s. 8d. a quarter. What was intended to be done by these measures was to keep corn near to that price, and to lessen the variations from year to year; the price was obviously one which was high enough to give a good profit to the farmer. In 1534 import was prohibited except with leave of the king, but this was frequently given. Through the reigns of Elizabeth and the Stuarts export was allowed at a certain rate, and though this rate was raised, the rise was not due to a desire to prevent the farmer from exporting when prices at home were low, but to the general rise in prices that prevailed during the seventeenth century owing to the silver from the New World. From this time till the end of the eighteenth century the principle remained the same, though the actual limits fixed at which export and import were allowed varied widely. The policy was sometimes moderate and sometimes extreme, as, for example, when during part of the seventeenth century import was forbidden altogether, or when in 1689 a bounty was given on export if the price went below 48*s*. a quarter. But the result which it was desired to attain was the encouragement of English corn-growing; that in ordinary years there should be plenty; that when owing to very good harvests there was a great supply it should be easy to find a market abroad; and that in years of scarcity the large area of corn-land which farmers were induced to cultivate should still yield enough to feed the people.

For a long time the policy was on the whole successful. There were occasional years of scarcity when importation was necessary, but in the main England was able to supply herself with corn in spite of the temptation to land-owners to inclose and begin pasture farming. In the early part of the eighteenth century there was even a considerable export trade in corn. According to the policy of power this was extremely desirable. The fact that by the Corn-laws the price of corn was raised to the English consumer was perceived, but the evil of it was held to be more than balanced by the economic gain of having a vigorous agricultural population; the rise in rents caused by high prices excited less condemnation than one might have expected. It was true that the landlords were the chief gainers, but it was felt that this was in a certain degree fair, as a much larger share of taxation fell on land then than does now, and it was further argued that if rents were high and landlords rich, there was a larger fund from which revenue might be drawn. As a method of taxation this seems strange to modern ideas; but there was an obvious convenience in having a class from whom it was simple to collect taxes, and the whole system must not be condemned, as we should condemn it from a modern standpoint, because it is not fair to put out of sight the fact that the Government then aimed at a different object, keeping the country strong, instead of making commodities plentiful and cheap. Legislators had not at that time to consider the necessity of feeding a giant population.

Precisely the same spirit inspired the protection of home industries. The restrictions placed by Richard II. on aliens who interfered in retail trade have already been noticed,[2] but it was not long before similar complaints were made about their wholesale dealings. Amid all the old accusations of regrating, taking money out of the realm, interfering in retail trade, and so on, a great point was made of their exporting wool and tin which, if not exported, would give employment to English artisans. The Italians, especially the Venetians, were blamed for this export, and the more so as the goods which they imported in return were luxuries, such as spices, or fine manufactured goods which gave no employment at home, but only provoked a waste of money. Silk goods imported by Lombards were prohibited in 1455, and Edward IV. went further with the same policy. In 1463 an act was passed to exclude an immense variety of foreign goods, woollens, silks, iron, steel and metal articles, leather goods, hats, embroideries, and small luxuries such as tennis-balls, playing-cards, and purses. The special articles excluded provoke a smile at the

[2] See Chapter VII.

apparent pettinesses of the protection, but the principle was clear enough; the prohibited goods were all manufactured articles, things which gave no employment at home, but which in the popular opinion might well be made in England. Hence the prohibition. The question asked about foreign trade was: how does it affect the English artisan? If the answer in the mind of Parliament was that the trade either carried off English manufactured goods, or that it brought raw materials which could be made up in England, then the trade deserved encouragement. If, on the contrary, it took away from England raw material, or brought manufactured goods that might have been made in England, or goods which displaced English goods in popular favour, or which were purely luxuries and were therefore unnecessary, it was injurious. Somewhat the same canons of criticism were applied to alien immigrants, although the case was hardly so simple; but, speaking generally, if they brought with them new industries, or introduced improvements in such matters as the finishing or dyeing of cloth in which England was behind her rivals, then they might be tolerated, although even then they would probably have to encounter much local jealousy. If, on the other hand, they interfered in industries where the English artisan was already proficient, or tried to take a share in retail trade, they were prohibited.

The key of the whole policy is to be found in the legislation about money. As has been said, pains had always been taken to preserve the coinage, both to stop the importation of bad money from abroad, and to prevent the money of the country being taken out. A serious fear had been felt in Edward III.'s reign that the country might be denuded of its money. We know now that it is impossible that this should happen altogether, for if money leaves the country, prices will fall, and foreign traders, being attracted by the low prices, will come to buy in England, but will not sell; if they do not pay for their purchases in goods, they must pay in money, and so money will flow into the country again; yet for this law to act rapidly and easily, international commerce must be well developed. Before this was the case, when commerce was of small volume, it was quite possible that if a good deal of money was taken out of the country by foreign merchants, what was left might not be enough to act as a circulating medium. Not only would prices fall sharply, which is always discouraging to trade, but there might even be difficulty in getting money at all, and it might be some time before the money would, in the natural course of things, come back. It was well to guard against this, and it was also reasonable to take precautions against the bringing in of bad and debased coin and foreign coin of dubious value and fineness, for thus the coinage of the country would get into an unsatisfactory state. Hence the rules that foreign merchants were to spend in England at any rate some part of the money they were paid for their wares, and that Englishmen who exported wool were to bring 40$s.$, or, as was ordered later, 13$s.$ 4$d.$ in plate into the country, in the hope of securing plenty of bullion for coinage. The object was to keep up a plentiful supply of currency.

THE MERCANTILE SYSTEM. 163

The mercantile policy about money was based on a different principle altogether. The argument ran thus: Money was the most visible and most desirable form of wealth; if a man who had plenty of money was rich, then a country was rich under the same circumstances; to be rich was to be powerful; money was the most convenient form of wealth; if the country had not a good stock of money it would be at a disadvantage in its rivalry with other nations, it would have a weak spot in its armour. Nor was this reasoning without a good deal of force in it. There is no doubt that in any sudden emergency the possession of a large sum of available specie is a great power to a country; some countries feel this to be so still,[3] and in days when communication was less easy, and industry less active, and the collecting and storing of supplies so much more difficult, the advantage of having ready money was still more marked. In the days when the Mercantile system took a definite shape, Englishmen looked abroad and saw their great rival Spain in possession of a supply of silver that seemed boundless, and nothing could be more natural than to take precautions that, so far as possible, England should be as well equipped as her enemy. Hence the mercantilists aimed at the accumulation of a great treasure in the kingdom. In their eyes it was unfortunate that England did not possess either gold or silver mines, so the money could not be got from them. But failing mines at home, money had to come from abroad. To that end the mercantilists wished to

---

[3] The German Government keeps a large sum in gold, stored at Spandau, for use in war.

keep what money there was in the country, and to get as much as possible from outside. Direct regulation was first tried, and again the beginnings of mercantile doctrine are to be found in the reign of Richard II. In 1381 the export of gold or silver oversea was prohibited, as "if it should longer be suffered it would shortly be for the destruction of the realm". There is here no very clear distinction as to whether Parliament thought the realm would suffer by the withdrawal of coinage or the dwindling of treasure, but the fact that not only money, but plate is mentioned, seems to show that something more than care for the currency was in men's minds. During the next century the idea of keeping money in the country inspired much legislation, aliens being required to give security that they would not export bullion, the papal merchants being especially watched and suspected, while in Edward IV.'s reign the offence of exporting coin became a felony.

But the results of all these measures were clearly not very satisfactory, for it was almost impossible to prevent money being smuggled abroad; so long as merchants wished to send it abroad, some would continue to be sent in spite of laws. Thus men were led to ask, "Why do merchants wish to export money?" If the desire or necessity for export could be done away with, then there would be no further need for legislation; all would of itself go well. Accordingly trades were scrutinized to see whether they required an export of money or not, and this conclusion was soon reached. Transactions between Englishmen, involving English goods, clearly did not affect the supply of money in the country at all, and could be left out of account; what the foreigner brought us we paid for; what we sent him he paid for. As it was assumed that the payment in each case was made in money[4] an import trade was believed to take money out of the country, while exports caused it to flow in. It is here that the Mercantile idea about money forms the bond of union for all the other branches of its policy. To encourage corn-growing meant that there would sometimes be corn to export which would bring in money. At the worst, if England did but supply herself, that was better than sending money abroad to pay for foreign corn. English ships saved our paying the foreigner to carry our goods. To help English industries was again a saving; if English goods were ousted by foreign ones, money would leave the country to pay for them; to export them and sell them to the foreigner meant a double gain, not only to the seller, who made a profit, but to the nation, which was enriched by more treasure. It is scarcely an exaggeration to say that in the eyes of the mercantilist the exporter was a patriot and the importer an enemy; with this qualification however: to export raw material was not praiseworthy, for it was better to have it made up at home and then export the still more valuable product; hence the prohibition of the export of wool. On the other hand, to import raw material, such as silk, which could not be obtained at home, and which could be manufactured and sold again, was permissible. It was not on the same footing with the injurious

[4] This assumption was one of the principal fallacies in the Mercantile theory.

practice of draining the country of money by importing either finished goods or luxuries.

The habit of regarding trade as a means whereby treasure could be amassed in the country was a step forward from the stage of trying to secure a treasure by direct regulation of the flow of bullion. But for a time the old regulations held their ground. The Government tried to insist that money should not be exported, that aliens who bought in England should spend their money there, that Englishmen who had debts to pay abroad should pay them in commodities. By degrees, however, it became clear that for some trades the export of bullion was a necessity. Such a trade, for example, was that with the East Indies. To the older view it was in every way a bad trade. It needed the export of bullion, and the goods imported were either unthrifty commodities, such as spices, which were not necessary, or manufactured silks or cottons, which displaced English woollens, and were also extravagant. But the trade was too profitable to be given up in accordance with these views, and its supporters urged that it not only encouraged shipping, but that it did not really drain away money, because it was possible to sell the goods from the East again to foreigners at such a profit that the money was replaced. Over this point a violent controversy was carried on in the earlier part of the seventeenth century, the "Bullionists", the party in favour of direct regulations of bullion, condemning the Indian trade, and the "Mercantilists", the party in favour of a measure of liberty in exporting gold and silver, supporting it. The dispute lasted long, but the younger party triumphed in the end, and with its triumph came the final view as to the right policy to pursue. This was to give up direct regulation, and to attend merely to the course of trade. So long as exports exceeded imports, then there was supposed to be a "Balance of Trade" in favour of England; if, as was assumed, this was paid in money, then all was well. It was the business of a wise government to keep trade healthy, and whether trade was healthy or not could be judged by the balance of trade, which was shown by statistics of export and import. If the balance was large, the country would grow rich; if it declined, the national wealth was supposed to be dwindling; if it turned on the wrong side, and the exports fell below the imports in value, then it was believed that the country would be in the position of a man spending more than he earned —on the way to bankruptcy.

Whichever plan was followed, that of bullionist or mercantilist, direct regulation or maintaining a good balance of trade, there was no alteration in the object to be attained. That remained clear and unquestioned; it was to amass treasure in the country, so that the country might be powerful. All were agreed that that was wise. If a trade was attacked, its supporters would defend it on the ground that it did not do the damage that was supposed to the balance of trade; the plea that it did not matter whether it affected the balance of trade or not was never put forward. That argument would have been at once fatal.

It was then under the influence of the policy of power, as applied to shipping, agriculture, industry and treasure that England was governed until far on in the eighteenth century. This policy did not indeed completely disappear until the nineteenth century, when the last relics of it, the Corn-laws, were destroyed by Peel. But for some time before that it was moribund; the central idea of the importance of money had been given up earlier, and the restrictions had taken the shape of indiscriminate protection, given to all English industries against the foreigner. To this period of decay it will be necessary to recur in a later chapter.

CHAPTER X.

ELIZABETH'S LEGISLATION.

From the standpoint of industrial and commercial history the reign of Elizabeth is remarkable in many respects. The Mercantile system was then reduced to a form which was strictly followed for many successive reigns. It is with Elizabeth, too, that we associate that outburst of the spirit of maritime adventure by which England has become a great power at sea, a power whose dominions lie scattered over the world, and whose commerce is even more wide-spread than her dominions. Trade at home benefited by the new fields opened to commerce abroad, and also by the policy of religious toleration, which attracted artisans from France and the Low Countries, to settle where they would not be persecuted. Another stroke of Elizabeth's was the reform of the coinage, which had been so much debased by Henry VIII. and Edward VI. that trade was hindered at every turn by uncertainty as to what money was worth. This reform by itself was of immense importance, and the success and moderation with which it was carried out were as much to Elizabeth's credit as the firmness with which she determined that at all hazards it must be done. It was in this same reign that capital began to play a more important part in industry and commerce. In a restricted sense there must always be capital where there is trade—capital, that is, in the form of stock devoted to one special use and not easily to be diverted to any other. The carpenter's tools, the weaver's loom and yarn, are "capital" in this sense. But there is another form of capital; capital in a less specialized and more widely applicable shape, of which the best example is money; and in the latter part of the sixteenth century, owing partly to the prosperity of England and partly to the new silver which came from America, there was a great plenty of money; it was easy to accumulate, to form capital ready to be applied to any enterprise which offered a chance of profit, and thus we have the beginnings of a familiar feature in modern times, namely, men trading with borrowed capital, and capital invested in companies where the investor has no share in the management. In a word, capital became more fluid. And with the fluidity of capital, there was, too, an increased fluidity of labour. The gild restrictions had largely disappeared, and men were more free to engage in what industry they pleased, wherever it seemed best to them to do so.

They did not, indeed, gain complete freedom in this respect; and as we shall see, the Law of Settlement in Charles II.'s reign diminished the moderate amount of liberty they had acquired. In spite of this, however, workers in the seventeenth century were much less hampered than their predecessors of the early years of the sixteenth century.

A complete system of policy as applied to trade, the growth of a maritime power, the foundation of Greater Britain, an expanding commerce, a reform in the coinage, and the beginnings of modern conditions in the growth and use of capital are all features of the Elizabethan age. But there was more than this. The reign contains two great legislative enactments, the Statute of Apprentices and the Poor-law, one at the beginning of the reign and the other at the end, which are enough of themselves to make it memorable. They mark the definite acceptance by Government of an increased sphere of duty. Both the statutes dealt with what is now called the labour problem, one directly, and the other indirectly.

There was more than one cause why a labour problem called for attention in the reign of Elizabeth. The progress of enclosure and the substitution of pasture for arable farming had displaced many from employment, and though the growing native woollen industry absorbed many evicted labourers, it did not absorb all. The dissolution of the monasteries and the forfeiture of their land along with that of the chantries and many semi-religious foundations also caused a great change in employment, while at the same time it did away with places where much had been done to relieve the poor, although not always in the wisest way. Further, the decay of the gilds had left industry unregulated just at a time when regulation seemed to be most required, for the whole conditions of industry were being thrown into confusion by rapid fluctuations in the value of money. These fluctuations were due to two causes, the debasement of the currency by Henry VIII. and Edward VI., and the spread over Europe of the silver which was brought into Spain from the mines of the New World. Both these causes led to a great rise in prices. It is necessary to follow a little more in detail what took place.

Currency may be altered in two ways, either by lessening the size of the coins without changing the fineness of the silver, or by actually using more alloy or base metal. Both of these things had been done. In Edward III.'s reign the weight of the silver penny had been reduced by about 10 per cent. This was comparatively trifling, but in 1412 and 1464 a further reduction took place, so that by the reign of Henry VII. the weight had decreased over 40 per cent from the original standard. This of itself should have led to a rise in prices, and to a certain extent it did so, but the effect was partly counteracted by the fact that Europe generally was in want of more money than there was to be had, and consequently the increased amount was readily absorbed. Further, Henry VII.'s hoards withdrew a good deal from circulation. But Henry VIII. speedily dissipated his father's treasure, and went further on the path of debasement. He lowered the weight of the penny to 10 grains, and Edward VI. lowered it further to 8 grains; and not content with this, the fineness of the coinage was altered. Whereas in 1527, 12 oz. of metal, consisting of $11\frac{1}{12}$ ozs. of silver and $\frac{11}{12}$ oz. of alloy, had been coined into 37*s*., in 1551 12 ozs. of metal, containing 9 ozs. of alloy and only 3 ozs. of silver, were coined into 72*s*. This, however, was not all. From the date of the discovery of the New World silver began to flow into Europe. At first it went mainly to Spain, and it was some time before English prices were affected by it at all. But from 1545, when the riches of Potosi were discovered, an immense quantity of silver came to Spain, and Spanish wars disseminated it over Europe. According to one calculation the total amount of money in Europe increased 50 per cent between 1491 and 1545, and had quadrupled by 1600. It is easy to understand that, at the beginning of Elizabeth's reign, with a coinage depreciated to one-seventh of its old value, and with a rapidly-increasing amount of silver, the change in prices and the consequent uncertainty must have been very great. For example, comparing the average prices in the decades 1511–1520 and 1541–1550, wheat rose from 6*s*. 8*d*. the quarter to 10*s*. 8*d*., barley from 4*s*. to 6*s*. 2*d*., oats from 2*s*. 2*d*. to 4*s*., an ox from £1, 3*s*. to £2, 2*s*., a sheep from 2*s*. 6*d*. to 5*s*. This is striking enough, but it was worse when the full effect of the debasement that went on from 1545 to 1551 became more widely felt. The currency was so discredited that the country began to retrograde towards barter, goods being often exchanged for goods, and wages paid in food. Where money was used the price of necessaries rose at least 100 per cent. Had the rate of wages risen proportionately, the evil of so sudden a change would have been less felt. But up to 1550 wages had in most cases risen less than 30 per cent, and even after this they did not rise above 50 per cent; in the face of a 100-per-cent rise in the price of necessaries this meant that many labourers were unable to exist on their wages at all. Consequently, men left the employments in which they could no longer gain a living and became beggars, trying to subsist upon charity.

Elizabeth then had to deal with a labour difficulty, the result of many forces acting in combination; the enclosing of lands for sheep-farming, the dissolution of the monasteries and religious foundations, the debased and discredited currency, the decadence of the gilds, all had helped either to throw men out of work, or to make work unremunerative, or to destroy the means by which the poor had been relieved from their distresses. As the trouble was many-sided, the remedies were many-sided too. The measures taken to relieve agricultural depression by checking enclosure and encouraging the growth of corn at home have already been described. We must now trace what was done for those who were out of work, or working under such conditions that their lives were an incessant struggle for mere existence. They were of different kinds. There were men who were out of work and anxious to find it, men who were out of work and preferred to remain sturdy beggars living upon charity, and, finally, the aged and impotent poor who could not work. All these classes were dealt with in turn.

The first measure was the restoration of the coinage. The confusion existing when there were three different shillings and four different sixpences, besides various kinds of smaller pieces in circulation, admitted of no minor remedies. It was necessary to call in the whole coinage, and this was done in 1560. The old coins were paid for in new coins at about their real value, while to encourage the old coins being brought in speedily a small bounty was offered on each pound's worth of silver paid in, and an order made that after a certain reasonable delay the old money would not be current at all. The whole operation was carried out with complete success. It is true that when it was done prices did not fall so much as had been expected, but this was due to the new silver from America that was now coming into the country in considerable quantity. It was this indeed that made the issue of the new coinage so easy. But if prices did not fall to their former level, the relief to commerce was immediate and great. Industry again took a step forward; in mercantile undertakings a time of rising prices, when the rise is not due to a debased currency, is generally a time of activity and expansion. Profits are high, and it is easy to accumulate capital and encouraging to invest it. Accordingly after the restoration of the currency the volume of English trade rapidly increased.

The new currency did much; it gave a sound basis on which trade and industry might grow, but it did not prove a complete solution of economic difficulties. Rising prices may be satisfactory to those who embark in commercial undertakings and gain the profits, but they press hardly upon those whose incomes are fixed, or change slowly and with difficulty, and in this class are the wage-earners. Even now when wages move more readily, they are generally slower to move than prices, and in Elizabeth's time the rate of wages lagged far behind the general rise in the price of necessaries. We are accustomed nowadays to the sight of workers trying to raise wages for themselves by combinations, threats, and strikes, when they think that a rise in wages can be obtained. But this remedy was hardly conceived in the sixteenth century, and had it been seriously proposed, the Government would have striven by every possible means to check any such combined action on the part of the workmen. The old remedy, the regulation of wages and prices by the craft gilds, had perished with the craft gilds; yet even before this came to pass, it had become necessary for the Government to do something. Elizabeth's enactment may be regarded as the completion of her predecessors' work in this direction.

The Statute of Apprentices passed in 1563 takes its name from what is its less important side in connection with the difficulties of the reign. The clauses which insisted on an apprenticeship in the case of those who wished to practise a trade only enforced generally what had been enforced piecemeal by the old gilds. There was indeed little doubt about the need of such rules; the mediæval idea was still strong that industry should be properly regulated, so that wares should be well made by competent workmen, in order that buyers might not be defrauded.[1] Elizabeth's statute did little more than reduce to a uniform system what had been in force with local variations before; in some few trades, especially in those connected with wool, which were spread widely over the country and more or less free from local control, there may have been a tendency to break away from the old system. The special provision in the act of 1563 that in the trades of a clothmaker, fuller, shearman, weaver, tailor, or shoemaker, one journeyman was to be kept for every three apprentices, seems to show that in these trades the apprentice system needed special regulation. Further, the act went upon old lines in making it more easy for an apprentice to enter agricultural employments or employments subsidiary to agriculture than trades in towns, in fixing the hours of labour, and in insisting on long hirings, and work from all those who were able-bodied.

This was all familiar enough in the rules made by gilds, or in the repeated Statutes of Labourers. We have already seen that under the exceptional circumstances produced by the scarcity of labour consequent on the Black Death, the Government had directly interfered in what had hitherto been

---

[1] Although mediæval regulation was almost unanimous in prescribing apprenticeship, yet it is clear that in many cases the apprenticeship was rather formal than of much value. It was required whether a man knew his trade or not; and in London at any rate a man was not bound to continue in the trade in which he had been apprenticed. Having served an apprenticeship in something, he could thereafter take up any trade he pleased. Such a regulation served more to hinder competition from those who were not free of the town, than to promote any efficiency among the craftsmen.

chiefly left to the gilds, namely, the regulation of wages. This had been necessary, because the agricultural labourers whose wages chiefly called for interference were not under gild control at all. The gilds could fix wages for their own members, but there was no gild of agricultural labourers. Indeed at the time the gilds had mostly gained their powers, the bulk of the labourers were only beginning to emerge from a servile condition, and till they were free from this, no question of wages could arise at all. We have seen, too, that the action of the Government was unsuccessful, not from any innate impossibility, but because for wages to be kept down prices had to be kept down too; as the Government failed in the latter object, the former came to nothing also, so that after a period of much friction the rise in wages had to be accepted as a fact which no amount of legislation could make away with. Having once stepped on the scene, however, Government did not leave it. It proposed to regulate the rise in wages, and keep it, so far as possible, in bounds. In the thirteenth year of Richard II.'s reign there is the first instance of a new policy, that of delegating the task of dealing with wages to a local authority, but no longer tacitly to the gilds. The Justices of the Peace were chosen, and bidden to fix the wages which labourers in husbandry and artisans were to receive in their districts; but they were not left with an entirely free hand, for Parliament laid down limits which wages were not to exceed. Acts of this kind often went into great detail, one in Henry VI.'s reign giving amounts for numerous callings; a hind or shepherd was to get 20s. each year, with 4s. for clothing, a common servant 15s. and 3s. 4d., a woman servant 10s. and 4s., while artisans were divided into classes, being paid 4d., 2d., and 1½d. a day, with 1½d. added in each case where board was not given. The retention of a limit that was not to be exceeded should not be interpreted as an attempt by Parliament to depress wages, for this was not intended; the limit was to prevent wages rising above what was regarded as reasonable. But the practical effect must have been to make the statutes somewhat unyielding; justices may well have thought that wages should be kept below the statutory limit, and though now and again Parliament raised the rates, yet the measures were not easily adaptable to changing circumstances. Elizabeth's Act of Apprentices gave up the limit altogether, and placed the matter entirely in the hands of the justices. They were to meet each year, to summon to help them such grave and discreet persons as they thought fit, and, taking into account the scarcity or plenty of the time, to fix wages for every kind of employment, agricultural and domestic as well as industrial, whether by the day, week, or year, in their district for the year.

How far this measure was carried out is difficult to say. An act of 1604 speaks as if it had not been generally acted upon, and provides for making it more effective, but evidence of its enforcement is scanty. On the other hand, assessments of wages by the justices were sometimes made, and the minuteness of detail into which they go, seems to show that they were to be observed. An assessment made at Bury St. Edmunds in 1630, mentions about 80 different employments, which are mostly grouped into large classes, and lays down the wages which they are to receive, according to whether they were employed with or without meat. Thus freemasons and joiners, wheelwrights, carpenters, sawyers, rivers of laths, rough masons, bricklayers, tilers, slaters, plumbers, carvers, thatchers, and reeders, being master workmen, got 8*d.* a day with meat and drink, and 16*d.* without, while knackers, lime-burners, basket and fan makers, coach-menders, cobblers, tailors, painters, saddlers, coopers, tinkers, brickmakers, tilemakers, gardeners, moletakers, and makers of deep grips in meadows and marshes got 6*d.* and 12*d.* respectively. Servants and apprentices were to be paid on a lower scale, partly according to age. Day labourers got 6*d.* and 12*d.*, except from Michaelmas to Ladyday, when their wage was 4*d.* and 8*d.* Mowers, threshers (5 kinds and all at different wage), woodcutters, farm-servants, bailiffs, maidservants and dairymaids, clothiers, servants, tanners, cutlers, blacksmiths, farriers, bowyers, and many others, are provided for, and the justices also fixed the rates for piecework. Such an elaborate regulation can hardly have been isolated.

The Act of Apprentices was not a measure intended to keep down wages for the advantage of the land-owners. It is possible that the justices may not always have administered it fairly; they may not have considered the plenty or scarcity of the time as they should have done, and they certainly failed to understand or allow for the rise in prices due to the new silver. Owing to the selfishness or the mistakes of those who administered the law, it may at times have acted hardly. But this was not intended by those who framed the measure; the fact that punishment was laid down for those who gave less than the assessed wages, but none for those who gave more, is sufficient proof that the intention was to raise rather than depress wages. And it is extremely doubtful whether the working-classes would have been better off, had they been left to their own resources. A period of rising prices is always hard upon the wage-earner, at any rate at first, till his wages rise proportionately, and there is no reason to think that the Elizabethan workman would have found it easy to secure this rise for himself.

Further, putting aside the disputed question whether the act was generally enforced or not, it was an eminently workable measure. There was nothing unreasonable about it to its own time, nor was it unduly rigid. A hard-and-fast measure goes soon out of date; even at first it may be fair in one part of the country and unfair in another. But the Act of Apprentices, by continuing the plan of temporary and local regulation by men who were on the spot, and giving them a free hand, overcame these difficulties. The best testimony that the measure was on the whole satisfactory may be found in the desire of the wage-earners in the eighteenth century, whose lives were made miserable by the new machinery and the Industrial Revolution, to return to the Elizabethan plan and fix a minimum wage.[2] The fact that early in the

[2] Motions for fixing a minimum wage were proposed in Parliament in

eighteenth century much misery occurred in the trades[3] which had sprung up since Elizabeth's day, and were, therefore, not subject to the act of 1563, also goes to show that trades where less government regulation was in force were not conspicuously more prosperous than the others.

With the restoration of the coinage and adoption of a plan to secure fair wages, it might be hoped that all that remained to be done was to provide for those who could not work. But this hope was not fulfilled. Thirteen years after the Act of Apprentices, Parliament had to include among the list of vagabonds those who refused the "reasonable wages fixed and commonly given" in their districts. Thus the task was not only to provide for the impotent poor, but also to check the vagabonds and tramps who found begging a more profitable occupation than work. The second of these duties was a familiar one; from the time of the Statute of Labourers onward there had been continual legislation against "valiant beggars", but that the State should provide for the impotent was a new idea. This task hitherto had been left to charity.

In passing in review the Tudor statutes which lead up to Elizabeth's Poor-law of 1601, it is convenient to begin with 1536. An act passed in that year marks a step forward. Hitherto there had been statutes enough against sturdy beggars

---

1795, 1800, and 1808. The wages clauses of the Act of Apprentices were repealed in 1813.

[3] Known as the incorporated trades: the stocking-frame workers are an example.

who refused work when offered, and vagrant rogues who imposed upon the charitable; but it had always been assumed that there were some who must of necessity live by begging—not indeed those who were out of work, for it was supposed that there was work for all if they were only willing to do it—but those who were impotent or past work, and certain privileged classes, poor clerks of the university, soldiers and sailors, who held licenses to beg. An act of severe repression was passed in 1531, prescribing that able-bodied and unlicensed beggars were to be whipped at the cart-tail and sent back to the places of their birth. But the act of 1536 went further, and prohibited open begging altogether; the valiant beggars on showing a testimonial that they had been duly whipped, were to be helped on their way to their native place by gifts of food and lodging every ten miles; if they loitered on the way their ears were to be bored, and the penalty for the third offence was death. It is true that there was no very definite provision for setting them to work in their homes when they did arrive there, beyond a suggestion of the use of alms from the parish; and this is practically an admission that there might be some who wished for work and could not find it. But besides this, and here lay the novelty, the impotent poor were not to beg either, but be succoured by their own parish. Alms were to be taken for this purpose at definite seasons, and the clergy were bidden to exhort all to give. Common doles[4] were forbidden,

---

[4] A distribution of alms to all applicants, made by monasteries or great houses.

and all contributions were to go to the parish funds. These funds were to be used for relieving honest distress among the impotent.

Close on the heels of this prohibition of begging came the dissolution of the monasteries, followed by the further confiscations of Edward VI.'s reign. The estimate of amount of charity given by these religious bodies may have been exaggerated; the influence of the indiscriminate charity which they gave, alike to sturdy and impotent, rogues and honest men, may have been bad; there may have been cases where charitable bequests to found hospitals and almshouses were carelessly administered, and did more to benefit the masters and wardens than the poor, so that a contemporary could say " the fat of the whole foundation hangeth on the priests' beards"; the relief granted may have been excessive in rich districts and too small in poor ones. But when all this is granted, when it is admitted that the charity of the religious foundations was none too wisely administered, and apt at times to create beggars instead of relieving distress, even so the abolition of these foundations was at the moment a severe blow to the poor. The monasteries had relieved the poor, although they had failed to draw a line between deserving and undeserving; almshouses and hospitals had sheltered some, though not perhaps as many as they should have done; gilds had lent a helping hand to widows and orphans, or to poor brethren. It is true that in some cases the funds of the hospitals and almshouses were, after the dissolution, still applied to charity, being merely transferred to new hands. But there was a great diminution of sources of relief, just at the time when it was wanted most. From 1527 to 1536 came an exceptional succession of bad harvests, and the dissolution of the monasteries cast an immense number of persons adrift on the world. Many of these joined the ranks of the beggars, some by necessity, some by choice. And thus a heavier strain was placed on the alms of the charitable by the very measure which did away with one great source of charity.

We may pass over the legislation of the reigns of Edward VI. and Mary, merely noticing that the sudden increase of vagabondage called forth in 1547 the most ferocious act of the whole series against idle and vagabond persons; the preamble complains that previous acts had been useless because of the "foolish pytie and mercy" of those charged with putting them in force, but this act certainly did not err in the direction of sentimental charity, for it prescribes for men and women alike branding with a hot iron as the first penalty, to be followed by slavery, and death on the third offence. It was repealed in 1549, and the laws of Henry VIII. re-enacted.

So far the State had relied on voluntary charity either private or parochial, but the first Poor-law of Elizabeth's reign shows that voluntary charity was no longer adequate. Edward VI. had provided for special "collectors" for the poor, who were bound to take office under a fine of 20s. and collect alms; persons refusing to contribute were to be exhorted by the parish priest, and if they still were obstinate, by the bishop. The act of 1563 raised the penalty for refusing to collect to £10, and provided that those who did not contribute might in the last resort be taken before the justices and imprisoned. Thus for the first time contribution was made compulsory; giving to the poor was no longer a charity, but a duty. The State had taken the charge of the poor upon itself, instead of leaving them to chance benevolence. Other measures consolidating the new system soon followed. The act of 1572 repeated harsh measures against vagabonds, and included among them the "proctors" and "fraters" who went round collecting alms for hospitals unless they had licenses from the Queen, and also fencers, bearwards, minstrels, jugglers, players in interludes, palmists—persons who were not strictly speaking beggars, but whose occupations were distasteful to the growing spirit of Puritanism in the House of Commons. Children of vagabonds were to be removed from their parents' charge and apprenticed to prevent them from growing up as idle as their parents. Habitations were to be built for the aged poor, and a register of the poor kept. And, finally, the amount of the contribution was fixed; a regular charge was to be made, and though this might be appealed against at Quarter Sessions, refusal to give would be punished by imprisonment. In 1576 provision was made for setting the poor to work on materials such as hemp, wool, and flax, to be paid for by a rate levied for the purpose, or by voluntary subscription. For this work the poor were to be paid and the goods sold by the collectors. If they refused to work they were to be sent to houses of correction, where they were to be whipped, put in irons, and then set to work.

In the acts of 1597 and 1601, which repeated and codified the whole, we have all the features of the Elizabethan Poor-law: succour for those who could not work, provided in their own parishes by a compulsory rate which might be levied by distress; punishment for the idle who would not work, also administered by the local authorities, either by whipping, or in the houses of correction; apprenticing of pauper children; and finally work to be found for those willing to work but unable to find it. On this last point the statutes give general directions about "setting the poor on work", and a little advice about providing stocks of hemp and flax for the purpose; it is not however surprising if Elizabeth's legislators found it difficult to make satisfactory regulations, for even in our own day the question of what to do with the unemployed cannot be said to have been met. But in other respects the system was certainly satisfactory; throwing the responsibility upon the local authorities made each district exercise care which would have been wanting in a central authority; the number of vagabonds decreased rapidly, the complaints of the impotent poor became fewer. And the whole system being flexible, was durable. No better proof of the wisdom and the efficiency of the Elizabethan Poor-law can be found than the disasters which followed when, in the latter part of the eighteenth century, men began to depart from its principles.

The place occupied by the reign of Elizabeth in the history of the industrial development of England is thus an important one. The Government undertook to put an end to the troubles which were the legacy of Henry VIII.'s dishonesty with the coinage, and of the breakdown of the old mediæval system of industry and charity, and upon the whole it met with success. The reform in the coinage made it possible for commerce and industry to expand with the widened conditions of the time. The Act of Apprentices did something to secure good work and also proper payment for labourers, while the Poor-law diminished the number of idle and vagrant men who were in the habit of committing endless thefts, assaults, and occasionally graver crimes, and admitted the broad principle that the poor, who through accident or the burden of age were no longer able to work for themselves, had a definite claim to be protected by the State and relieved by their more prosperous brethren.

CHAPTER XI.

THE TRADING COMPANIES AND THE BEGINNING OF COLONIAL EXPANSION.

On January 6th, in the year 1558, Calais surrendered, and when a fortnight later the neighbouring fortress of Guisnes fell, England was left without a possession on the Continent. Mary was so overcome as to say that at her death the word "Calais" would be found graven on her heart. But the loss, though humiliating, was not so great as it seemed, for even before this English ambition had entered a new field. Instead of being a military power striving for dominion in France, England was to become a naval power, and to spread her dominions over the east and west.

In the development of Greater Britain two stages may be distinguished. Roughly speaking, the first covers the reigns of Elizabeth and the Stuart kings, and the second the eighteenth century. The acquisitions of the first period came mainly from private effort, the voyages of the Adventurers, or the expeditions and colonies sent out by trading companies, such as the East India Company or the Plymouth Company. The Crown indeed took an interest in their doings, Elizabeth privately encouraging Drake, and accepting a share of the plunder while she publicly disavowed responsibility for his acts, and the Stuarts granting charters to the colonists of the new world; but colonization and the acquisition of territory had hardly become a national policy. For example, the treaties of the time say little or nothing about colonies; the only important gains are Bombay, which, together with Tangiers, formed part of Katharine of Braganza's dowry on her marriage with Charles II., and New York, which was ceded by the Dutch. Cromwell indeed committed England to a repetition of the struggle with Spain for dominion of the New World. His expedition, though beaten off from St. Domingo, took Jamaica from the Spaniards, while the fleet repeated on a national basis the exploits of the buccaneers against the Spanish treasure-ships. Nor was Spain our only rival. Holland also was attacked by the Navigation

Act, and the enmity to the Dutch continued through Charles II.'s reign. But in this reign we are in the transition from private to national undertakings. And how marked is the contrast between the two! Compare the barrenness of the treaties of the seventeenth century with the luxuriant harvest reaped in the eighteenth century. Here, almost every treaty that ends a war is marked by colonial gains. From the Treaty of Utrecht, when England got Nova Scotia and St. Kitts, secured her rights to Newfoundland and the Hudson Bay Territory, and set up a naval station in the Mediterranean, till the Peace of Paris, by which Tobago, St. Lucia, Mauritius, Ceylon, and the Cape were left in English hands, the same tendency appears and reappears, namely, a widening of our colonial dominions at the expense of France, Spain, and the Dutch.

To this eighteenth-century phase of the expansion of England it will be necessary to return. We may, however, remark some other features which distinguish the early period from it. The earlier is a time of occupation mainly of territory previously unoccupied, or occupied only by savages, the later a time of capture from European rivals. Our rivals themselves were different; at first they were Spain and Portugal, and a little later Holland, but afterwards the struggle was mainly with France. The original idea was to get precious metals from colonies, although England perhaps did not cling to this as closely as did Spain; in the eighteenth century colonies were valued for the trade which they brought.

In 1492 Columbus sailed across the Atlantic to the New World, and in 1498 Vasco da Gama, rounding the Cape of Good Hope, discovered the sea route to the East Indies. The effect of these two discoveries was to move commerce onwards from the "thalassic" stage, the stage when it goes mainly over inland seas, to the "oceanic" stage, when it extends over the oceans, and so all round the world. The highway of commerce had been the Mediterranean, and the Mediterranean ports, Venice, Genoa, Barcelona, Marseilles, the great trading centres. But when the Atlantic became the highway, the countries that looked out on it, Spain, Portugal, France, Holland, and England, were given new opportunities. Commerce did not at once abandon the Mediterranean; much of the eastern trade went on the same lines as before, for it was not, indeed, till the rise of the Dutch power that the mass of eastern goods came to Europe by the ocean route; consequently the decay of the Mediterranean ports was gradual, but none the less it was inevitable, for the Mediterranean countries could not compete with those on the Atlantic in the trade with the New World.

It was long before England began to take advantage of the new conditions. Spain had spread her power over the West Indies and Central America, and Portugal had established herself in Brazil and in the East Indies some time before England became a competitor for the New World. One expedition which set sail from England seemed to show that we did not mean to be left behind. In 1497 John Cabot and his three sons put out from Bristol with letters patent authorizing them to discover and annex any new-found heathen lands. After a two-months' voyage they sighted land, probably Labrador, and thus anticipated Columbus in the discovery of the mainland of America. In 1498 another voyage was undertaken, again to the west. But this early effort, which, after all, was led by a Venetian and not an Englishman, remained isolated. Newfoundland, indeed, was visited by English ships for the sake of the fishery in the early years of the sixteenth century, while William Hawkins reached Brazil in 1530, and there were voyages to the west by Thorne, Tison, and Hore. But English enterprise during these years cannot be compared with what was done by Spain and Portugal. Cortez had subdued Mexico, and Balboa had crossed the Darien Isthmus to the Pacific, and so led the way to Peru, whither he was followed by Pizarro. Meanwhile Magellan[1] had sailed into the Pacific, and from there round the world, adding the Philippine Islands to Spanish territory. Cabral had found Brazil, and the Portuguese, settling there, formed the first permanent European colony. In eastern traffic, too, the Portuguese were far in advance of all others, trading with south-east Africa, China, Japan, and the Spice Islands. Alexander VI.'s famous bull dividing the world between Portugal and Spain seemed to be in a fair way of becoming actually justified in fact.

Two things combined to retard English enterprise. For the first half of the sixteenth century

---

[1] Magellan, a Portuguese in the employ of Spain, died during the voyage. His ship, the *Trinidad*, completed the first voyage round the world.

England was occupied with the Reformation. The excitement of the religious struggle kept men's attention at home, while other nations were looking abroad. And secondly, when the spirit of enterprise grew, it turned at first into the wrong channel. The idea of the territoriality of the sea[2] was strong. Not only were the west and the east Spanish and Portuguese, but the routes across the Atlantic, and round the Cape of Good Hope, were Spanish and Portuguese also. Not only did Spain and Portugal strive to prevent others from trading with their new settlements, but they regarded vessels sailing in these waters as poachers on their preserves. Hence English ambition strove first to discover a new route to the east which should be exclusively English, and here is the explanation why so much time and so many lives were lost in voyages to the north-east or the north-west. A North-east or North-west Passage, if discovered by Englishmen, would be English, and English only; further, it would possess the added advantage that, passing by cold lands, the inhabitants would be ready to buy the staple English export, cloth, which found no market in the hotter climates whither the Spaniards and Portuguese went. The pursuit of this chimera of a North-west Passage went on long. Frobisher sailed to the north-west in 1576, and again in the the next year " for the further discovery of the way

---

[2] The phrase is borrowed from the technical language of International Law. The sea for a certain distance round the coast of each nation is regarded as territorial, and under the jurisdiction of that nation, as opposed to the high seas where no nation has jurisdiction, save over its own ships. In the sixteenth century nations made wider claims, based on the claim of discovery.

to Cathay". Ten years later Davis was struggling with storms in the same icy latitudes, having "a perfect hope of the passage", which was doomed to be disappointed. In 1607 Henry Hudson sailed to find a North-east Passage, without, however, getting east of Nova Zembla. In 1610 he changed his ground to the west, and sailing into Hudson's Bay was buoyed up with hope that the passage was at last found. His melancholy fate[3] did not deter Baffin (1615), Fox, and James (1631) from adventuring their lives in the same seas, with as little result as before. In fact northern voyages have added much to the glory of English navigators at all times, but it has been the barren glory of the explorer, not the profit in gold, silver, and spices sought by the Elizabethan adventurers, or the merchants at home who sent them out.

The only one of the early voyages in search of an English trade route which was important commercially was almost the first of the whole series, and as it was further an expedition exclusively English, it marks the entrance of England upon the struggle for a share in the commerce of the world. In 1553 Sir Hugh Willoughby and Richard Chancellor started with three ships from the Thames for the "intended voyage to Cathay", by the North-east Passage. The ships separated in a storm off the Norwegian coast. Willoughby and his men, after driving about in Arctic waters, landed late in the summer in Lapland, where they made up their minds to winter, but perished through cold and

---

[3] Hudson's men mutinied and set him adrift in an open boat in the great bay which is called after him. He was never heard of again.

starvation. Chancellor, with the *Edward Bonaventure*, was more fortunate. He sailed into the White Sea, and, reaching land where Archangel is now, came upon inhabitants who owned the rule of Ivan the Terrible. Chancellor eventually made his way overland to Moscow, and found the Czar willing to encourage trade with England. From this beginning came the visit of the first Russian Ambassador to England, and the founding of the Muscovy Company.

A new direction was given to English enterprise by the long-drawn-out hostility between Elizabeth and Philip II., that culminated in the Armada. It was owing to the fact that Spain, a colonial power, was the champion of the Catholic Reaction, that Englishmen were led, in defence of their religion, to create for themselves a maritime empire. Of course so long as Mary was on the throne she discouraged any trespassing on her husband's western dominions. But even before Mary died Spain was hated. Persecution at home, and the sufferings of Englishmen who fell into the hands of the Inquisition abroad, accounted well enough for this. As Philip's hostility to Elizabeth became more clear, so the desire to do Spain an injury in her western possessions grew stronger and stronger. It was patriotic, and it was likely to be profitable, for after the discovery of the South American silver mines masses of treasure came to Spain across the Atlantic. Hence raiding in the Spanish Main grew into a regular commercial enterprise. Merchants at home found the money, and equipped ships for a voyage to the New World, and the dream of every adventurer was to intercept the Spanish Plate fleet. Such conduct stamped the adventurer as a pirate, but he felt that if he brought back enough silver bars, or pieces of eight, for the Queen to get a substantial share, he might snap his fingers at the complaints of the Spanish ambassador. Elizabeth might promise redress and punishment of the offender, but her promise would not be fulfilled.

In this "Age of the Navigators" the central figure was Francis Drake. He was associated at first with William and John Hawkins, sons of William Hawkins who had voyaged to Brazil in 1530. Of these, the elder stayed mostly at home and looked after the financial part of the adventures, while the younger has gained an evil notoriety as the first English slave-trader to the Spanish Main. In 1562 he had taken a cargo of 300 negroes from the West African coast to Hispaniola and sold them, bringing back hides, ginger, sugar, and pearls. The adventure was so profitable that the Queen lent the *Jesus*, a royal ship, as part of his second expedition. Having collected negroes, Hawkins again made off for the Spanish Main. This time, however, he found the Spaniards unwilling to buy; they had, in fact, received orders not to do so. But Hawkins, by landing "a hundred men well armed", overcame their scruples, and got rid of his cargo, part at Burburata in Venezuela, and part at Rio de la Hacha. In reality the Spaniards were mostly willing enough to buy, and the show of force gave a good excuse for disobeying orders. On the third trip, in 1567, Francis Drake accompanied Hawkins. Six ships made up the fleet, two of them being from the royal navy. When a cargo of 500 slaves had been collected, the squadron sailed westward as before, and again the Spaniards were forced to buy. This time the end of the venture was less fortunate; the squadron was attacked at Vera Cruz, treacherously, as Hawkins said, and only two vessels got home, Drake himself having a narrow escape. As the *Jesus* was lost, and little plunder brought, the Queen was angry, and Hawkins in disgrace, not because he had been fighting with Spain, but because his venture had failed and he had lost two of Elizabeth's ships. In 1570 and 1571 Drake was again in Spanish waters, and in 1572 he led seventy-three men to an attack on Nombre de Dios, "the Treasure House of the World". The town was taken by a *coup de main*, but could not be held, nor was Drake able to carry off the treasure he found. In spite of all the Spaniards could do, however, he remained off the coast, and later, with eighteen men and thirty Maroons, crossed the Cordilleras to the gates of Panama— thus being the first Englishman to see the Pacific— and cut off a mule train loaded with treasure for Nombre. After a series of escapes that read like a fairy tale, he succeeded at last in getting to sea with his booty, and returned to England in August, 1573. One glimpse of the Pacific was not enough for Drake. He had a mind to see more of it, and accordingly, in 1577, he sailed again with five ships on the famous voyage that took him round the world. Reaching Brazil, he kept southward, went through Magellan's Straits, and appeared off the coast of Chili and Peru, where no Englishman had ever appeared before, and where, consequently, the Spaniards were least able to resist him. He plundered Valparaiso and Callao, captured the great Spanish treasure galleon the *Cacafuego*, sailed up the coast of North America to latitude 42° N., and then, crossing the Pacific, made his way home past the Moluccas, Java, and the Cape of Good Hope, after an absence of about three years. Not only was the voyage the most successful of all raids in the amount of treasure brought back, but it opened to Englishmen the whole field of the South Seas.

It is unnecessary to tell the story of Cavendish, who followed Drake round the world a few years later, or of John Oxenham, who was hanged by the Spaniards as a pirate, or of Andrew Barker, or Walter Raleigh's quest for El Dorado. One or two examples may well stand for the whole, especially as the importance of them lies not in the ships each man plundered and sank, or in the towns he sacked, or in the treasure he brought home, but in the maritime spirit that sprang up over the country. If it is true to say that Britons are at home on the sea, the taste for maritime adventure came to them in Elizabeth's days. In the voyages to the Spanish Main there was formed the love of the sea, the self-reliance, the disregard of odds, that made "Aquinez" and "El Draque"[4] names of terror to the Spaniards, and enabled us to turn aside the weight of the Armada. And as Drake was the master-spirit in this struggle, it is interesting to notice how clear to his mind was the importance to England of sea-power. He pressed

[4] The Spanish names for Hawkins and Drake.

continually to be allowed to destroy the Armada as it came out from port, or at any rate fight it in open sea and not in the Channel. And after the Armada was gone and the chief danger over, he proposed a plan of maritime retaliation upon Spain and her colonies, which the Queen's hesitation and parsimony prevented him from carrying out to the full, though what he did in burning Corunna and Vigo, threatening Lisbon, and taking nearly a hundred ships in Spanish waters, showed how formidable a weapon of offence a fleet could be when resolutely handled. Drake's Armada had a much closer resemblance to the exploits of the navy in the eighteenth century than anything else till Cromwell took up the same policy.

We have so far concerned ourselves with the growth of England as a maritime power. But Drake and Hawkins were destructive rather than constructive. They plundered Spain for England's benefit, but they were essentially rovers. English possessions did not arise from their captures. The opening scene in the history of English colonies lies elsewhere than in the Spanish Main.

The beginning was singularly discouraging. Having obtained a patent from Elizabeth "for the inhabiting and planting of our people in America", Sir Humphrey Gilbert set sail with five ships in 1583. The expedition reached Newfoundland and took possession of it in the name of the Queen, but going on to the mainland, was overtaken by a great storm off Cape Breton. Here the flagship ran aground and was lost, and Gilbert turned homewards. On the way back he met with terrible weather; Gilbert himself went down with his little ship the *Squirrel*, and one vessel only got back to England. Raleigh, however, persevered with the task. An expedition of his took possession of Virginia in 1584, and in the next year Sir Richard Grenville, being also sent out by Raleigh, founded the first English settlement in the New World, leaving the settlers under the charge of Ralph Lane. The settlers were at first enthusiastic about the natural wealth of the country, but soon got into difficulties with the savages, and were glad enough to accept Drake's offer of a passage home in 1586. Grenville, arriving soon after, found them gone, but left fifteen men to hold the colony. In 1587 Raleigh sent a fresh expedition of 150 men under John White, but this also ended in disaster. White himself returned home for supplies, leaving 118 persons; when he came back to the colony in 1590 he found that the colonists had moved inland, where they perished.

Thus, in spite of these efforts, by the end of Elizabeth's reign England had acquired nothing on the mainland of America. The failure of the Elizabethan expeditions was due in the main to the fact that the right sort of colonists did not go. Those who went were too strongly imbued with the notions of the buccaneers. They were largely gentlemen adventurers, anxious for gold, filled with ideas that the new colonies were places where wealth could be had for the gathering; they were not prepared for the work that was needed before the richness of the soil would yield its increase. "The nice bringing up" of most of those who went produced impatience and disappointment at the hardships which had to be undergone. The painful lessons of experience were learned by degrees. By the reign of James I. men began to see that the New World was no place for idlers. Bacon, too, gave a practical piece of advice to intending colonists when he bade them "Moile not too much underground". As soon as the idea of getting gold was deposed in favour of cultivating the soil, progress was possible. Further, a new motive began to aid emigration. This was the desire of getting a home where men could follow their own religion in peace. Settlements like those of the Pilgrim Fathers in New England, or the Catholics in Maryland, had a permanence unknown before, for the settlers had no wish to fill their pockets with money and return home to spend it. Home was to them where they could live with brothers, undisturbed by penal laws or persecution, worshipping God together after their own fashion. Hence while Elizabeth's colonists had failed, their successors under the Stuarts, seeking a home and content to work for a plain living, were more prosperous.

The first settlement, the germ of the United States of to-day, was sent out by the London Company, and settled in 1607 at Jamestown. It was fortunate in its leader, John Smith, who saw, as no colonist had seen before, the true principles of success in colonial enterprise. Firm alike in keeping his colonists obedient and cheerful, he made it clear that it was useless to waste time in harum-scarum searches for gold, or a North-west Passage, but that, on the contrary, "nothing was to be expected but by labour". The infant colony had its ups and downs. It was nearly abandoned in 1609, and again in 1611, but the evil days passed, and prosperity came with the lapse of time. The original 105 emigrants had increased by 1619 to 600, and in the next year the number rose to 2000. In 1619 the first general assembly was held, and from that time progress was steady. The next year (1620) saw the sailing of the *Mayflower* and the settlement of the "Pilgrim Fathers". These men were mostly Separatists, who, in 1607, had left England sooner than conform, and had lived for some time as exiles in Holland. They established themselves at Plymouth, naming their new home after the port whence they had sailed, and so formed the nucleus of the New England states. From this time onward colonies grew fast. In 1629 the colony of Massachusetts Bay was established by charter, in 1630 Boston was founded, in 1633 Connecticut was settled in defiance of the Dutch, and in the same year the colony of Maryland was founded for Roman Catholics by Lord Baltimore. In 1643 Connecticut, New Haven, Plymouth, and Massachusetts Bay united in an alliance for mutual defence; Pennsylvania, a refuge for the oppressed sect of Quakers, was started by William Penn in 1680. In the islands, too, settlements were common. Barbadoes and the Bermudas were colonized early in the seventeenth century, and by the aid of sugar-planting and slave labour the planters made large fortunes. All this indicates a great activity in foreign settlements, but what was done was mainly the work of individuals or companies. The Crown granted charters, and in some cases sent governors, and it also meddled in the trade of the colonies when once started. But as a rule the Government took little interest in the expansion, save so far as it affected the course of English trade under the Mercantile system. The royal forces were not employed; colonies were not the subject of treaties. The Committee of Trade and Plantations, the first definite sign that Government was beginning to recognize its responsibilities in the matter, was not appointed until 1668; far-seeing men like Shaftesbury and Locke took much interest in its deliberations.

The story of the trading companies instinctively turns English eyes towards the East. Our Indian empire is the abiding memorial of the work of such a company. But though the East India Company was incomparably the most important of these, it was not the earliest. The system of company-trading was familiar enough in England. Even before the Norman conquest a body of alien merchants, the men of the Emperor, had had their establishment, the Steelyard, in London. There had been Hanse merchants, and merchants of the Staple. In fact, when any freedom in trading with aliens was unusual, when such privileges as were given were obtained by treaties between the rulers, it was necessary that the trade should be put in the hands of known and responsible persons. From 1407 onwards the English Company of Merchant Adventurers traded in English cloth, not necessarily to a fixed port, as had been the case with the Staplers, but "venturing" where they pleased. By the end of the fifteenth century they sent ships to Spain, Holland, Venice, and other Mediterranean ports, and to the Baltic. We have already noticed how Chancellor's voyage, which opened the Russian trade, resulted in the foundation of the Muscovy Company to carry it on. The Prussian or Eastland merchants were incorporated by Elizabeth in 1578; the Levant Company, trading overland with the East, got its first charter in 1581; there was a Barbary Company and a Guinea Company, and in James I.'s day we have seen the London Company and the Plymouth Company, which helped to colonize the New World. In fact they were common enough. What distinguishes the East India Company is the extraordinary and altogether unexpected success of its operations. The others faded away by degrees and left little or no mark; the East India Company acquired for us our Indian empire.

It is not enough merely to wonder at this unique trading company, which has added to our dominions a country roughly equal in size and population to Europe without Russia; we must examine why it was possible, and how it was done. That will fall to a later chapter; at present we are dealing with the beginnings. No thought of territorial dominion appears in the policy of the Company till the eighteenth century. To secure liberties to trade and build factories, to oust the Portuguese, to keep in check the Dutch, and, if possible, get from them a share in the spice trade, to protect the Company against "interlopers"—persons not members, who desired to poach on the Company's ground—to pay good dividends to the shareholders, these are the early objects of the Company. But even here the Company was different from its predecessors. The Levant and Muscovy Companies were what is called regulated Companies, that is to say each member traded with his own capital at his own risk and for his own profit. But the East India Company was a joint-stock company; the Company, or rather its board of directors, traded with the common capital, and divided the profits according to each man's holding. The difference may seem trivial, but it was not so. The Company as a unit was much more powerful than any set of individual traders could be; as a corporation it was permanent and did not die; it had a larger capital; it could afford to undertake wider operations; its policy possessed a unity, a common aim, which isolated ventures lacked. In fact a regulated company could not have founded an empire, as we know this joint-stock company did.

Its beginnings were humble enough. The Queen granted a charter in 1600, and in the new year Sir James Lancaster sailed with the first fleet of five ships. Much doubt was felt as to what were the best goods to take; iron, cutlery, broadcloth, and glass formed the bulk of the cargoes, but under their charter the merchants were allowed to export bullion —a thing generally forbidden. A share in the spice trade was the chief aim, and Lancaster accordingly made a treaty with the King of Achin in Sumatra. In the Spice Islands, however, the Dutch were beforehand with us, and soon began to complain of our interference in what they regarded as their monopoly. Fighting took place in 1612 and 1615, while in 1623 the Dutch, getting wind of what they believed to be a plot to seize the fort of Amboyna, arrested some servants of the English Company, tortured them, and acting on the evidence thus gained, put to death all the English in the island. The "Massacre of Amboyna" aroused great enmity in the East for a long time; but the Dutch were on the whole well able to look after their own interests, and English enterprise made little headway in the Spice Islands during the seventeenth century.

On the mainland we were more fortunate. In 1612 Best obtained leave to set up a factory at Surat, under an arrangement with the Mogul emperor. In 1615 Thomas Roe went as the first ambassador to the Mogul's court, and got a fresh privilege, giving leave for more factories and a wider trade. In 1612 the Company itself was reorganized,[5] its capital increased, and its operations placed under a board of directors. Its trade spread fast; settlements at Madras in 1620 and on the Hoogly in 1642 were followed by the gift of Bombay by Charles II. in 1668. Fort St. George and Armegon were built to protect Madras and the settlement on the Coromandel coast in 1639 against either Dutch or Portuguese. The latter were not dangerous, but it was far otherwise with the Dutch. They had begun before us; they had been openly at war with Spain, while England had been ostensibly at peace, and in consequence there had been none of the hesitation which Elizabeth had showed. When Portugal had

---

[5] At first there had been a joint-stock fund for each venture, to which a member could subscribe what he liked, his interest and liability ending with the venture. Under the later constitution, each subscriber took his proportionate share from all the profits made by the Company.

been absorbed into Spain, the Dutch had found the Portuguese factories in the East an easy prey. The Dutch East India Company, founded in 1591, made Amsterdam the great centre for Eastern produce during the seventeenth century, and the Bank of Amsterdam gave facilities for commerce which England did not possess. By 1650 the Dutch were recognized as our most dangerous rivals. Spain had ceased to be formidable; France had not yet become so. Holland, however, was at the height of her power, and seemed likely not only to eclipse English efforts in the East, but also to absorb the carrying trade of the world. During the Civil War almost all the trade of the English West Indian colonies passed in Dutch ships. The Navigation Acts of 1651 and 1660 were designed to check this, by forbidding importation or exportation of goods between Africa, Asia, America, and England, save in ships built and owned in England, with English crews, by preventing aliens being merchants or factors in our colonies, and by prohibiting the bringing of Eastern goods from Dutch ports. This was likely to lead to war, but none felt any hesitation on that account. From 1650 to 1674 the Dutch were "our natural enemies", and the furious fighting in the Channel between Blake, Monk, and the Duke of York on the one side, and Van Tromp and De Ruyter on the other, was really a struggle for the carrying trade and dominion in the East. Chatham said later that he would conquer America in Germany, but it might have been said, with equal truth, that in the end of the seventeenth century we were warring for the East Indies in the Channel.

The contest was a stern one, and, so far as mere fighting went, the Dutch had none the worst of it, but in the end the gain was England's. Holland, a smaller power, was less able to bear the strain of a naval duel with England followed by two continental wars with France; and when the eighteenth century came she was exhausted, and unable to compete on equal terms with her stronger rivals, France and England.

A century and a half saw England learn first to plunder and then despise Spain, saw her explore the North in search of a trade route, occupy the eastern coast of America with settlers, and lay the foundation of her empire in the East. It was a great result; more so, if we remember that it was mainly due to private enterprise, and astonishing when we consider the smallness of the means by which the great result was attained. Spanish and Portuguese vessels were, as a rule, much larger than the English, their men more numerous, their expeditions more carefully planned. In Eastern voyages the disparity is not so marked. Lancaster's ship, the *Red Dragon*, in which he led the East India Company's first venture, was of 600 tons, a large ship for the time, but she was inferior in size to some of the Portuguese ships. But the ships that went to Western and Arctic waters were very small. Frobisher's fleet was made up of two small barques of 25 tons, and a pinnace of 10 tons. Drake started in 1572 with the *Pasha* of 70 tons, and the *Swan* of 25 tons: men and boys together, the crew was only seventy-three, and yet these took Nombre, plundered the Spanish treasure train, and from first to last overhauled 200 vessels on the Caribbean Sea. The expedition that started for the Pacific was on a somewhat larger scale. The *Pelican*, renamed the *Golden Hind*, was 100 tons, and the *Elizabeth* of 80 tons. But the *Christopher* of 15 tons was not thought too small to go with them. Hudson in his first investigation of the North-east Passage had but ten men and a boy, and though the number finds a modern parallel in the history of the latest Arctic exploration,[6] yet the conditions differed so widely that one may as well admire the courage of the earlier explorer as of the later. The *Squirrel*, which foundered with Gilbert, was only 10 tons. Nor was it that larger ships were unknown. Henry VIII.'s *Great Harry* was about 1000 tons, and carried 700 men, and though this was the largest ship in the English navy at this time, yet when the Queen lent ships, as she often did, to the Adventurers, they were almost always larger than the private vessels. To appreciate, as they deserve, the energy and hardihood of the Elizabethan seamen, we must remember that their ships were smaller and their crews less numerous than their enemies; their advantage lay in superiority of manœuvring and sailing, and above all in the daring which refused to reckon the odds against them.

[6] The crew of the *Fram* numbered thirteen.

CHAPTER XII.

A SURVEY OF ENGLISH INDUSTRIES. 1640-1700.

The latter part of the eighteenth century is marked by that vast expansion of industry and commerce which has made England the great manufacturing country of the world. To appreciate the main features of this Industrial Revolution, as it is sometimes called, requires some knowledge of industrial conditions before the introduction, first of all, of machinery, and later, of steam-power, changed the old order for a new one. And if the history of industry in the eighteenth century is remarkable as giving us the beginnings of our modern system, yet the seventeenth century has an importance of its own, quite distinct in character from what came after, since it was in the latter part of it that England received her last and greatest benefit from the immigration of foreign artisans.

To relate the whole tale of what England has gained in this way would take us far back. It would take us to the colony of Flemish weavers who came into England soon after the Conquest, and were protected against native jealousy by Matilda of Flanders, William I.'s wife. This policy of granting royal protection to foreign artisans appeared again in Edward III.'s reign, when a fresh body of Flemish weavers driven from their homes by oppression took refuge in England, bringing their crafts with them. As we have seen, it was to this immigration that we owe the great stimulus to the weaving industry that went on hand in hand with the enclosures of the fifteenth century and the beginnings of our export trade in cloth. As the English industry grew, that of Flanders declined, but in the dressing and dyeing of cloth, and in the making of the finer kinds, England was still behind. But the injury which the Count of Flanders and Philip of Valois had begun in the fourteenth century was turned into ruin by the Duke of Alva in the sixteenth. The religious persecution drove Flemish Protestant weavers in hundreds from their homes; the long war which followed utterly disorganized the industry of those who remained. That Spain should have been the power to destroy the Flemish weaving industry, and thereby leave England without a rival, is a curious example of the irony of history. At the outset of the competition between England and Flanders, Flanders was at a disadvantage, for England was the only great wool-producing country, and by stopping the export, England could and did throw her rival's trade into confusion. But during the fifteenth century Spain began to be renowned for her wool—some said by the foolish generosity of Edward IV., who sent a present of English rams to the King of Aragon— and Flemish weavers were no longer dependent solely upon England for raw material. When the Netherlands and Spain came under one king, one would have been prepared for a close commercial union between countries which had so much to gain each from the other. Yet things fell out quite otherwise. Spanish persecutions ruined the Flemish industry and thereby spoiled the market for their own wool. Persecution led to rebellion, and her rebellious subjects were foremost in stripping Spain of her New World riches; while heretic England, as hateful in Spanish eyes as the heretic Netherlands themselves, harboured the refugees and reaped the advantage of their technical skill.

We have already seen something of the exclusive spirit in trade which grew up again in the fifteenth century,[1] after the work of Edward III. had been swept away. Jealousy of aliens was one of its most marked features, and though immigration continued on a small scale throughout the century, alien artificers were not well received either by the Crown or its subjects. A statute of Richard III. complained that "a great number of artificers and other strangers" came and used the "making of cloth and other handicrafts . . . to the great impoverishment of the King's subjects", not suffering the King's subjects to work with them, and forbade the using of "any handicraft the occupation of any craftsman in this realm of England". The hostility towards aliens found expression in the great riot of Evil May Day, 1517, when, stirred by a sermon of Dr. Bell's at the Spital to the effect that the land was given to Englishmen who ought "to cherish and maintain themselves, and to hurt and grieve aliens", a mob of apprentices and journeymen assembled, to the number of near a thousand, broke open the jail and rescued some who had been imprisoned, and then maltreated a number of foreigners and wrecked their houses. The rioters were severely dealt with by Wolsey, but they got a good deal of

[1] See page 124.

sympathy from native merchants and workmen. Even when Englishmen and alien refugees were united in hostility to Rome, the Government did not at once receive the strangers heartily. Henry VIII. had no mind for toleration, and though Thomas Cromwell protected the Lutherans, and Somerset encouraged them, they suffered much in the Marian persecution. It was not till Elizabeth's reign that the immigration, especially from the Netherlands, assumed its largest proportions. By 1568 there were nearly 1500 Flemings and Walloons in Norwich, and the next year saw the number doubled; there were similar colonies of refugees in Colchester, London, Southwark, Canterbury, Southampton, and Sandwich. The reception which they met varied; the common folk disliked them, and the weavers were jealous; but the Queen, and those who could put aside national prejudice and consider the good of the realm, welcomed them, for they brought those very arts which England had hitherto lacked. They were skilled in dressing and dyeing cloth, and also in making those finer fabrics, bays and says, moccados, arras, fine kersies, and "such other outlandish commodities as hath not used to be made within this our realm of England". Thus rose the "New Drapery"[2] of Elizabeth's time, the bombazines, so fashionable in James I.'s reign, which restored the prosperity of Norwich, the bays and says, which were the toast of the town at Colchester, and which had become of such importance that when the town was besieged by Fairfax, Parliament offered to buy what the manufacturers

---

[2] Called so in distinction from the "Old Drapery" of Edward III.'s time.

made during the siege. These and other new kinds of cloth were made by the new-comers, not only to their own profit, but to the profit of many of the poorer folk in England who learned the new trades, and to the advantage of the realm.

Under these circumstances cloth-making became more than ever the staple industry of the country. In addition to the foreigners, mostly settled in the east, there were other manufacturing districts in the west of England, and in the north, particularly the West Riding of Yorkshire. Serges were made in Exeter and Taunton; kerseys, bays, and frizados in Tiverton, Barnstaple, Torrington, and Crediton, the last of which was celebrated for the fineness of its thread. Coarse cloth was made in the West Riding; Wakefield, Halifax, and Keighley were clothing towns. A complaint from "many thousands of poore clothiers" of Leeds in 1626, in spite of a suspicious fondness for large round numbers, serves to show that the industry was at any rate considerable. But we must guard against misunderstandings in applying such words as "centres of trade" and "clothier". The industry was mainly domestic, and very widely spread. There were a few mills where weaving was carried on under the roof of a master, but this was rare; such enterprises had been discouraged by Elizabeth.[3] As a rule the wool was carded, spun, and woven in the workmen's own homes. The appliances, the spinning-wheel and the hand-loom, were practically of the same type as had been used for centuries. The shuttle was passed from

[3] See p 148.

hand to hand, which made it impossible for one man to weave cloth wider than about three-quarters of a yard. Wider cloth needed two weavers, one to pass the shuttle to the other. In some districts the work was done for a "clothier" who bought or provided the wool, put it out in succession to carders, spinners, and weavers, paid each for their work, and sold the cloth when completed. But this was not invariable. In Devonshire, each man worked for himself, the husbandman or gentleman farmer bringing the wool to market, where it was bought by the comber or spinner. They worked it up and sold the yarn to the weaver, who would bring it as cloth to the weekly market, where it was bought by the "clothier", who sent it to London, or by the merchant who, after sending it to the fuller, and sometimes to the dyer, shipped it abroad. Here the "clothier" is a cloth dealer, but not an employer, while a third sense of the term appears in the Leeds petition where clothier means cloth-worker.

While this stage of scattered industry offers one striking contrast to the modern concentration in factories, the action of Government affords another. The attempt to force every one to make cloth of the same length had been given up, but Government still strove to ensure good quality. Aulnagers and searchers of cloth were to certify that it was properly made; proclamations were issued against dishonest practices of stretching the cloth, or using inferior warp for the middle, or thickening with oatmeal, tallow, and flox. Dyeing also called for regulation; it does not appear that even as late as

1668 English dyers were as skilled as those on the Continent, for in that year fifty Walloons were brought into England, who taught a better system of dyeing, whereby 40 per cent could be saved. The use of bad materials, such as slip alderbark, iron filings, galls, " gummes, sirropps, or deceiptfulle stuff" was forbidden.[4] And while care was taken to prevent the customer being deceived, and the trade falling into disrepute, the Government did not neglect to foster the trade. One curious example is Charles II.'s[5] Act providing that people should be buried in woollen, instead of the linen that was commonly used.

Many other industries were practised by the refugees, and though it is impossible to be sure in all cases that these were unknown before in England, yet the industrial stimulus was great. In the seventeenth century silk weaving, ribbon weaving, linen weaving, glass engraving, printing and bookbinding, the making of combs, buttons, jewellery, baskets, gallipots, parchment, needles, and thread, all engaged their attention. Foreign names are common among those occupied with canvas, paper, soap, saltpetre, wire, and cutlery. The "cottons" of Manchester were probably of alien origin, and the refugees introduced considerable improvements in mining and in the manufacture of ordnance. From foreigners, too, came the engineering skill required for the draining of the fens. In such efforts in this direction as were made in Elizabeth's reign, as well as in schemes for improvements in harbours and water-works, foreigners were always

[4] This more particularly in dyeing of silk. [5] 18 and 19 Ch. II. c. 4.

consulted, sometimes Italians, but generally Dutchmen. One of these, Cornelius Vermuÿden, employed Dutch workmen to drain Hatfield Chase in Yorkshire, and reclaimed 70,000 acres of ground. Similar work was carried out in the Isle of Axholme and in the great Fens, though Vermuÿden was much hampered by the fenmen, who thought the improvements would rob them of their old commons and common rights, and frequently assaulted the alien workmen, and broke down their dykes, thus undoing much of the work. When by degrees a more temperate view was taken, the benefit of the drainage schemes came to be appreciated.

Hitherto it had been mainly from Flanders that skilled artisans had come, but Charles II.'s reign saw a fresh influx, this time from France. The Revocation of the Edict of Nantes in 1685 made hundreds of Huguenots leave their country sooner than change their religion, and those whose natural way of escape was by sea came mostly to England. They included many of the best workmen in France, whose principal industry had been silk weaving. Now this was precisely one of the trades which, in the opinion of the time, it was most desirable to establish in England. It would have been best, according to economic ideas of the seventeenth century, to wear nothing but English woollens, and to abstain altogether from foreign silks, but this was too much to expect. If silks were to be worn—and it was clear that they would be—then they should be English silks. But though under James I. some attempts had been made to improve the English industry by importing silk weavers, dyers, and throwsters from Italy, and also by encouraging the rearing of silkworms, the English silks were inferior to the French in quality, variety, and design. Here, however, as in the case of Spain, our rival came to our assistance by religious persecution. In 1681,[6] encouraged by a grant of naturalization from Charles II., over a thousand persons came bringing their merchandise, tools, implements, and above all, skill. So continuous and so great was the exodus that between 1670 and 1690 80,000 persons came to England, about a third settling round London, especially in Spitalfields, and the rest spreading to Canterbury, Sandwich, Norwich, Southampton, Bristol, some even going as far as Edinburgh and Ireland. As a majority of the immigrants were silk workers, the impulse given to the industry can easily be understood. In 1689 we hear of 40,000 families living by it; in 1694 there were a thousand looms at work in Blackfriars. It was calculated at the beginning of the eighteenth century that the trade had increased twenty times since 1664. The new goods included alamodes, brocades, ducapes, black and coloured mantuas, black velvets and lustrings, the makers of the last being incorporated in the Royal Lustring Company. Before the Revocation England had imported £200,000 worth of lustrings annually, but by 1698 it was found possible to prohibit importation altogether, the native supply being sufficient. The designs and

---

[6] An edict of June 17, 1681, lowering the age at which the conversions of the children of Protestant parents were accepted from twelve to seven years, led to the first great exodus of Huguenots from France during this period.

finish of brocades and figured silks were enormously improved, and save that the fashions still came from France—"France has the first of the market and England the fag end"—English goods could compete successfully in a trade in which they had seemed hopelessly behind. It is unnecessary to dwell upon England's gain. A striking proof of the evil of an intolerant policy is that in Tours there were 70 mills where before the Revocation there had been 700.

The Huguenots practised other industries besides silk weaving, some of them new, some of them introduced into England by previous immigrants. To them we owe the manufacture of sailcloth, taught by a Huguenot named Bonhomme, who set up at Ipswich. The secrets of tapestry were revealed by an ex-Capuchin monk, and the industry established at Fulham. The hat trade was also much improved, if it was not altogether set up afresh, the refugees being skilled in preparing the beaver and sticking it to the hat. It is said that for the time France lost the trade so completely that Protestant England had to supply the Roman Cardinals with hats from the factory at Wandsworth. The refugees also taught the art of paper-making. Prior to their arrival the only English paper was of the coarse brown kind, and the finer kinds had been imported; but immigrants from Bordeaux and the Auvergne brought their skill, and before long England was able to supply herself. Watch-making and clock-making and kindred mechanical arts, such as the manufacture of locks, roasting-jacks, and mechanical toys, came from abroad at this time, while the plate-glass industry benefited largely.[7] Not all these industries were equally prosperous. After a time France, recognizing her loss, made efforts to bribe her workmen to return. The sailcloth business was much hindered in England by this, so much so that by George I.'s reign we were still unable to produce as much as we wanted at home; similarly some hat makers were tempted to return to France and revived the lost art there. But upon the whole the economic gain to England was enormous. At a time when there was little or no machinery, the most important things were skill and trade secrets. These in an ordinary way were most jealously guarded at home. But the French persecution had thrown the economic ideas of the time to the winds. Recklessly driven from their homes, the French artisans who gathered in England[8] brought with them their skill, their processes, their trade secrets, and by using them in England taught them to Englishmen, and what was done could not be undone; the immigrants themselves might return or die, but the results of what they did survived. The stimulus to English manufacture given by the alien immigration at the end of the seventeenth century was not so vast in amount as that given by the introduction of machinery a century later. But it certainly was considerable. There is, however, this difference: in the first case the improvement was mainly in skill, in the second in speed; but in

---

[7] Many of the technical terms used in glass making are derived from the French: the melted glass is the "found" (*fondre*), and the place where the crucible is put is called the siege (*siège*).

[8] Many went to Brandenburg, which, like England, owes a vast industrial advance to them.

each the result was a commercial advantage over her neighbours.

While the seventeenth century saw England receive the last and greatest impulse to her industrial prosperity from immigrants, native industries were by no means idle. Three things are especially noteworthy: the first experiments in smelting iron with coal, the planting of the linen industry in Ireland, and the discovery of rock-salt.

Coal had been used for fuel in the neighbourhood of the pits since the thirteenth century, and a good deal was sent by sea to London and other towns, but even when sea carriage was used the price was extremely high. In 1638 a chaldron cost 19*s.* in London; an excise of 4*s.* the chaldron, and the restriction placed on the trade by the Newcastle corporation, who would permit none but freemen of their body to engage in it, were largely responsible for the high price; but the difficulties of loading, unloading, and carrying it over very bad roads also had much to do with it.[9] In the coal districts, however, it was cheap enough and much wasted. In Staffordshire, where in some cases it could be dug from the surface, or, in any case, without taking the mines deeper than eight to twenty yards, there was plenty to be had. It was estimated by Dudley that in 1660 2,000,000 tons were raised, and not less than 5000 tons of slack were thrown away every year as useless. While coal was thus wasted, wood was getting scarce. Two loads of wood were required for a load of char-

---

[9] Before Brindley's canal from Worsley to Manchester was made, the only way of bringing coal to the latter town in winter was on horseback.

coal, and two loads of that to smelt a ton of iron; indeed the chief use of labour in ironworks was cutting the wood and making the charcoal. Thus at Coote's three works in Ireland 2500 men were employed, principally in preparing the fuel. In Sussex, where the iron trade centred, there were over a hundred furnaces and hammers, and in Surrey several glass-works, some of them burning three or four loads of charcoal a day. There was, in fact, a serious danger that the iron workers would disforest the country altogether, and even as it was, fuel was so dear that Irish bar-iron fetched £15 to £18 a ton. The woods dwindled, and Parliament, fearing that the shipbuilders would be left without timber, had to interfere by ordering that those who cut down should plant, and by limiting the building of new furnaces.

Cramped and restricted in this way, iron-founders naturally enough turned to coal for a substitute. In 1612 Sturtevant had a patent for using coal for smelting, but turned it to no account. The next attempt by Dudley was more successful. According to his own account he made bar-iron at £12 a ton of such good quality that fowling-pieces could be made from it. But he got into many difficulties. His first works were destroyed by floods, and when he set up again at Askew Bridge, and was turning out seven tons a week, he was attacked by the jealous charcoal men and his works wrecked, on the specious ground that when monopolies were abolished his patent was void. Legal proceedings ended in his being imprisoned for debt, and when he was released some new partners swindled him.

Then came the Civil War, and as Dudley was a Royalist the Parliament transferred his patent to some of their own side. Altogether he was no more fortunate than most inventors, but he had the gratification that if he could not use his process, others could not wrest it from him. No one succeeded even as well as he did, though experiments went on to the end of the century. One difficulty was that the impurities of sulphur and phosphorus in the iron made it brittle either when hot or cold. Dudley said he was able to correct this. Another source of failure seems to have been that a strong enough blast was not used, and though such a blast could have been perfectly well obtained by water power,[10] it was not, as a matter of fact, till the steam-engine had become fairly well known that a good blast was used; and so, in spite of Dudley's transient success, the iron trade languished for want of cheap fuel until the days of Abraham Darby[11] of Colebrookdale and Roebuck of Carron.

The linen business set up by Strafford in Ireland went through similar vicissitudes. It owed its origin to political considerations. Owing to the cheapness of living in Ireland there was a movement among English clothiers to set up cloth weaving of the finer kinds, in addition to the old manufacture of rough cloth (frieze) that had always gone on among the natives. But the English

---

[10] The blast for the furnaces at Carron in 1760 was worked by water-power, although a steam-engine was used to pump the water.

[11] There were three well-known iron-founders of this name, the eldest of whom died in 1717. He introduced improvements in casting, and was one of the earliest to use coke. His son and namesake succeeded to the management of the works in 1730 and developed his father's improvements.

weavers were violently jealous of Irish rivalry, and cloth weaving in Ireland [12] was suppressed. Linen weaving was not open to the same objections; it did not threaten a great English industry, and Strafford's policy in planting it showed much foresight. For a time the new industry was very successful. Strafford wrote: "The bearer I send to buy some flax seed, which I find by this last year's trial to take extremely well in this country, and very ambitious I am to set up a trade of Linnen clothing in these parts, which if God bless so as it be effected, will, I dare say, be the greatest enriching to this Kingdom that ever befell it". He relied on women to do the spinning, sowed £1000 worth of flax seed, set up looms, imported workmen from Holland, and believed that he could undersell France or Holland 20 per cent. But this early promise was doomed to disappointment; the great rebellion swept away most of his work, and when in more peaceable times the industry revived, it remained in the north, and did not, as Strafford had hoped, spread over the country.

Besides Ireland, the country that made most progress in linen working was Scotland. There Charles II.'s policy in regard to wool was copied in an act of 1686 prescribing that all were to be buried in linen. Measures were taken to provide flax, and instruction was given all over the country in spinning and weaving. Both before and after the Union, Scotch linen was regarded with peculiar jealousy by the comparatively small body of linen makers in England. The English desire

[12] Except the original native industry, frieze making.

was to restrict the Scotch to importing linen yarn which the English manufacturers might make up themselves, a restriction which was reasonably disliked in Scotland. Linen leads naturally to cotton, and the more so because at this time the trades were actually connected. When Lewis Roberts, writing in 1641, speaks of Manchester and Bolton buying cotton wool from Cyprus or Smyrna and working it into fustians, vermillions, and dimities, we might imagine that we have mention of a true cotton manufacture. But this was not so; "cottons" of the seventeenth century were all mixtures of linen and cotton, or wool and cotton, for cotton could not at that time be spun in England strong enough for use as warp, and consequently these fustians and dimities were of linen warp and cotton weft. The same kind of fabrics were made in Scotland and in Devonshire, where they were disliked as unworthy rivals of woollen cloth, men saying, "Woe unto you, Piltonians, that make cloth without wool". The industry, though not true cotton manufacture, was at any rate wide-spread and considerable in size. If, as is stated in petitions from the town, the population of Manchester rose from 10,000 in 1578 to double that number in 1635, the increase may very probably be attributed to the new industry. Such cottons as there were, calicoes and chintzes, came from the East, and were resented as displacing English-made woollens. Even calicoes printed in England were so unpopular that rioters threw aquafortis at the wearers of them. Anne's reign saw them heavily taxed, and in 1720 they were prohibited altogether. This interference in favour of an English industry is thoroughly typical of the mercantile and protective spirit, for the obnoxious goods paid a heavy duty, and even so were much cheaper than the woollen goods which they replaced. But the supposed good of the English weavers outweighed considerations of revenue or individual advantage.

The story of the salt trade furnishes another illustration of the jealousies which arise in protected trades, and the difficulties to which they lead. Before 1670 salt was made in two ways in England; the older industry, bay-salt making by evaporating sea-water went on at many sea-coast towns, and principally at Shields, Bristol, and Southampton; the younger, brine-salt, at the salt-pits in Worcestershire and Cheshire. The two put together could not supply all the salt that was needed, and a good deal had to be imported from France. Even so the English salt-makers trembled and complained at any hint of competition. The French bay-salt was, they said, "one seventh dirt and nastiness, putrefied human bodies, dead fish, and carcasses". They grumbled at the admission of Scotch salt, and declared they were ruined when Cromwell exempted it from duty. This captious spirit might pass for patriotism so long as it showed itself against foreign salters, Frenchmen and Scotchmen only, but in 1670 a discovery opened a fresh source of supply, ample enough for all English wants; a person boring for coal near Northwich to his surprise cut into a substance "hard as Allom", which proved to be rock-salt.

When the shaft was sunk, the vein of salt was found to be twenty-five feet thick. This would make an end of all need to import salt from abroad, and those good patriots, the native bay-salt and brine-salt makers, who had been loudest in condemning foreign import and in declaring the need of supporting English industry, should have rejoiced, if they were prepared to stand by their principles. But of course they did nothing of the kind. Pockets came before patriotism. The rock-salt promised to be a more dangerous rival than French or Scotch salt, and accordingly they declared that "the rock-salt of Cheshire had so many bad qualities that most certainly Nature could never have intended it to be used". They urged that mining rock-salt would diminish the supply of brine, that the rock-salt could be manufactured anywhere and so cheat the excise, and they petitioned Parliament to put a heavy tax on the new industry, because of its natural advantages over themselves. Here we have protection at its worst. Trades which begin by assuming that they are to be saved from foreign competition, end by imagining themselves to be so sacred and so important that they are to be protected from any change or novelty which they think likely to injure them. The strength of the country, the original idea of Mercantilism, is pushed out of sight; every improvement is a foe; instead of English industries being united against the foreigner, they are at war among themselves; having been taught to look for rivals, they find rivals at home even more dangerous than rivals abroad. When feelings such as these grew common we are in the decadence of Mercantilism. Instead of being an intelligible national policy, it was becoming a scramble for protection of everything that was established, and an enemy to all industrial progress.

CHAPTER XIII.

THE RISE OF BANKING.

We think of a modern bank, such as the Bank of England, as fulfilling not one, but a number of functions. For example, it takes money on deposit for customers, and lets them have it as they want it; it lends money on bills, discounting them, and so receiving interest on its loans; it issues notes which are legal tender; it remits money from place to place. These are some, though by no means all, of the uses of the bank. But it is obvious, if we are concerning ourselves with the history of banking, either in England, or if we go further afield and include Europe, that no bank began by doing all these things from the first. With what, then, did they begin? Was it by lending, or by taking deposits, by issuing notes, or by remitting money; or did they begin in none of these ways, but with some other object, which has now fallen into the background? These questions cannot be answered simply with Yes or No, for banks originated in different ways in different places. A history of banking must be at first a history of the system in each country, and even in some cases a history of individual banks. As time went on, banks copied and learnt one from another, and so they grew to a common type. But their beginnings were distinct and often very different.

A little consideration of these main duties fulfilled by modern banks will reveal which of them is the most likely to have afforded a promising beginning. When we go back to early days we do not, of course, expect to find the same confidence in banks as exists now, but there must have been some sense of security in a country for banking to exist in any form. Until a money economy has replaced a natural economy to some considerable extent, until there is some accumulation of wealth, some opportunity for investment, some foreign trade and intercourse, banks will not exist at all, because there is nothing for them to do. But presuming that a nation has reached this stage of progress, is accustomed to the use of money, carries on a certain volume of trade, and is beginning to accumulate wealth, it is natural to ask which of these functions, safe-keeping, the issuing of notes, remitting money, or lending money, calls for the minimum of confidence. For till the minimum for these, or some similar object, is reached, banks cannot start at all.

Now, the taking of deposits, and the circulation of bankers' promises to pay, demand a good deal of confidence on the part of the public. But as Bagehot has pointed out, they are not quite on the same level. For a bank to get a number of private deposits, it is necessary that a number of people should make up their minds to do the same thing, and it is not hard to see that the advantage must be very plain and very real before a great number of people will agree thus to act together in showing confidence in a banker. Each man will prefer that some one else should make the experiment; if it turns out a success, well and good; he will think then about doing the same. But with notes, it lies with the banker, and not the public, to make a start. "To establish a note circulation a large body of persons need only *do nothing.* They receive the banker's notes in the common course of their business, and they have only *not* to take those notes to the banker for payment. If the public refrain from taking trouble a paper circulation is immediately in existence."[1] The note issue in fact advertises the banker's credit, and when this is established, the deposits will come after. As banking spreads and becomes more familiar the liabilities on notes fall compared with the liability on deposits. In Scotland, the note issue, which was at first the main source of profit, has now become trifling compared with the deposits. In England, till 1830 notes were the main thing and deposits secondary, but now it is the other way about. But in countries where banking is relatively backward, the liabilities on notes far exceed those on deposits. Deposit banking then may be led up to by a note issue. To banks formed in this way it will be necessary to recur; but there are other ways also.

Quite different objects led to the foundation of the Bank of St. George at Genoa, and other Italian

[1] Bagehot, *Lombard Street*, p. 88.

banks which copied it, and of the Bank of Amsterdam. For convenience we will deal with the last first, although in doing so we are departing from chronological order, for the Italian banks are the earliest of all, and were flourishing centuries before other nations followed the Italian example. But the Bank of Amsterdam can be described without taking into account any considerations about usury, whereas it is the change in ideas about the question of usury and interest that will form the most convenient line of connection to lead us from the early Italian banks to the rise of private banking as carried on by the goldsmiths in England.

When Holland rose to importance as a commercial state, it had, in company with other small states which carried on a great foreign trade, to meet a difficulty from which larger states were more or less free. Its currency did not consist in the main of its own coin, but was largely mixed with coins of the states with whom it traded. Under any circumstances this would breed confusion, but when this foreign coin was clipped, or light, or in some cases debased, a very serious difficulty arose. If this mixture of coin were used to pay foreign bills of exchange, then the uncertain value of it would turn the exchange very much against the country.[2] And since, as is stated by Gresham's law, bad coinage will drive out of circulation good coinage, good coin being hoarded, or melted down, or exported, the state of the currency tended to get worse, and the

---

[2] A bad currency always has this result. Thus in William III.'s reign, before the old coinage was called in and the new coinage issued, the rate of exchange was so much against England that we had to pay between £120 and £130 for every £100 sent through Amsterdam.

exchange more unfavourable. It was to remedy this evil that the Bank of Amsterdam was founded,[3] and it did so by receiving money of all sorts at its real value in good coinage, giving credit to the payer for this amount in what was called "bank-money". As all bills over a certain value had by law to be paid in bank-money, every merchant had to keep an account with the bank; but as the bank-money was of known and uniform value, and always in demand, the unfavourable rate of exchange disappeared. Although the bank did not pay out coin to those who wished to draw their bank-money, yet since it took bullion on credit, giving receipts for it, any one who, having bank-money, wished to get bullion from the bank, had only to bring one of these receipts, and the bank would issue the bullion to him, on condition of his transferring to it an amount of bank-money equal to that which had been originally advanced on the bullion. Thus the Bank of Amsterdam came to discharge several functions of the ordinary bank; it remitted money, and in a roundabout way it took money on deposit, but its primary object was to improve the currency.

Let us now return from this digression, go back more than three centuries, and take up the story of the Italian banks. With them currency, though an object, was not a primary object. The Bank of St. George at Genoa, and the banks founded in imitation of it, were finance companies, who supplied Governments with money. They were not, at first, concerned with individuals at all; they made loans to states. But their field of operations

[3] In 1609.

widened, and their bills of exchange and letters of credit were used in remitting money from one country to another. Italian merchants from Genoa, Lucca, Siena, and Florence, among whom the best known houses were the Peruzzi and the Bardi —men who caused the name of Lombard Street to be given to the banking street in London—combined the business of buying wool with that of collecting and remitting the papal revenue by means of bills of exchange. Henry III., Edward I., and Edward III. all borrowed from them in order to provide money for their wars, and the last-named, by delaying payment, ruined a number of Italian houses, among them the Bardi, and so caused a panic in Florence. These loans to the Crown were secured on the taxes or customs. Consequently we find the business of collecting, or farming the taxes, often in the hands of these Italians, who were part merchants, part bankers. But they did not confine themselves to dealing with sovereigns; they lent also to monasteries and ambassadors, and sometimes, too, to the King's subjects. Here they were upon dangerous ground, for though, undoubtedly, they gave facilities for business which England would otherwise have lacked, yet they grew extremely unpopular as soon as they were understood to be concerned in the taking of usury.

An understanding of the ideas about money-lending, and the wickedness of taking usury, must precede any account of the rise of banking in England, and it is particularly important, for if the moral objection to usury be not grasped, it would be natural to suppose that banking began with money-lending, which obviously calls for no confidence on the part of the public. But banking did not begin with money-lending, because for a long time money-lending for a profit was illegal, or if not actually against the law, was held to be immoral. The prohibition of usury was a Christian precept based on the Gospel command, "Lend, hoping for nothing again". As early as the Council of Nicæa churchmen were forbidden to take usury on pain of degradation, while in the ninth century the prohibition was extended to the laity. Since, however, the Roman civil law permitted usury, the spread of the study of it gave a stimulus to money-lending, which the Church exerted itself to stop. "Manifest usurers" were not to be admitted to communion, nor given Christian burial.[4] In 1274 Gregory X. ordered that none were to hire houses to usurers or harbour them, and these censures were made more effective by the command that the wills of usurers were to be invalid. As ecclesiastical courts administered wills, usury was thus brought clearly within their scope. Usury being thus unchristian, the monopoly of money-lending fell, as has already been observed, to the Jews.[5] Christian opinion did not touch them, and though Christian courts put difficulties in the way of their recovering debts, yet the Jews were under the special patronage of the King in England, and it was not his interest to let them be defrauded. In 1290, however, Edward I., pressed by ecclesiastical opinion and by the dislike which his subjects felt

[4] 1179. [5] See p. 81.

for the Jews, and irritated by the way in which they thwarted his schemes for a better coinage, drove them out. Henceforward money-lending for usury, if done at all, would have to be done by Christians.

At first we are inclined to say that if Christians did do it they acted wrongly, according to the opinion of the time. This, however, would be an over-statement. There was no wavering in the idea that taking usury was wicked, for it was against the teaching of the Gospel. If a man suffered no loss by lending the money, if he could have made nothing with it had he not lent it, if he got it returned as agreed, then usury was taking advantage of another's necessities; it was making a gain where no gain was deserved. This was true enough when these conditions held good, but only so long. When there was a field for investment, or when it could be shown that the lender suffered actual loss, then it was unreasonable that he should not be recompensed.

From the thirteenth century onwards it is plain that such a field for investment was gradually opening out. Merchants made profits on their ventures, and if they could borrow money and trade on a larger scale they would clearly make more. But when it was once of common occurrence to get a return for money in this way, then the lender might reasonably urge that he was a loser by lending, or that at any rate he might become so if he was not promptly repaid. Hence it was recognized as fair that a penalty (*pœna conventionalis*) should be inflicted on the borrower who was unpunctual in repayment. It might be justified on the ground that actual loss had been incurred by his default (*damnum emergens*), or that gain which was probable had not been made (*lucrum cessans*). And if the payment was long delayed, then it was reasonable that the penalty should increase in amount. Contracts of this kind were not condemned[6] as usurious, provided (1) that the loan was first made gratuitously, (2) that the loss incurred was real and not fraudulent. At first, proof had to be given of this, but later, in the case of merchants and those accustomed to trade, proof was no longer required. The loss was presumed. In these payments we have the germ of "interest", "that which is between" the position of the lender had his money been returned punctually, and his position when repayment was delayed.

But the whittling away of the usury prohibition did not end here. A man might purchase a rent-charge on an estate; that is to say, for a sum down he bought the right to receive a fixed annual income[7]. Contracts of this kind were not held usurious, provided they were attached to property which did bring in a *bona fide* revenue. As this

[6] Fourteenth-century opinion was opposed to compensation for *lucrum cessans*, but only on the ground that the gain was doubtful. By the fifteenth century it was generally held justifiable.

[7] Generally in money; but in some instances payment was made in kind in return for the transfer of a holding. Thus, for example, "Surrender by John Lewyn to John Honewode of a messuage and land in Pynnor, under the condition that the aforesaid John Honewode shall find for the aforesaid John Lewyn every other year a new woollen garment, and in every year one pair of boots and one pair of shoes, one pair of woven linen sheets for the term of the life of the aforesaid John Lewyn. And in case the aforesaid John Lewyn shall survive Joan his wife then the aforesaid John shall find for the aforesaid John Lewyn, the food for the term of his life, and one bed chamber as is fitting."—*Harrow Manor Court Rolls*, 7 Richard II., 1384.

principle was extended from land to include shops, houses, and trading rights, it was not difficult for a merchant to borrow money in this way. Further, partnerships were legal enough, even where one partner found the money and another did the work, provided only that each shared in the risk, and that payment was not made for the use of money when no profit was gained. Loans on bottomry, the earliest form of marine insurance, offered another way in which money could be lent. These were loans on the security of the ship or goods to be repaid with profit, or interest, on the completion of the voyage. Originally used by ship-masters in distress in foreign ports, these loans became a favourite form of commercial investment. As the interest and capital had to be repaid only when the ship reached port safely, these loans were not held usurious, for the lender ran a risk of the ship sinking, in which case both capital and interest disappeared. Thus in all these contracts the fact of the lender taking a risk sufficed to clear him from the charge of taking usury.

These considerations may seem over-refined and unimportant, as being concerned with antiquated commercial proceedings, and in any case somewhat far removed from the story of English banking. But they are not so; they show, first, that a clear distinction was drawn between what was usury and what was not, between lending money on the chance of gain, or with the certainty of it; secondly, that the prohibition of usury properly so called did not seriously hamper the investing of capital, for there were plenty of ways in which money could be employed that were not usurious; and thirdly, that the lending which banks do now, namely, stipulating for interest from the first whether a profit was made or not, was clearly usurious according to the mediæval ideas, and that accordingly banks would not have been permitted to carry on such business.

As the condemnation of usury was in the main the work of the theologians, it was naturally affected by the Reformation. Catholic opinion became for a time more stringent, and took a step backward in making the prohibition more vigorous. The reformers, on the other hand, inclined rather to favour greater liberty, and Calvin did not see his way to "visit usuries with wholesale condemnation", although he still disapproved of usury which took advantage of a man's needs. But a more practical view of the new conditions prevailed with Henry VIII. His act of 1545, which permitted the taking of 10 per cent, gave up all attempt to distinguish the character of the transaction, and tried merely to prevent oppression. The act was repealed in 1552, but re-enacted in 1571. And though English opinion was by no means unanimous in favour of the new principle, the old prohibitions were never put in force again. By the seventeenth century Catholic theologians too had practically admitted the justice of taking interest on money lent, even where the lender did not share the risk. Modern conditions had superseded the ancient ones, and had brought new ideas with them. Neither sentiment nor law any longer placed obstacles in the way of such lending as banks carry on now.

The first persons to take advantage of the new

state of the law were the goldsmiths. As they had valuable property of their own to guard, people were inclined to think that what would be trusted to them was safe. Accordingly the practice of depositing money or bullion with the goldsmiths became a common one, the more so after 1640, when Charles I., then in great straits for money, had seized the bullion of private merchants left for safe-keeping in the Tower. The amount certainly was repaid later, but depositors were nervous of trusting the King any more, and considered the goldsmiths safer; they were less likely to find themselves tempted by political necessities. When the goldsmiths thus obtained deposits, they naturally were ready to lend at interest. Cromwell borrowed from them on the security of the taxes, and paid them back when the taxes came in; Charles II. continued the plan, paying the goldsmiths 8 per cent for what they advanced. As, however, they had to pay their customers 6 per cent on their deposits, the profit was rather steady than large. In 1672, however, the system received a rude shock. The King, who then owed the goldsmiths £1,328,526, announced that the sum would not be repaid, but that his creditors would have to be satisfied with interest. Even this crumb of consolation was denied till 1677, when 6 per cent was at last paid. Payment stopped again in 1683, but in 1701 it was arranged that 3 per cent should be paid.[8] Later still, the South Sea Company took over the debt, and on the failure of that body the sum was included in the National Debt, of which indeed it formed the nucleus.

[8] This was a very low rate for the time.

This fraudulent action of the Crown gave a serious shock to the goldsmiths, but it did not cripple their banking business permanently. The interest which they gave attracted deposits, and their bills circulated freely, so much so that at the end of the seventeenth century it seemed likely that a system of private banking would spread over England.

Another turn in the political wheel brought a change which has had the greatest consequences in the commercial development of England. In 1694 William III. was at his wits' end for money to carry on his continental war. His advisers proposed to raise a loan, but the credit of the Government was not good, and either very high interest would have to be offered, or the money would not be obtained at all. Yet money there must be, or the Channel would be left without a fleet. The Government asked for £1,200,000, and offered eight per cent interest, while as an additional bait the lenders were allowed to incorporate themselves as the Bank of England, and have a monopoly of note issue as a corporation. The bait was successful. Before eleven days were over the whole amount was subscribed.

The Bank was at first much disliked; as it owed its support to the moneyed interest, the land-owners feared it; having been promoted by the Whigs, it was hated by the Tories. The bill authorizing its creation got through the House of Lords only with the very greatest difficulty. Nothing but the fact that without the money the war must stop persuaded the Lords to pass it. The Tories found in this Whig financial company a menace to the monarchy. Banks, they urged, were republican in character; they flourished at Amsterdam, Genoa, and Venice, but they did not exist in monarchical France or Spain; why then establish one in England? Whig opponents to the scheme saw the bank as a worse engine of tyranny than the Star Chamber. Such a bank would enable the king to raise money without consulting Parliament. So great was the clamour that a clause had to be inserted prohibiting the Bank from lending to the Crown without leave of Parliament. The Bank, however, survived these onslaughts, as it survived the more dangerous attacks of its rivals the goldsmiths. These chose their time well. In 1697, when the old coinage was withdrawn from circulation, and before the new had been issued from the Mint in sufficient quantities, the goldsmiths suddenly presented at the Bank a number of its own notes, which they had been industriously collecting for this purpose, and demanded payment in cash. Owing to the scarcity of coin, the Bank was of course unable to pay, but it was not insolvent. All it required was time; it refused to pay the goldsmiths, as it declared their demands were malicious, but it offered to pay fifteen per cent of all *bona-fide* demands at once; and it was able, by degrees, to pay in full. And so this attack failed also, and the Bank survived.

Temporary expedients have often lasted on to become permanent institutions with wide-reaching results, but there has been no more conspicuous example of this than the Bank of England. It was created by a party to finance a government; now it has nothing to do with party, nor with financing, though its connection with the Government has remained a close one. It keeps the Government balance, and this alone has given it great stability. What the Government sees fit to trust, individuals will trust. It is to the Government that it owes its monopoly of note issue as a joint-stock company in London; and while in England and Wales there are still sixty-nine banks issuing notes, no new bank of issue can be started, and the circulation of Bank of England notes tends to increase. And, further, it was believed that by its charter the Bank had a monopoly of deposit banking against all other joint-stock companies. This belief was not correct; the monopoly was a monopoly of note issue only. But the practical effect of this belief was that the Bank was the only joint-stock company doing deposit-banking in London until 1833, when the mistake was found out and other London joint-stock banks started.

Just as the Government helped the Bank, so the Bank helped the Government. More than once it found loans when the Government was in want of money, and could obtain it no other way. But this plan of borrowing had far-reaching results. The "funds", the debt of the nation to those who had lent money to it, united the Government and the moneyed men in the city against the Stuarts. Just as the gifts of monastery land had bound the nobles to uphold the Reformation and resist the revival of Papal authority, so the loans which formed the National Debt confirmed the loyalty of the rich class to William and the Hanoverians. If the Stuarts returned, there was little reason to think that they would be zealous in paying interest on money borrowed and used against themselves by kings whom they regarded as usurpers. So far as the Bank and the National Debt inclined men to uphold the Revolution settlement, the verdict of later years is in their favour without qualification, but in another respect there is more room for doubt. Borrowing was no doubt an easy way of meeting difficulties, especially when the money had not to be paid back. By the foundation of the Bank, William's government got £1,200,000, and only paid £100,000 for it in interest. But that interest had to be paid every year; and thus the burden of William's wars, instead of being discharged in his time, was shifted on to the shoulders of those who came after. Hitherto expenditure had been met by taxation, Government paying its way as it went. When borrowing became a common resource, this was no longer so. Taxpayers now are still paying for the wars of the eighteenth century, without having any choice in the matter. And more than this, the interest paid has exceeded the amount of the debt.

It is fairly open to question whether a Government is justified in pledging the national credit, in binding future generations to pay for its actions. On the one hand, to repudiate the debt is impossible; on the other, it is hard that expenditure, which may be seen later in its true light as extravagant or even unnecessary, should fall, not on those who authorized or encouraged it, but on later generations who have gained nothing from it. Such expenditure cannot be criticised on general grounds; each case must be considered on its own merits. Where, as in the Napoleonic war, the nation was threatened by foreign invasion, where its very existence as a nation was at stake, it is easy to justify a policy of borrowing. Payment will have to be made in the future, but it will be payment for substantial benefits. On the other hand, where a war is the outcome of pique or jealousy, or of a mistaken policy by which the nation gains nothing, then it is clearly unfair that the Government which advised such a war should be able to escape the unpopularity of the high taxes necessary to pay for it, by contracting loans and leaving the task of paying interest to those who come after. For example, whether we hold that the gains of England balanced the expenditure of the eighteenth century, depends upon how high we are inclined to place the value of colonies. This is a political question, and the view which a man takes of the British empire as it stands, will dictate the answer.

Whether the new system of banking and national finance has been always used well or not, the commercial capabilities have been immense. They stand revealed in the industrial and commercial progress of the eighteenth century at home, and the power of the nation abroad. Merchants, manufacturers, and the Government alike were able to extend their operations; the manufacturers by taking advantage of the new inventions and working on a scale hitherto unknown, the merchants and shipowners by spreading British-made goods over the world, and the Government by thwarting French colonial ambition, by colonizing America, by establishing British rule in India, and by building up a naval power which destroyed its competitors, and was left at the last without a rival; and this was largely done by using credit to get command of money. And it was the banks, and especially the Bank of England, that made it possible for individuals and Government alike to carry out these vast undertakings.

CHAPTER XIV.

THE GROWTH OF GREATER BRITAIN—THE TRADE WARS OF THE EIGHTEENTH CENTURY.

There is a remarkable contrast between the colonial expansion of the seventeenth century and that of the eighteenth, some features of which have been mentioned already. We have seen, for example, that our rivals in world-dominion were first Spain and then Holland. In the eighteenth century, however, France took their place. It is true that our gains were not made entirely at the expense of the French, for we took much from Spain and Holland. Yet this was not because these countries fought with us of their own choice, but because each successively became entangled in French alliances, or dominated by French policies, and so England, in combating her prime enemy France, stripped the enemy's allies. In fact, the eighteenth century saw the beginning of a Hundred Years' War with France, just as the reign of Edward III. had done, but for very different objects. Fourteenth-century ambition looked to a conquest of France itself, or at any rate a valuable portion of French territory; in the eighteenth century the struggle was for colonial power. Marlborough, indeed, threatened an invasion of France, as did Napoleon an invasion of England, but between these two there are three wars between England and France in which direct measures of attack on each other are hardly contemplated. The old engine, invasion, is superseded by new methods; war goes on in India and America and the West Indies, while French and English fleets strive for the command of the sea, for it is felt that this command will lay the colonies of the enemy at the mercy of the victor. Another point of difference is that, in the main, we have continued to hold the gains of the eighteenth century, but the American colonies, the great monument of seventeenth-century enterprise, have been lost. It is true that India still remains to us, and the beginnings of English connection with India date back to 1600. But this connection was a trade connection. The epoch of conquest, of territorial power in India, did not begin till the eighteenth century was half over, when a Frenchman showed that native troops might be used to secure something more than mere liberty of trading, and Englishmen were not slow to copy their rival's method.

It was, no doubt, a momentous discovery that native soldiers, when drilled and officered by

Europeans, would enable French and English traders to compete, and compete successfully, against Mahratta chieftains in the general scramble for power in India which followed the break-up of the Mogul empire. It led direct to the British rule in India, as we know it. But the policy of acquiring colonial dominion by force was only new as applied to India. What happened there was that the East India Company changed from being mere traders, to being sovereigns and conquerors, possessing an army, and able to use force where milder methods failed. But precisely the same change had taken place in English colonial methods elsewhere, even earlier. We have seen that the Crown took very little interest in the foundation of the American colonies, save by bargaining for a share in any revenue that might be gained. Statesmen of the seventeenth century did not feel any absorbing interest in the growth of a Greater Britain. To Cromwell, indeed, we owe Jamaica, but its capture was not a deliberate act of policy; on the contrary, it was a hasty stroke delivered to distract attention from the failure of his expedition against San Domingo. His policy was of an old type: it was directed against Spain, an old antagonist, and indeed nearly exhausted; it was carried out on the old Elizabethan buccaneering model, and with the assistance of England's yet unrecognized rival in the colonial struggle, France. It was essentially an old-fashioned policy. The Navigation Acts were certainly directed against a commercial rival. They were intended to destroy Dutch carrying trade and Dutch fisheries, and to exclude the Dutch from sharing in the profits of existing colonies; they were not deliberately designed to spread English power over new lands. Treaties tell the same tale; the diplomatic arrangements of the latter part of the seventeenth century do not yield either in number or complexity to those which ended the wars of the Spanish Succession, or the Austrian Succession, but they take little or no heed of colonies. The only mention of them in the great Treaty of Ryswick (1697) is a stipulation that commissioners were to be appointed to settle the limits of English and French territory in Hudson's Bay. The fact is that our colonies were still largely private affairs. They had been founded by private enterprise and supported by private resources. The State had granted charters and a vague general protection; the colonists indeed remained Englishmen, and now and again, as after the massacres at Amboyna, the Government had stepped in to get redress for injuries to its subjects; but, as a rule, England had maintained a less close connection with her colonies than either Spain or Portugal, and had scarcely recognized them as national concerns, or paid much attention to them in her international agreements.[1]

---

[1] A general statement of this kind is, of course, subject to exceptions. That it is, however, true as a whole, is shown by the following list of the chief English settlements down to 1690, and the method of their foundation:—

COLONY.	DATE.	FOUNDERS.
Virginia,	1607.	London Company of Virginia, under charter from James I.
Bermudas,	1612.	Offshoot of Virginia Co., incorporated as Governor and Company for Plantation of the Somer Isles, 1615.

The eighteenth century, however, shows the change definitely established. As early as 1701 two treaties mark clearly the new interest that was felt in possessions abroad. In the Treaty of Lisbon between Spain and Portugal, Spain promised not to make peace until the Dutch restored to Portugal their captures of Cochin and Cananos, and agreed to try to recover and hand back to Portugal any possessions which she had lost, while in the same year on the other side, England and Holland

Colony.	Date.	Founders.
Gold Coast of Gambia,	1618.	Company of Adventurers of London Trading to Africa.
New England,	1621.	Pilgrim Fathers, under license from Virginia Co.
Nova Scotia,	1621.	Sir Wm. Alexander, under patent from Crown.
Maine,	1622.	John Mason and Ferdinando Gorges—grant from Crown.
St. Kitts,	1623.	Thos. Warner, sent by Ralph Merrifield. The other Leeward Islands, mostly offshoots from St. Kitts.
Barbados,	1624.	Sir William Courten.
Massachusetts,	1629.	Formal establishment of Co. of Massachusetts Bay under charter from Crown.
Maryland,	1632.	Lord Baltimore.
Bahamas,	1646.	William Sayle: afterwards further colonized by Carolina Proprietors in 1666.
Jamaica,	1655.	*Captured.*
Carolina,	1663.	Carolina Proprietors.
Hudson's Bay,	1670.	Hudson Bay Company.
Pennsylvania,	1682.	William Penn.

To these must be added all that was done in India by the East India Company, and it becomes obvious that company and private efforts far exceed those made by the State. On the other hand, the war between France and England in 1666, spread into the West Indies, and led to hot fighting between English and French colonists there: the Declaration of Breda (1667) makes some colonial stipulations. The fact is that as regards colonies the latter part of the seventeenth century is a period of transition from the days of private enterprise to the policy of deliberate acquisition by the State.

arranged that any conquests made by either party in Spanish America were to be retained at the end of the war. And when the war was ended by that Treaty of Utrecht, so much abused as giving England much less than after the successes of Marlborough she had a right to expect, England gained undisputed possession of the Hudson Bay Territory and Newfoundland, save that some fishing rights were reserved for the French; France gave up all claims on Nova Scotia and St. Kitts, while Spain ceded Gibraltar and Minorca, and assigned to us for thirty years the Asiento, that is to say the right, under treaty, of importing slaves to the colonies of Spanish America. This was a most lucrative concession. By it English slave-traders made large sums of money, and as it had hitherto belonged to a French company, the transference of it to English hands was a great gain over a commercial rival. Thus, taken as a whole and looked at from a modern point of view, the Treaty of Utrecht was by no means barren. It is true that the war had been undertaken to exclude the Bourbons from the throne of Spain, and that this object was not attained; but the union of the power of France and Spain turned out to be much less disastrous for England than had been imagined; and so long as Spain remained a French ally, England had an excellent opportunity of plundering a country which, though rich in colonies, could do little to defend them.

A short résumé of the wars of the eighteenth century and the treaties which ended them will serve to emphasize the fact that the Government had taken over from private enterprise the business of acquiring territory in the East and West, and how steadily successful the new policy was. Till the beginning of the eighteenth century England had never embarked in a war for the sake of colonies; but under the Hanoverian kings every war has a close connection with some colonial question or other. The first war, that which broke out with Spain in 1727, was partly caused by Spain's recognition of the Ostend Company, a dangerous rival of our own and Dutch trade in the East. Short and indecisive as it was, it preluded more serious contests. In 1739 we were again at war with Spain, nominally on account of an outrage committed on a certain Captain Jenkins, who had had his ear cut off as a punishment for illegal trading in Spanish waters, but the real reason was that the Spaniards refused to allow English vessels to trade with Spanish America. This "war of Jenkins' ear" was absorbed in the war of the Austrian Succession, France joining her ally Spain, and promising to obtain the restoration of Gibraltar and Minorca, and the destruction of the English colony of Georgia. When peace was made, each power restored its conquests, so that England's gain lay rather in the damage she had inflicted on Spain than in any acquisition of territory.

The peace, however, lasted but eight years, and was only a peace in Europe. French and English interests were continually in collision in India and America. During the last war La Bourdonnais had captured Madras, while Dupleix had beaten off an English attack on Pondicherry, so that it appeared as if the French would succeed in driving us out of the South of India altogether. This success, however, was due to the French Sepoy troops, and Sepoys were a force that either side could use. Clive imitated the example which Dupleix had set him, enlisted and drilled native troops, seized and held Arcot (1751), staved off the attack on Madras which Dupleix was planning in defiance of the peace, and established the English supremacy. Slight as was the regard paid to the peace of Aix la Chapelle in India, it was even less respected in North America. Here the French were strong on the St. Lawrence and Lower Canada, while the English owned the Atlantic seaboard—what is now the Eastern United States. The question was who should possess the great basin of the Mississippi and its tributaries: were the English to spread westwards over the Alleghanies, or the French to descend the Ohio, join hands with their settlement in Louisiana, and confine the English to their strip of sea-coast? Bickering between the colonists of the two races on the head-waters of the Ohio led to the building of a French fort, Fort Duquesne; Braddock was sent with a force of regulars and colonists to destroy this, but was himself taken in an ambush and his army routed on the Brandywine river (1755). In revenge Hawke seized some French ships, and the two nations were again at open war in 1756, striving for supremacy in India and America. The truth is that they had never been at peace. But, just as in 1739, a colonial war became absorbed in a European one. The magnitude of the

Seven Years' War, the overwhelming forces collected against Frederick the Great, his desperate struggle against odds, are apt to distract our attention from the true import of the war to England. What, we are apt to ask, did it matter to us whether Frederick kept Silesia or Maria Theresa recovered it? It mattered indeed very little. England was engaged in a colonial struggle with France; the European war was largely of France's making, and primarily of slight concern to England. But if we fought France in Europe, she would be less vigorous in resisting us abroad. This is what Pitt meant in his famous statement that he would conquer America in Germany. France with her hands full in Europe could not find enough men to resist Wolfe in Canada, or Clive and Eyre Coote in India; Spain only joined in the war to see England capture Cuba and Manilla. When the war was ended by the Treaty of Paris, England gained Canada, Cape Breton, Grenada and the Grenadines, St. Vincent, Dominica, Tobago, Senegal, and Florida, being thus left without a rival in America, while in India, though Pondicherry was restored to the French, their power was shattered, and the ultimate spread of English influence over the peninsula assured.

This treaty marks the high-water of English colonial power in the eighteenth century. The next war, in its origin purely colonial, ended in the loss of our American colonies. France, by helping the revolted colonists, managed to deal a heavy blow at our supremacy, though, thanks to Rodney and the English navy, we were able to hold our other possessions.

One of the chief difficulties in making peace (1783) between England and Holland lay in the Dutch claim to reserve for themselves the right of trading in what they regarded as their own East Indian waters, a claim they were obliged to give up. In spite of the loss of the American colonies, England continued her policy of fighting for commercial and colonial advantages. Three years later we were on the verge of another war with Spain about a fresh colonial question, the possession of Nootka Sound on the Pacific coast of North America. Spain gave way, and peace lasted till the outbreak of the revolutionary war in 1793. At the beginning, this war bears less of a colonial look than those which precede it; England appears to be fighting because the French had overrun the Netherlands, or to avenge the treatment of Louis XVI. But the colonial character soon supervened. On the Continent, indeed, England for a long time could do little that was effective; here the French appeared irresistible. But at sea England was supreme, and supremacy there meant that what remained of Greater France lay at our mercy. And as France absorbed Holland, so Dutch colonies went the way of French colonies, into English hands. Other nations fought, were beaten, made peace, rose and fought again; England alone went steadily on with the war. Napoleon realized clearly enough with whom and for what the real contest was. He made an expedition to Egypt to embarrass English affairs in the East; he stirred up Tippoo Sahib, "Citoyen

Tipou", against us in India; he planned a direct invasion to strangle the power whose fleet had foiled him at the Nile, and was again baulked by the inefficiency of his own navy. Then he fell back on indirect attack. As England throve by her trade, he would cut off that trade, and accordingly he set up the Continental System, forbidding his subjects or allies from trading with England; but here again his plans failed because he had no power at sea to enable him to enforce his decrees; his disastrous expedition to Russia was partly due to a desire to force Russia to join him in refusing to trade with England. When the end came, England had added to her dominions the Cape of Good Hope, Demerara, Essequibo, Trinidad, St. Lucia, Malta, Ceylon, while under Wellesley the work of Clive and Warren Hastings had been carried so far in India, that the East India Company, instead of being a trading company, content with permission to trade here and establish a factory there, and trembling before the disapproval of native princes, had itself become a sovereign more formidable than its rivals, with as large a revenue, a wider territory, and a more effective army than any of them.

It is unnecessary to dwell upon the means by which this world-power was built up. War with the other European powers who possessed colonies gave England the opportunity to absorb them, and sea-power was the weapon which proved so effective. The one war in which our command of the sea wavered, namely, the war of American Independence, was on the whole disastrous. Sea-power was of little use against the colonists, and for a time the French fleets seemed to be as good as ours. Hughes could gain little advantage over Suffren in the East Indies; De Grasse, by blockading Cornwallis, brought about the surrender at Yorktown; Guichen was able to take some English islands in the West Indies. Not until Rodney broke Grasse's line, on April 12th, 1782, was the English supremacy restored, and it was that battle which made the Peace of Versailles so much less disadvantageous to England than seemed at one time probable.

If England during this century awoke to a sense of the importance to her of sea-power, her enemies realized it also. The Armed Neutralities of 1780 and 1800 were designed to resist English claims to extend her effective force at sea, and to capture enemies' goods wherever she found them. When the Armed Neutralities demanded that enemies' goods in neutral vessels should be exempt from capture, that the list of contraband articles should be restricted, that neutral convoys should be allowed to pass without being searched, that blockades should only be binding where adequately enforced, they were attempting to limit the power of the English fleet against its enemies, and to give neutrals an opportunity of enlarging their trade at the belligerents' expense. But though England accepted some of these rules for a time, yet, in the end, they were overthrown, and carrying-trade as well as colonies became the prize of the victor at sea.

At the beginning of the eighteenth century England was a colonial power, but she was only one among others. The subjects of Spain, of Portugal, of Holland, of France, were all of them also busy in colonial and foreign possessions, some seeking gold and silver, others trade, others a home from religious persecution. Various alike in object and method, what till then had been done by Englishmen was the work in the main of individuals, not of the State. But during the eighteenth century this was changed. Spain and Portugal had from the first treated their colonies more as State affairs than England had done. When France began to pursue the same plan it became necessary to call in the force of the nation to supplement the efforts of individuals against the rival colonial power. So effectively was this done, that by 1815 Greater Britain was not only consolidated in itself, but had swallowed up most of Greater France and Greater Holland, while, by the revolt of the Spanish-American colonies, most of Greater Spain had disappeared. England had, in fact, risen from the position of one of many rivals for colonial territory to be the one great colonial power of the world.

We have seen how this came about. It remains to see why; and the answer is given by the old colonial theory. Men hold widely different opinions about the value of colonies to us nowadays, but they would mostly agree that colonies are useful as an outlet for our surplus population. But in the old colonial theory this idea had no place, for the best of reasons, namely, that there was no surplus population. On the contrary, grumblers at home complained that colonies weakened the mother-country by withdrawing men who could ill be spared. Colonies were valued for a widely-different reason, for the opportunities they gave for trade.

One is tempted by what seems plausible to say, "If that is all, why then did we make war for colonies with which we might trade; why not trade with the colonies of others?" The answer is that no country permitted foreigners to engage in trade with its colonies. It was on this very ground that Spain went to war with us in 1739; and we, though ready enough to resent exclusiveness on the part of Spain or Holland, had taken considerable pains to prevent the Dutch interfering in our colonial trade. Further, when France, owing to the predominance of the English at sea in time of war, was unable to keep up communications with her own colonies, and carry on the trade which she usually reserved jealously for her own subjects, and therefore, as a last resort, threw the trade open to neutrals, in the hope that her colonies at any rate would profit by the protection of a neutral flag, England declared that all neutrals engaging in the French colonial trade were rendering the enemy service, and that, accordingly, such vessels might be captured.[2] In fact, it was a general belief that colonies must trade with the mother-country only, for from this the mother-country was repaid for the trouble and expense which the colonies cost her.

Naturally, then, English statesmen strove so to regulate colonial trade that the greatest benefit should be conferred on England. From what we have seen of Mercantilist ideas, it is easy to lay down the principles applied. Colonies were encouraged to send home raw produce, such as sugar, tobacco, cotton-wool, indigo, and dyes, which could

---

[2] By the "Rule of War of 1753".

not be produced in England. But as colonies were to be used for the advantage of the mother-country, this advantage would be greatest if these goods were cheap and plentiful; accordingly these articles were "enumerated", and prohibited from being sent to any but English ports. On the other hand, colonial export of such manufactured goods which could also be produced at home was held to be mischievous, and even those manufactures by which the colonies supplied their own wants were stopped. Thus the American colonists were not allowed to make beaver hats, though they could make them at little over one-third of the cost of the imported hats, because by doing so they diminished the market for English goods. Similarly the colonists were allowed to send bar-iron to England for a time, because the English iron industry was languishing through the scarcity of charcoal, and to encourage it would have led to further destruction of forests, yet they might not make up their iron into nails or any form that interfered with English export. Thus hampered by restrictions as to what they exported, and where they sent it, prevented from selling in the best market, and forced to buy dear for the sake of a mother-country which many of them had never seen, the allegiance of the American colonists was exposed to a strain. It is fair that we should recognize this: but it is also fair that we should remember some considerations on the other side. It cannot be disputed that the colonies cost England much, and except what they yielded indirectly by their trade, they paid us nothing. If they valued the protection which England gave—and without it they must have fallen victims to France—then there is much to be said in favour of their paying for it. Further, we must beware of looking at the dispute from the modern standpoint of Free-trade. Mother-country and colonies alike were familiar with Mercantile ideas; there was nothing new about them, nor were the American colonies alone subject to them. The West Indian colonies were treated in the same way, and remained loyal. And lastly, it is not impossible for the mother-country to remain on excellent terms with great colonies, in spite of one protecting its industries against the other, for that is exactly what our colonies do against us now. The American colonists had reasonable grounds for complaint, and these complaints were not met in a conciliatory spirit; our action may have been as unwise as that of the colonists was ungrateful; there are times when it is good policy not to stand too much upon rights, and this may have been such a time. But in the abstract matter of rights, England's case was certainly as strong as that of the colonists.

Unfortunately rights on one side or the other soon became of little importance when compared with feelings. Yet, however aggrieved the colonists imagined themselves, there was no real danger of rebellion so long as the French held Canada, for to break with England would have been to fall into the jaws of France. When, however, Canada had been conquered and the French driven from the mainland altogether, then the English regulations were felt to be more oppressive and more unreasonable. Hitherto the colonists had put up with them for the sake of the protection which the mother-country gave in time of war; when the obvious need for protection grew less, the gratitude for it waned also, and men began to ask what England did for them in return for the advantages which she exacted. They argued that they supplied her with cheap raw materials and bought her manufactured goods, and she repaid this by checking their enterprises, repressing their manufactures, and keeping them in a backward condition, because she believed that if they were allowed to grow they would grow to do without her. Colonies and mother-country alike saw their own interest, and were blind to all beyond it; in English eyes the colonies were ungrateful children, who forgot the benefits conferred on them in the past, while to the colonists England was an unnatural mother, who treated her children as if they were her servants. The essential fact that they were mother and children was overlooked altogether. Hence when England went further, and tried to raise a direct revenue from the American colonies, irritation speedily grew into hatred, and rebellion followed. The blame must not be laid solely upon Grenville, Townshend, and North, who imposed the Stamp Act and the import duties. Their action was terribly unwise; they were pouring vinegar into wounds instead of oil; but they did not inflict the wounds; that was the work of the old colonial system, the outcome of the Mercantilist idea that everything should be sacrificed to making England strong at home.

The old colonial system lost us our American colonies. Much, however, was left, and more was speedily added. In 1768, one year after Townshend had returned to the foolish policy of taxing America, Cook sailed on the first of his great series of voyages, which were to add so largely to English dominions. The year 1770, which saw Lord North take up the Government during which the American colonies were to gain their independence, saw Cook reach the coast of Australia and take possession of it in the name of King George. It was long before the value of Australia and New Zealand was realized. More immediately fruitful seemed to be the spreading of our supremacy in India, the growth of Canada, the capture of the Cape of Good Hope from the Dutch. By the time, too, that this second expansion was complete, Mercantilist ideas were becoming effete, and with them went the old colonial system. A new policy based more on patriotism and sentiment, and less on material considerations of actual monetary profit and loss, took its place. Colonies began to be governed, or allowed to govern themselves, according to their own ideas, instead of being managed as if they were branch establishments of a great trading firm. Of this new policy we shall have to see more in a later chapter; meanwhile we may notice that, so far, it has been attended with great success, so much so that little regret is expressed for the loss of our first colonies. We marvel at the extraordinary spectacle of one small island owning dominions all over the world, and are almost inclined to be thankful that we have been relieved of the responsibility for the enormous state which has developed from the beginnings which we made in America. This view may be reasonable; it may be that independence was inevitable, though there is no proof of it. But it was not inevitable that the colonies, which had been England's children, should become her enemy. The sense of injustice, which began with commercial disadvantages, and which was aggravated by futile attempts at taxation, led to rebellion, separation, and independence for the colonists. But it did not end there; there remained a national hostility, which was deepened by the war of 1812, and aggravated during the war of Secession. This attitude of suspicion and jealousy, with which the two great English-speaking races of the world have generally regarded each other, is in a great measure a legacy of England's commercial policy in the eighteenth century. Recent events, indeed, have led to a warmer feeling between the two countries, but whether this is likely to be permanent it would be idle to discuss here.

CHAPTER XV.

MACHINERY AND POWER.

We have seen in the last chapter the growth of Greater Britain, the building up of an empire so wide that it is a national commonplace to say that the sun never sets upon it. Wide, however, as the empire is, British trade spreads still wider. Originally our colonies were prized because they gave us larger markets; restrictions might be placed on our trade with European nations, or with their colonies, but with our own colonies we could deal as we pleased. If we had persisted in this policy, and done nothing beyond it—if we had built up a colonial empire so great as to dwarf the work of any other nation, and had confined ourselves to trading in the main within the bounds of this empire—England would even then have been the greatest commercial country in the world, with more ships, more industries, and a greater volume of trade than any other. But England has done more. She has not been content with supplying the multiple needs of her own dominions, vast as they are, but she has gone further, and invaded the field of the world's trade. To a great extent she has become the world's factory, the world's money-market, and the world's carrier. Not that other nations have been contented to sit idle and see their industries supplanted and their wants supplied by British enterprise. On the contrary, they resented the intrusion and tried to check it by a protective system, but on the whole their efforts failed. For a time we seemed to possess a natural commercial advantage which gave us a monopoly of many of the greatest branches of the world's trade, and British goods were so much cheaper that even with the aid of protection Continental manufacturers were hardly able to compete. It is true that in some respects the advantages seem nowadays to be waning, and the monopoly less complete. But even if England is no longer the only workshop of the world, she is still incomparably the greatest. And this is a national characteristic quite distinct from our world-wide colonial dominion. The two indeed grew up together, and each has helped the other. But one was not a consequence of the other. England might have been a great colonial power without gaining any predominance in manufacture—such indeed was Spain in the sixteenth century; or she might have been rich through her trade and industries without possessing colonies of much account; Belgium is of this type now. England, however, has grown great in both respects. She is both a great colonial power and a great industrial power. And she has been fortunate in possessing the natural conditions necessary to success.

For industry and commerce, no less than the the command of the seas, are limited by natural conditions. Modern manufactures cluster round coal-fields, where power can be had cheaply; the possession of good harbours is essential to maritime trade; a country where broad and gently-flowing rivers act as natural canals will have advantages in internal communications over a country broken up by mountain ranges. If we go into details we find the same thing; the wet climate of Lancashire gives it an advantage in the cotton manufacture, since for many processes damp is essential; the dry limestone ranges of the Yorkshire hills give the best grass for grazing, and we find the woollen industries gathered at the foot of these hills; the iron ore of Staffordshire is worked and that of Sussex neglected, because coal lies close at hand in the one case and far away in the other.[1] It is unnecessary to heap up examples of the importance of natural advantages; everyone admits it. Yet even when we recognize that England is rich in these advantages, that she has coal and iron lying close together, that her sheep give the best wool, that her harbours are plentiful, that she is not ill-off for rivers, and that no part of the country is farther than some seventy miles from the sea, we have not said all. It is a remarkable fact that though England has always had her natural advantages, she has not always been accustomed to use them. The industrial history of the eighteenth century tells us how the nation discovered the value of her resources, and, above all others, of her coal-fields. The story is told that Boulton, James Watt's partner, remarked to George III., "I sell, Sire, what all the world desires—power", and the observation was true, for it was during the latter half of the eighteenth century and the beginning of the nineteenth century that England discovered and revealed to the world what could be done by machinery driven by power. England was first in the field, and her natural resources have enabled her to remain first, although rival nations, following the same lines of development, are now to some extent making up their lost ground.

The story of the amazing development of English industry in the eighteenth century is mainly the story of mechanical inventions. The first step was taken in the staple English industry, weaving. The main conditions of the woollen trade have been

[1] For example, if the Kent coal-fields come to anything, the southern counties' iron ore may again become valuable, if it is of sufficiently good quality.

described already; it was a domestic industry; the weaver worked at his loom in his own cottage, sometimes for a "clothier", who supplied him with yarn, and took the cloth off his hands when woven, sometimes for himself; in this case he would have to get yarn for himself, and this was not always easy, for it took ten spinners to spin yarn enough to keep a weaver at work. This did not create as great a scarcity of yarn as might have been expected, because spinning was a widespread bye-industry, practised by women and girls at all leisure times. In rural districts whole families busied themselves with spinning in the long winter evenings, and so the supply of yarn, with a struggle, kept up with the demand. But what is most important to notice for our present purpose is that, mechanically speaking, the whole business of spinning and weaving had progressed very little. Improvements had been made in the kinds of cloth manufactured, but the machines in use, the spinning-wheel and the loom, were of the same type as they had been for years out of mind.

In 1733 came the first step in the long course of invention, when Kay of Bury patented the flying shuttle. Hitherto the weaver had passed the shuttle carrying the weft through the threads of the warp from hand to hand. This was naturally a very slow process, and it further limited the width of cloth which one man could weave to the span enclosed by his arms when meeting in front of his body.[2]

---

[2] Roughly speaking, about three quarters of a yard. The fact that this is still the common width for many fabrics is a survival from the days before the flying shuttle.

For wide cloth two weavers were employed, one to hand the shuttle to the other and to receive it back again. Kay's invention, by which the shuttle was mechanically propelled from side to side, not only enabled the weaver to work wide cloth as easily as narrow, but it more than doubled the pace at which work could be done.

This improvement in the hand-loom completely upset the relations between spinners and weavers. Up till then it had been difficult for spinners to keep pace; now it became impossible. So scanty was the supply of yarn that it was common for a weaver to start his day's work by walking three or four miles and calling on a round of spinners before he could collect enough yarn to last him the rest of the day. Under this great pressure spinners searched for mechanical improvements, and no long time passed before they were successful. In 1764 a hand-loom weaver, James Hargreaves of Blackburn, whose spinning-wheel, overturned on the floor, went on revolving while the thread remained in his hand, worked out from this idea the spinning-jenny. The machine as first made worked eight rovings in a row, but it was speedily discovered that it could work far more than this, and as children could work it, the productiveness of the spinner was enormously increased. Hargreaves was followed by Richard Arkwright, who was the first to make a practical success of spinning by rollers which, revolving at different velocities, drew the roving to the requisite fineness. Arkwright's machine, which was worked by water (hence the name given to his yarn "water-twist"), produced a harder and stronger yarn than was made by the jenny. Finally, Crompton, by combining the principles of Hargreaves' jenny and Arkwright's water-frame in his "muslin wheel" or, as it was afterwards called, "mule", was able to spin a much finer yarn than any hitherto made in England.

These three inventions had very remarkable consequences. In the first place, though they all applied at first to cotton spinning, yet sooner or later they were adapted for use in the other textile trades. Thus the advantage of the weaver over the spinner disappeared, first in cotton, then in linen, and lastly in wool. By the end of the century hand-spinning in cotton was practically extinct, and the more widely-diffused industry of woollen spinning was feeling the competition of machinery as an increasing evil. The inventors shared a common lot in that they all suffered from mob-violence. But each invention had its separate result. Hargreaves enabled the cotton spinner to keep pace with the work done by the flying shuttle. Arkwright's "water-twist" first made the manufacture of true cotton goods possible in England; hitherto none had been able to spin cotton strong enough to be used as warp, and linen yarn had to be used for this, and consequently the "cottons" made were composite, half linen and half cotton; but the "water-twist" or throstle spun yarn was firm enough to replace the linen for warp.[3] And just as a pure cotton manufacture was made possible

---

[3] Arkwright's cotton goods, curiously enough, infringed an act of Parliament passed in 1736, which prohibited goods consisting entirely of cotton, on the presumption that these could not be of English make, but must be Eastern. The act was repealed in 1774.

by Arkwright, so Crompton's fine yarn started the manufacture of muslins in England.

The jenny, the water-frame, and the mule were all capable of being worked by power, and the power first applied was water. This led to the rise of the beckside mills in Lancashire and Yorkshire, to which it will be necessary to return in another chapter. But meantime the loom was still dependent on man's force. A clergyman, Edmund Cartwright, incited by a visit to Arkwright's mill to an expression of his belief that a machine could be made to weave, and being received with ridicule, proceeded to justify his opinion by making the first power-loom. The machine was wonderfully clumsy, but experience enabled him to make improvements, and in 1791 a Manchester firm contracted to take 400 of his power-looms. His first power-loom was worked by a bull, but in 1789 his Doncaster factory was fitted with a steam-engine. He also invented a machine for wool-combing, a process hitherto done by hand combers so slowly that the difficulty of getting wool combed had hampered the woollen weavers almost as much as the want of yarn. Other men went on with Cartwright's work; Radcliffe and Horrocks especially improved the power-loom, so that by 1815 the machine was coming into fairly general use, and enabling the weavers in their turn to catch up the spinners. Other inventions in kindred processes came quickly one upon the other. A Scotchman named Bell invented cylinder printing of calico goods, which replaced the old plan of printing with a hand block some ten inches by five, and enabled one man to do as much with the machine as a hundred men had done in the old style. Heathcoat's machinery for lace making was an object of wonder for its complexity and success; Murray's machines for heckling and spinning flax led the way for the introduction of machinery into all branches of linen working; Benjamin Gott adapted the inventions first applied to cotton for use in the woollen industry.[4] In fact, in all the textile industries machinery began to take over what had previously been done by hand. There was an enormous increase in the amount of the goods manufactured, and a corresponding fall in prices. To take one or two statistical examples, there were in 1813 2300 power-looms in use, in 1833 there were 100,000. In 1740, roughly speaking, a million and a half pounds of cotton was imported, in 1815 close on one hundred millions. In 1742 somewhat over 100,000 pieces of cloth were milled in Yorkshire, but in 1815 the number had risen to 500,000, and each piece was double the former length.

The effect of this extraordinary progress upon the working-classes must be deferred to a later chapter. At present the fact to be remarked is that machinery was busily engaged in taking over one process after another which had previously been done by hand. All this mass of machinery called for power. Wind was too fickle, water-power was good where it could be obtained, but this was not everywhere; the flat eastern counties lay at a hope-

---

[4] The adaptation of machine spinning to linen and wool dates from the last decade of the eighteenth century.

less disadvantage in this respect. But England had undeveloped stores of power in her coal-fields, and the first man to show how they could be used effectively was James Watt. Momentous as Watt's inventions were, it is a mistake to speak of him as the inventor of the steam-engine. The steam-engine contains many inventions, and when Watt took it up in 1763, it was no longer a toy. As soon as Newcomen[5] introduced the use of the cylinder and piston, the steam-engine, or "fire-engine" as it was called, became useful for pumping. In 1775 Smeaton made a gigantic engine with cylinders 6 feet in diameter and 9½ feet stroke; but such a monster as this consumed at least £3000 worth of coal in a year. Still, even with all their defects, "fire-engines" were much used in mining—there were 57 at work round Newcastle in 1767—and Roebuck used one at Carron to work the blast for his furnaces, though the power was indirect; the engines pumped water to turn a water-wheel and this worked the bellows; the plan of turning the longitudinal motion of the piston-rod into the rotary motion of the wheel was not yet adopted.[6]

The engines were expensive for two reasons: the workmanship was very bad; the principle was bad also. Steam was used to fill the cylinder under the piston, and being condensed there, a vacuum was formed under the piston, and atmospheric pressure forced it down. The engine did not go by steam-power at all. This plan of condensing steam in the cylinder was most wasteful, for after

---

[5] About the beginning of the eighteenth century.
[6] It was known, however: the crank had been used at a much earlier date.

each stroke the cylinder was cooled and then had to be heated again. Watt's first great invention was the separate condenser, by which the need of cooling the cylinder was avoided. He afterwards made his engines double-acting, that is, he used steam pressure to raise the piston, and then, by admitting steam above it, forced it down again, thereby making the engine independent of atmospheric pressure at all; he was also the first to use steam expansively, and he employed iron for his gear and cog-wheels, and by many similar devices made the steam-engine effective and economical. But though he was an inventor of great fertility, yet some of the credit for his success must be assigned to his partner, Boulton, who, besides supplying the keen-sighted business ability which Watt lacked, provided Watt with much better workmanship than he had hitherto known. While Watt, at Kinneil, was struggling with his engine—"Beelzebub", as he called it—and thinking himself fortunate if the cylinders bored by the Carron workmen were not more than three-eighths of an inch out of truth, success was impossible; but Boulton and Wilkinson of Bersham worked accurately. The new power soon attracted popular attention. In 1781 Boulton wrote to Watt, "The people in Manchester are all *steam-mill* mad", and the course of the next twenty years saw Watt's engines set up in many factories all over England. Steam-power rapidly superseded water-power, and mills and factories, hitherto lining the streams, began to collect into towns where coal was cheap. The value of our coal-fields was thus recognized; they alone, independent of other mineral wealth, would have given England the lead of countries where coal was less abundant.

But the value of coal in providing power was not the only, nor indeed the first, important discovery about it made in the eighteenth century. We have seen that as early as the seventeenth century Dudley was experimenting with coal for iron-smelting. Whatever measure of success he attained, it is clear that nothing of permanent value survived him; if he had a secret he kept it. But during the eighteenth century a succession of iron-masters—the Abraham Darbys at Colebrookdale, and Roebuck at Carron—showed first that coke and afterwards that raw coal could be used for smelting; the real improvement appears to have lain chiefly in the use of a better blast, and for this the new steam-engine was much in demand by all iron-masters. The effect of this change alone was enormous. As late as the middle of the century the amount of pig-iron imported into England was increasing annually, because the charcoal masters could not get enough fuel for their furnaces, and an average charcoal furnace yielded under 300 tons in the year; England, in fact, could not supply her own wants. But after the use of coke and coal became general, the output of each furnace leaped up at once to 1500 tons in the year, and by 1815 the annual export of iron stood at 91,000 tons. Still greater results came from Cort's discovery,[7] that malleable iron could be made with coal instead of charcoal by "puddling". This new process, combined with his patent for using rollers instead of the hammer

[7] 1784.

to get rid of impurity, revolutionized the malleable-iron trade as completely as the use of coal instead of charcoal had changed the pig-iron trade. Cort himself, like so many of his race, got nothing from his invention, but he laid the foundations of great fortunes for others. The end of the century saw the growth of gigantic iron-works all over the country. In 1784 Colebrookdale had sixteen steam-engines, eight blast-furnaces, and nine forges. In 1765 Anthony Bacon had got a ninety-nine-years' lease of mineral rights over forty square miles of country round Merthyr Tydvil for £200 a year, but in less than twenty years he retired with a fortune, and from the sale of his rights began the great works at Cyfarthfa, Dowlais, and Penydaran. Crawshay of Cyfarthfa, who in 1787 had made forty tons of malleable iron in a month, was, by 1812, turning out twenty times as much.

Here, then, was a second use for our coal-fields hardly less important than the first. They yielded power to drive machinery; they also provided iron cheaply and plentifully from which the machinery could be made. A far-seeing man, Wilkinson of Bersham, was laughed at for his belief in the future which lay before iron. When he spoke of iron bridges and iron vessels and iron houses, he was called "iron mad", but he lived to prove his own sanity and the folly of those who laughed, by assisting at the opening of the first iron bridge,[8] and by launching the first iron vessel.[9] The improvements he introduced in machinery have been already noticed; others followed him in the same field,

---

[8] Over the Severn, 1779.   [9] In 1790.

especially Maudslay, who carried accuracy of work to a point hitherto unknown, and thereby not only made better machinery, but gave confidence in its use, because if one part broke, another could be supplied to the same pattern. It is easy to understand that men were apt to shrink from using complicated machines in days when, if a screw broke, it was considered better to bore out a fresh thread in the nut to fit the fresh screw, rather than attempt to fit a screw to the existing nut. By the work of such men as Maudslay and his followers, Clement, Murray, Whitworth, and Nasmyth, order and standard patterns took the place of the former confusion.

So far we have been dealing with the expansion mainly of industries that used or supplied machinery and power, for this is the feature that marks the industrial history of the end of the eighteenth century. But the expansion was not confined to these industries; it was natural that activity in one branch, caused by the new agents, should lead to activity in others, even supposing that they did not use power or machinery. And in industries of this kind there was more than activity; there was great progress owing to new discoveries. The latter part of the century was an era of inventions. If we take, for example, the china and earthenware business, we have the increased use of Astbury's invention of the use of flint for glaze, and Cookworthy's discovery[10] that Cornwall could yield abundant supplies of the china clay, and the consequent beginnings of the manufacture of hard-

[10] His patent is dated 1768.

paste porcelain from native materials. Transfer printing on china and earthenware was first practised about the middle of the century, and the best-known name in ceramics, that of Josiah Wedgwood, belongs to the same period. Wedgwood, indeed, patented little, for he felt that the best protection against the rivalry of others was to make goods that defied rivalry. He bestowed an infinity of pains on his business, and occupied himself alike with improving tools, material, and designs, reaping in the end an abundant reward, for he prospered in everything he undertook. From his works at Etruria came a vast variety of goods which set a standard for others to strive after; and he was not without competitors, for there were busy factories at Derby, Coalport, Worcester, Liverpool, Bristol, and elsewhere.

It is impossible in the space at command to give even a glance at all the new processes and labour-saving inventions that mark this period, or to estimate the effect which they have produced. When one reads, for example, that by the discovery of chlorine gas and its compounds the process of bleaching was reduced in duration from six months to a few days, the magnitude of the improvement is scarcely realized, when compared with the more striking achievements of Arkwright or Watt. Yet an invention of this nature was of very great importance, for just as the strength of a chain is the strength of the weakest link, so the output of a complicated industry, such as linen or cotton, is limited by the speed or slowness of its slowest branch. The application of the new process of bleaching, which was perfected by Tennant of Glasgow, is not the only instance where Scotland took the lead of English manufacturers. Watt has been already mentioned, and another compatriot, Muir, made the first engine used to work machinery in Glasgow; Miller of the same town patented a power-loom not long after Cartwright; Mackintosh began the water-proofing process that has made his name familiar; the manufacture of Turkey-red was also introduced into Scotland by the aid of a French emigrant, and dyeing in all branches flourished. Between 1785 and 1818 Glasgow more than tripled its population, and at the later date had fifty-four cotton mills in full work.

In speaking of the natural advantages of a country, stress was laid upon the importance of easy communication. Though England is small and distances consequently short, yet for the most part of the eighteenth century means of communication were bad. Many even of main roads were not properly "made"; in 1750 the average pace of coaches on long journeys did not exceed six miles an hour. On many important routes there was no turnpike, merely a narrow causeway, with soft unmade road on each side. Arthur Young, who in the course of his tours had ample opportunity of becoming acquainted with the badness of English roads, speaks of ruts four feet deep on the turnpike between Preston and Wigan, and of wagons stuck fast in Essex mire, utterly unable to be moved till a team of thirty or forty horses was attached to them. Under these circumstances it was hardly possible to send goods except on pack-horses, and the cost of carriage was enormous. In winter coal was sent from Worsley to Manchester in panniers on horseback, 280 lbs. being the usual load; road carriage from Liverpool to Manchester cost 40*s.* a ton; pot waggons carried goods from Burslem to Bridgnorth at £3 per ton. Reform indeed came slowly. Smeaton and Rennie built bridges which replaced dangerous fords, and Telford constructed nearly a thousand miles of good roads in Scotland; but substantial improvement dates from 1815, when Macadam taught that roads could best be repaired with stones broken into angular fragments and more or less of a size, instead of the pebbles and flints which had been cast down hap-hazard in the hope that the broad-wheeled waggons would crush them into some sort of a surface.

But road-carriage, even over good roads, could not suffice for the increasing amount of goods sent about the country, and long before the road-makers had arisen to a sense of what was necessary, another means of transport had taken over much of the heavy work. The Duke of Bridgwater owned coal-mines at Worsley, only a few miles from Manchester, yet the cost of sending coal thither exactly doubled its price. Accordingly he determined to make a canal between the two, and employed as his engineer a millwright, James Brindley. Brindley was rough and almost without education, yet he possessed a natural shrewdness which made all his work sound and practical. Although much use had been made of canals in France and Holland, in England they were almost unknown; all that had been done had been to deepen the beds of existing rivers. This was good in its way, but for canal making Brindley saw that it was best to keep clear of rivers altogether. River water meant the danger of floods, and involved all sorts of elaborate precautions against a giant power that might upset all of them. Brindley aimed at having long level stretches of water which floods would not affect, and on these lines he built the first canal from Worsley to Manchester, and carried on a branch to Runcorn. The Duke of Bridgwater had the greatest difficulty in raising money to pay for these canals, but he was speedily repaid when they were opened; nor did he alone profit, for the price of coal in Manchester fell exactly one-half owing to the new means of transport.

A more important undertaking followed, namely, the Grand Trunk Canal, which, when completed, ran from Runcorn through the salt and pottery districts, joining the Trent at Wilden Ferry, and amounting, with all its branches, to 139 miles in length. Wedgwood was one of the chief promoters and cut the first sod; and indeed his confidence was justified, for no industry profited more from canals than pottery. Not only did the potters use quantities of clay, lime, and coal, that had to come from some distance, but their goods when made, being both bulky and brittle, were ill suited for conveyance by land. The Grand Trunk Canal reduced the old rates to one-fourth of their previous amount, a ton going from Etruria to Liverpool for 13*s.* 4*d.* instead of 50*s.*, and a quarter of wheat, instead of costing 20*s.* per hundred miles, now going for 5*s.* As a consequence of the success which attended the first canals, a canal mania, only comparable to the railway mania forty years later, seized the nation. Between 1790 and 1794 eighty-one canal acts were obtained, and though some of the canals were afterwards shown to be unnecessary, yet upon the whole the trade of the country gained enormously by the new and cheaper means of communication which they afforded. Nor was the direct gain the only gain. The canal engineers demonstrated what could be done to overcome natural obstacles. Brindley's great tunnel at Hare Castle (2880 yards long), the Barton aqueduct which carried his canal over the Irwell, the embankment at Stretford, remained as examples to the railway engineers, while the sturdy workmen, the "navigators", were the first of that race of English "navvies", as we have come to call them, the value of whose labour, endurance, and rough-and-ready skill is appreciated by engineers and contractors, not only in England, but all over the world.

One other feature of this period calls for notice, and that is the growth of population. During the first half of the eighteenth century the increase was about 18 per cent, in the latter half not far short of 50 per cent. This increase was mainly in the towns of the new manufacturing districts. Whereas in density of population in 1700 neither Lancashire nor the West Riding appear in the first twelve counties, and the next three places after the metropolitan counties were held by Gloucester, Northampton, and Somerset, in 1750 Lancashire stood fifth and the West Riding eleventh. At the end of the century they had advanced still further, as had Durham, Stafford, and Nottingham. While towns such as Norwich, York, and Exeter were comparatively stationary, the new great centres of manufacture, Liverpool, Manchester, Birmingham, Glasgow, Leeds, Sheffield, Newcastle, were rapidly overtaking their older rivals.[11] In the twenty years from 1801 to 1821, the increase of Liverpool, Manchester, Glasgow, and Bradford was 75 per cent, and even more remarkable still was the progress of manufacturing and mining villages in the North of England. This vast growth, accompanied by a great displacement of population, had important consequences upon the course of events which will next claim our attention.

CHAPTER XVI.

THE AGRARIAN REVOLUTION.

If from what we have already seen of the conditions of the eighteenth century we were to argue deductively about agriculture, we might suppose that it enjoyed a period of prosperity. It would be natural to infer that the rapid growth of population, which went on from 1750, created a demand for agricultural produce; and further, as this increase of

---

[11] Between 1700 and 1760 the increase of Liverpool was tenfold, Birmingham sevenfold, Manchester fivefold, Sheffield sevenfold.

population was mainly an artisan population living in towns, we might argue that the new demand was great, and brought with it high prices and high profits. Repeated wars, and especially the long struggle with revolutionary France and afterwards with Napoleon, also contributed to increase the demand for home produce, since it was almost impossible even in famine years to get much corn from abroad. Of course with a rise in prices we are prepared to find a rise in rents, but a rise in prices always precedes a rise in rents, so that though the landlord would, in the end, profit most by the new conditions, the farmer would profit too: and in the case of the man who farmed his own land we should be prepared to find a condition of unusual prosperity, for he would profit both as land-owner and as farmer.

Such conclusions appear at first sight quite reasonable, but when we come to consider the history of agriculture in the eighteenth century we find once again how dangerous is such a course of deductive reasoning, for the conclusions which appear natural are largely false; and they are false, not because the facts on which they are based are inaccurate, but because other sets of facts have been left out of sight. It is true that there was a period of high prices and prosperity; but only some farmers were able to benefit by them. To many the new conditions only brought hardships. Some were not able to avail themselves of the opportunities offered; others, and these largely the small owners, whom we were tempted to picture as more prosperous than the tenants, since their gain could not be absorbed by an increase of rent, were so injuriously affected by the new conditions, that as a class they disappeared, leaving a few survivors scattered here and there instead of the numbers who, at the beginning of the century, had formed the bulk of the agricultural population of England. How this "Decay of the Yeomanry"[1] came about, how the small owners were dispossessed and large farmers took their place, is one of the most interesting features in the history of English agriculture.

In an earlier chapter[2] mention has been made of the enclosures which followed the Black Death. The difficulty of getting labour made land-owners find it more profitable to keep sheep than to work their demesne land, either with villein labour or by hiring men with the money dues for which this villein labour had been commuted. But the enclosing which consequently went on caused, as we have seen, alarm in Parliament, and statutes were passed to check it and to encourage arable farming. This legislation, combined with the fact that the new sheep farms soon met the existing demand for wool, while agricultural labour itself became less difficult to get, brought the enclosure movement to a standstill. And when in the seventeenth century a point of rest was reached, it appeared that, although much land had been enclosed, yet still more remained in open field. At the beginning of the eighteenth century three-fifths of the cultivated land in England was tilled in this way.

[1] This is the title given by Arnold Toynbee to one of the chapters in his *Industrial Revolution*. [2] Chap. VIII.

A system of cultivation which had survived unchanged since the Norman Conquest might be supposed to have real advantages about it to cause men to cling to it for so long. But the advantages were rather of the past than of the present; the plan of ploughing together had been good when each cultivator had been too poor to keep enough oxen to work his own plough; the simple unvaried rotation of crops made no call on the intelligence; the amount of produce might be small, but it was enough for each man to live upon, and that in the main was all that he expected. But what had made the system long-lived far more than any intrinsic advantages, was the difficulty, nay even the impossibility, of changing it. Among the cultivators thus working together there were no doubt some who saw that changes might be for the better; but there were many more, who through indolence, or mental sluggishness, or inherent dislike of any alteration, refused to allow any experiments. This being so, reform of the open-field farming was out of the question.

None the less a change was necessary, and the fact was shown still more clearly by the progress made by those who were not tied to the antiquated system. Clover and lucerne had been known in the seventeenth century, though their valuable properties of cleansing the soil and breaking it up with their deep roots were not realized at first. But in the next century they were introduced into a new and better rotation of crops, thereby saving the wasted year during which, on the old plan, open fields lay fallow. Turnips had also been common since the seventeenth century, but the right principles of cultivating them were neglected, as they were sown too thick and insufficiently hoed. Jethro Tull[3] first taught a better method. He made careful experiments as to the best soil, the right depth, and the best manner of sowing. Besides inventing a drill which laid the seed in furrows instead of the old plan of sowing it broadcast by hand, he saw that crops did best where the soil is well pulverized and hoed among the roots. Among the many landlords who adopted Tull's improvements in turnip-sowing and horse-hoeing was Lord Townshend[4], whose fondness for turnips gained him the nickname of "Turnip" Townshend. He began the Norfolk course, a rotation of four crops, interposing clover and turnips between his cereals; this avoided the disastrous plan of taking two corn crops in succession, which was entailed by the three-field course—a proceeding which, before the knowledge of chemical manure, was bound to impoverish the soil—and at the same time enabled the farmer to use his land instead of leaving it fallow after each corn crop, as he had been obliged to do if he followed the two-field course. Another pioneer in agricultural improvement was Bakewell[5] of Dishley, whose success in breeding sheep gained him a wide reputation. Before his time sheep had been chiefly valued for their wool, and the joints which they yielded when slaughtered had been thought a

---

[3] His *Horse Hoeing Husbandry* was published in 1733.
[4] Townshend began farming at Rainham in 1730.
[5] Born 1725; died 1795.

minor matter. But with the new demand for meat to supply the big towns where the new machinery worked, meat was more worth attention than wool. Accordingly by judicious breeding Bakewell produced something better than the old-fashioned ram, whose description ran: "His frame large and loose, his bones heavy; his legs long and thick; his chine, as well as his rump, as sharp as a hatchet; his skin rattling on his ribs like a skeleton covered with parchment".[6] Not only did Bakewell's "New Leicesters"—compact, short-legged, and well covered with flesh—yield an immense profit on the cost of their keep, but they showed other stock-breeders what might be done. From sheep, the impulse spread to cattle; these hitherto had been as gaunt and long-legged as the sheep, and with good reason, for they were the common beast used for the plough; long legs and great bones were of use in a heavy soil, or when cattle had to drag carts through miry tracks, and wander over waste country in search of food. Indeed until the better knowledge of root crops, cattle were never even moderately fat except at the end of the summer, while during the winter they were half starved. But turnips gave winter food and the opportunity for winter-fattening, while, owing to the cattle being either kept in stall or close at hand, the manure could be gathered and used, instead of being scattered over an immense area of ground and practically wasted. With the winter food afforded by the root crops, and the example set by Bakewell with sheep, the cattle breeders soon made a corresponding

[6] Marshall, *Rural Economy.*

advance, and the latter part of the eighteenth century saw cattle-breeding become both popular and profitable; Colling's Durham Shorthorns, Tomkins' Herefords and Lord Leicester's Devons made the roast beef of old England more worthy of the name. The progress made may be judged by the increase in the average weight of sheep and cattle sold at Smithfield between 1710 and 1795. Beeves increased from 370 lbs. to 800 lbs., calves from 50 lbs. to 148 lbs., sheep from 28 lbs. to 80 lbs., lambs from 18 lbs. to 50 lbs.

When we reckon up these improvements it is not difficult to see what class of farmers were reaping the benefits of the new demand caused by a rapidly-increasing population. They were those who could and did avail themselves of the new methods. On Townshend's Norfolk estates, light, sandy soil where hitherto "two rabbits fought for every blade of grass", a new prosperity set in. One farm of which the rent was £180, thirty years later brought in £800, another rose from £18 to £240; Arthur Young speaks of a general increase near Norwich of ten times the original value. One man who farmed 1500 acres made enough from it to buy an estate worth £1800 a year. We can well understand that to buy land under such circumstances was thought to be the best form of investment; we might even wonder that any were found to sell it.

This brings us to look at the other side. Hitherto we have seen prosperity, but it was not all prosperity with the farmers of England. On the contrary, there was in some quarters adversity, adversity that was all the harder to bear when contrasted with the brilliant prospects of the new school of farmers. These men were making fortunes by the use of new methods, better crops, and better stock. Nothing could be more tantalizing to the open-field farmer who had intelligence than to see others taking the chances which he was forced to let slip. It was useless to dream of clover and turnips, of winter food for beasts, of a better rotation of crops, by which one-third of his land would not be left fallow, producing nothing each year. Had he attempted to grow clover or roots, these would have only been devoured by his neighbours' cattle, when at the end of a harvest they were given the run of the common fields. His land was not fenced off from that of the rest, and he had to be treated as the rest. If, for example, he desired to drain it, there was every likelihood that the neighbour on to whose land he intended to direct the water would object, and block his drains; if he was dissatisfied with the usual slovenly weeding and hoeing, he might make his own strips models of well-cared-for land, but he could do nothing to protect himself against a lazy neighbour who let thistles and weeds grow wild and seed. A man may suffer much in this way nowadays, but it was worse then, when each man's holding was not compact, but scattered among his neighbours' holdings, when, instead of a fence, the only separation was a path or a strip of unploughed ground. And the way in which the holdings were intermingled and all marked off one from another had other results. Land was wasted by numerous footpaths in all directions; what was worse, neighbours lived in constant suspicion that their land might be stolen by an encroaching turn of the plough, or a furrow run at night; and, finally, everyone was forced to spend a serious amount of time in walking from one plot to another. Thus the individual could do nothing to break loose from the difficulties that hindered him in arable farming, and stock-farming offered no better prospect. Winter food could not be obtained in sufficient quantities; so long as the village cattle were turned out all together to get what food they could on the village waste, they were certain to be for most of the year in a miserable condition, while if any man wished to separate his own beasts from the rest, and raise a better stock by paying some attention to breeding, after the manner of men like Bakewell and Colling, he was hampered by the fact that he had no pasture land that he could call his own. His beasts, even if he procured a better sort, had to mingle with the rest, where the improved type would soon disappear, and were exposed to foot-rot and scab and all the diseases with which the ill-kept village herds were always infected.

Reform, then, among the open-field farmers had to be wholesale or not at all, and it was not for want of teaching that wholesale reform did not come; the farmers of the day had the advantage of a teacher who combined knowledge, enterprise, enthusiasm, and the gift of setting forth in the clearest way what ought to be done. Arthur Young undertook the task of urging agricultural improvement, and pursued it with a zeal to which it is not easy to find a parallel. Although he failed himself as a practical farmer, it was not from want of interest in his calling.

He travelled not only in Great Britain, but also in France, Spain, and Italy, minutely inspecting the methods of farming, noting what was bad, and suggesting what was better. His *Tours* record the results of his observations. The more he saw the more he became convinced that if our agriculture was to prosper, it must do so on the new lines and not on the old. Wherever he went he urged on the open-field farmers the absolute necessity of abandoning antiquated methods, and moving with the new ideas.

But as Arthur Young speedily saw, reform among the open-field farmers was well-nigh hopeless. The ideal that he aimed at was not theirs. They were contented if their farms gave them a livelihood in the old style. He wished to see farms become great producers of corn and meat for the new urban population. So long as it was in the power of a few obstinate or lethargic men not only to remain as they were, but to keep those associated with them in the same condition, progress was impossible; reform, indeed, would not meet the case; what had to be done was to get rid of the open fields altogether by enclosing them.

Enclosure might be carried out in two ways, either by mutual consent, or by obtaining a private act of Parliament. The first way, we have seen, demanded almost more unanimity than could be expected, yet this unanimity was sometimes attained. One of the causes to which Arthur Young put down the agricultural prosperity of Norfolk was enclosure without the assistance of Parliament. To obtain a private act the consent of the lord of the manor, the tithe owner, and four-fifths of the commoners was required. These private acts became more common as the century went on. In the twelve years of Anne's reign there were three, and in the thirteen years of George I. there were sixteen; so far progress was slow, but George II.'s reign saw 226 in thirty-three years. Still, at the accession of George III. the open-field system existed in half the parishes in England. The amount varied in different counties; some had been enclosed during the sixteenth century, while Norfolk and Essex had led the way in the enclosures of the eighteenth century; about half Berkshire was still open field; in Cambridgeshire the open fields took up about nine-tenths of the whole area under cultivation. But from 1760 the process of enclosure went on apace; in the first thirty-seven years of George III.'s reign the number of private acts rose to 1482, while from 1797 to 1820 there were 1727, as well as a general enclosure act in 1801. Describing the whole tendency in a metaphor, we may say that for the first quarter of the century there was a trickle, which by the middle of the century had grown to a strong current and turned at the end into a widespread flood.

Unlike the enclosures of the fifteenth and sixteenth centuries, which had been in the main enclosures for sheep-farming, these were enclosures for a better system of arable farming. But just as in the earlier period, the land enclosed was not all of one kind, so it is here. There was enclosure of the open fields, and with it of the wastes and commons belonging to the open-field farmers; but, beyond this, there was enclosure of a good deal of downland that had not belonged to the open-field farmers. This latter was a consequence of the increased demand for corn, by which it became profitable to grow corn on land which hitherto would not have repaid cultivation.[7] It was obvious that when prices fell, such land would again go out of cultivation, and this was what happened when free-trade in corn began.

In whatever way enclosure was carried out there was bound to be a certain expense. In re-arranging the old scattered holdings in a more concentrated form, careful measurements had to be taken; where the law was called in, lawyers had to be paid; and even if their charges were not really exorbitant, there was a wide-spread belief that they were, which found expression even in so strong a supporter of the enclosure movement as Arthur Young, who speaks of "the knavery of commissioners and attorneys". Then, in addition, there were hedges and fences to be set up at the cost of the farmer, while during the re-allotment there was a certain disorganization of agriculture. When the village waste was enclosed, the villagers lost their old rights of cutting turf and gathering wood for fuel, so that, altogether promising as the future might be, the immediate result on the small farmers was to land them in pecuniary difficulties.

Just at the time when the small farmers were struggling to keep their place, a change, which

---

[7] In the more technical language of political economy such land had hitherto been beyond the margin of cultivation; owing to the large demand and the higher prices it came within the margin.

was to them totally unexpected, made their position still worse. We have seen already how the inventions of Hargreaves, Arkwright, and Crompton altered the conditions of the spinning industry, and this in two ways: first, by furnishing an abundant supply of yarn instead of the scanty amount hitherto forthcoming; and secondly, by making yarn of a better quality, both finer and stronger, than the hand-spinners could produce. It is true that these inventions all applied to the cotton trade, and consequently at first only the cotton-spinners (mostly in Lancashire) were affected by them. But when, as was the case later, they were adapted for use in the woollen industry also, their competition began to be felt all over the country. The domestic stage of industry was doomed; it disappeared before the rivalry of machines driven by water or steam. What this meant to the rural population who had practised spinning and weaving in their own homes may be gathered from a picture of a Lancashire village (Mellor) under the old conditions. Here there were fifty or sixty farmers, of whom there were not more than six or seven who raised their rent directly from the land, "all the rest got their rent partly from some branch of trade, such as spinning or weaving woollen, linen, or cotton. The father of a family would earn from eight shillings to half a guinea at his loom, and his sons, if he had one, two, or three alongside of him, six or eight shillings each per week. But the great sheet-anchor of all cottages and small farms was the labour attached to the hand-wheel; and when it is considered that it required six or eight hands to prepare and spin yarn sufficient for the consumption of one weaver, this shows clearly the inexhaustible source there was for labour for every person from the age of seven to eighty years (who retained their sight and could move their hands), to earn their bread, say one to three shillings a week, without going to the parish." This example, dating from 1770, is drawn, as has been said, from Lancashire, where the bye-industries clustered most thickly; and here, in the midst of the new machinery, the hand-spinners in cotton were soonest driven from the field. These, indeed, were by no means widely diffused. Lancashire and Cheshire held the majority of them. But though the woollen-spinners escaped at first, the evil day was only deferred. The last decade of the eighteenth century saw machinery invade their province also, and when this came about, the injury to the small farmers was far-reaching, for woollen-spinning was an almost universal bye-industry in all the agricultural districts, bringing in every week small but steady earnings to supplement what the cultivator got either from his land or from his wages. What was first felt in Lancashire and Cheshire, spread over Scotland, Yorkshire, East Anglia, the Midlands, and the west of England; the hand-spinner was beaten in quality and speed, and after a period of desperate competition was forced to give up. When the "great sheet-anchor" failed, domestic industry was soon on the rocks, and the castaways had no choice but to abandon their trade or take refuge among the machine spinners.

It has been necessary here to anticipate one of the great social effects of the new system of machinery and power, to take it from what might seem its more natural place among industries, and transfer it to the chapter upon agriculture, for though in its nature the change was industrial, yet it reacted mainly upon the rural population. The loss of the domestic industries made it still more difficult for the small farmer to go on as he had done. In any case he felt the loss whether his lands remained in open field or were in the process of being enclosed. In the first case he found it still harder to make a living and pay his rent; in the second he was deprived of an addition to his resources just at a time when he needed it most.

Under the combined effects of the expense of enclosure and the decay of domestic industry, many small farmers failed altogether, so that the enclosures of the eighteenth century brought about in many cases the same result as the earlier enclosures, namely, the dispossession of a great number of small farmers. Some of these men migrated to the new manufacturing towns and became artisans, but the larger number sank into the condition of agricultural labourers, working under the new large farmers into whose hands the enclosed land passed. For the future lay with the large farmer; he possessed more intelligence, more initiative, more power of looking ahead, more capital. He was better fitted to succeed under the more speculative conditions that had begun to prevail, when, as a consequence of the growth of population, England had ceased to be a corn-exporting country, and was beginning to rely on foreign sources for some part of her supply. To get the best out of land more had to be put into it, and the small man could not afford expensive improvements. As Arthur Young points out, he was not able to marl his land at the rate of 100 tons to the acre, or spend £2 or £3 per acre in drainage, or £5 per acre to irrigate his meadows. He could not cart manure from towns long distances to his farm, nor buy expensive rams and bulls to improve his stock, nor import skilled labour or expensive implements. The man who had capital could do these things and be repaid for them. But the small farmer was really unable to take advantage of the new methods, because of the expense. It was because, to his mind, small farming meant bad or unprogressive farming that Arthur Young wrote so strongly against it. His declaration that the only remedy for the bad methods of the small farmers was to raise their rents, expresses his idea that they must either learn to farm better in order to pay the increased rent, or give place to better men. The high rents which he praises were not a panacea for agricultural distress; far from it; they were only a sign of an end, and that end the adoption of better methods. Where the rents were high, it was obvious that the better methods were in use; were it not so the rent could not have been paid.

The expense of enclosure, the decay of domestic industry, the competition of large farms, all played a part in the destruction of the small farms and the changing of the small farmer into the wage-labourer. Another cause was at work also, which acted not only on the small farmers who had paid rent for their farms, but on the yeomen or small freeholders whose farms were their own. This was the general desire on the part of the rich to buy land. It was not merely a good investment, for land brought in more than a money return. The possession of it conferred a social status, a sort of rank which the landless man had not. The old families were land-owners, with country seats, pleasant parks, far-reaching estates; the new families wished to have the same things, and they were well able to indulge their tastes, for most of the new families had made large fortunes in trade and commerce. How could they invest them better, they would ask themselves, than in land, which not only gave a good return, but also gave them the social prestige and position which they coveted? Besides the indefinite but very real gain in respect which a man got with the possession of a big estate, there were other advantages. If we take the case of the House of Commons and the franchise, it at once becomes clear how much importance was attached to holding land. Since the days of Anne, none could be a member of the House of Commons unless he possessed the qualification of owning some land; the county franchise was restricted since the days of Henry VI. to freeholders worth 40s. the year, and although under the Commonwealth persons worth £200 had been added to those qualified to vote, yet the main teaching of these laws was that the landless man was not fit to sit in Parliament, nor, unless he was a man of some means, could he vote in a county at all. If then a manufacturer was moved by ambition or by a natural desire to leave his busy town life and enjoy the pleasures of the country, his first step would be to buy land. Not only were there many such new men seeking to qualify as country gentlemen, but old families, too, by intermarrying with successful merchants and manufacturers had recruited their fortunes, and were striving to extend their influence by enlarging their estates. Many of the new large estates were formed by buying up small holdings which had been partitioned from the open fields. Nor was it only the small farmers holding their land at a rent who parted with their farms. The yeomen, the small freeholders, found it easier to sell their estates at the high prices which land commanded during the time of the Napoleonic wars than to work them at a profit. The buyer, anxious to build up a large domain and farm it on the newer style, could afford to offer a high price, since, putting aside the social advantages, he expected to get better profits than the small man could make. Hence the large estates tended to swallow the small estates and themselves grow still larger, and the yeomen and small squires disappeared. While at the beginning of the eighteenth century King estimated there were 180,000 freeholders in England, Arthur Young, writing after the wars against Napoleon, speaks of the small freeholder as practically extinct. Much as he had disliked the backward methods of farming followed by many of them, yet he regretted them, as they had "really kept up the independence of the nation". They were, indeed, the men who had triumphed over the absolutism of the Stuarts; but in the struggle of the next century, a struggle rather of brains and money than sword and musket, they were unable to maintain the dominant position they had held in the kingdom, and they dwindled in numbers and in political importance until they were bought out by the greater proprietors, who were to wield the main power in Parliament until the passing of the Reform Bill in 1832.

This agrarian revolution, the course of which we have been following, was in its results like other revolutions, neither wholly good nor wholly bad. The benefits must be set against the disadvantages. On the one side must be placed better methods of farming, larger crops, a wider area under cultivation, a greater plenty of corn and meat to supply the new demand of the increased town population. On the other side stand all the temporary hardships which any great change brings—men displaced from their old homes and old employments, and with difficulty finding new ones; the extinction of the class of small farmers working their own lands, who had in the past been looked on as the backbone of England, who had been protected by legislation of an earlier day as affording the best material from which to draw English soldiers, and who had often in battle given proof that the national belief in their courage and endurance was not misplaced. Instead of these we have the modern triple division of landlord, farmer, and labourer, where the first is often absent, and sometimes inconsiderate through his want of local knowledge, and the third, who does the hard manual work, no longer reaps a proportionate return from the soil, but is paid a wage whether his work is thorough or perfunctory. We have the "cash-nexus", the dependence of all relations on money instead of the old personal friendly feelings between landlord and tenant. When the small freeholder went, there went with him that spur to exertion that came from possession, from knowing that the land was his own, and the reward of his improvement was sure. The change that took place in agriculture was similar to the change in manufacture. Old conditions give place to the modern ones with which we are familiar. Just as domestic industry was overthrown by the growth of factories, so small farming yielded to capitalist farming. But the results in the end were not the same; both agriculture and manufacture remained for a time under protection, though the former gained far more from it than the latter. When Protection disappeared and Free-trade took its place, the manufacturers found themselves relieved of restrictions, and were able to compete on still more favourable terms for the world's trade; for a time indeed they had no serious rivals. But it was different with the land-owners. They had been helped by the plan, the outcome of mercantilist ideas, of making England a corn-exporting country, and when this had ceased to be, and a limited import had been allowed under a high duty, they still relied on the artificial advantage in English markets which the duty gave them; as, however, their advantage was artificial, so their prosperity proved artificial also.

CHAPTER XVII.

LAISSEZ-FAIRE AND STATE CHARITY. ARTISAN AND PAUPER.

The era of invention, when machinery began to take over from human skill and human labour many of the most important processes of manufacture, when England first took its place as the great manufacturing nation of the world, is sometimes called the "Industrial Revolution", but used in this way, the term is robbed of its full meaning; the progress of machinery and power is only a part of this revolution; beyond this, and of still deeper consequences, were the social effects of the new conditions. It was not merely that the output of the spinner was multiplied a hundredfold, that a weaver could weave many yards in the time hitherto spent in weaving one, that the output of ironworks for a month was as great as it had hitherto been for a year; a change in the volume of trade, however great, may not deserve the term "revolution"; that term implies a change not only in volume, but in nature and method. So far we have sketched the careers of the inventors and the direct results of their inventions upon goods and processes; now we may go deeper and try to estimate the indirect, and yet more remarkable results upon the artisans. To sum up these results in one simple statement is impossible. The natural complexity of economic history should make us distrust sweeping generalizations; on the other hand, the attempt to follow in detail, through each consecutive stage, the changes that sprang from the inventions would be beyond the limits of this book; we must be content to classify the main results as shown in each of the great industries, and then to draw with some hesitation what general conclusions may be drawn.

The period of the Industrial Revolution, especially during its later phase covering the first thirty years of this century, was marked by discontent and distress. We find numerous examples, of which the Luddite riots are the best known, in which machinery was wrecked and mills burnt, manufacturers threatened, and even in some cases shot; violent actions which called forth stern repressive measures on the part of the Government. The time was no doubt a troubled one, but the fault must not be laid entirely at the door of the Industrial Revolution. There were other disturbing causes to be borne in mind.

First of all, during much of the time England was at war, and had to bear the burden of exceptionally heavy taxation; and, in addition, owing to the policy of protecting the corn grower, food was generally scarce, and corn often rose to starvation prices; in 1800–1 the price per quarter was 116s. 8d., and though the average from 1802–1808 was 73s. 8d., in 1812 it was at 155s. Not only were the very high prices most oppressive to the poor, among whose available foods bread occupied so prominent a place, but the violence of the fluctuations disturbed all calculations, and brought in an element of uncertainty in the labourer's living. Wages that would support his family one year might six months later prove perfectly inadequate; it was of little comfort to him to think that the pressure would in all likelihood be but short, that if he could manage to tide over the bad time all would be well again. With men who are living near the margin of subsistence, present ills are so acute that future hopes hold out no bright prospect. Before the better time came the labourer or artisan would have been forced to go on the rates for support; the evils of that course will have to be dealt with hereafter, but plainly they cannot be laid at the door of the new inventions.

Similarly, the time was one of political and social unrest; the waves of the French Revolution beat indeed somewhat faintly on English shores, but they were enough to trouble our waters to some extent, and all the more that the working-classes, to whom the new ideas chiefly appealed, had no chance of making their voices heard, or their power felt, except by disorder. Smothered discontent is more dangerous and more alarming than open complaint; no one knows accurately what progress it is making, or where it may develop dangerous energy and break out. Hence the ideas of the few agitators who talked of the "rights of Man", and muttered of revolution and death to the aristocrats, were applauded by working-men angered at the high price of corn and the sight of machinery that threatened to take from them even the scanty wage that they had.

All these things—war, a protective policy that made corn dear, a vicious poor-law, a period of political discontent, were not the consequences, nor the necessary accompaniment of the Industrial Revolution. They had similar results; they brought industrial uncertainty and distress in their train, so that out of the whole total of misery and distress among the industrial classes at this period, some must be put down to causes which were accidental, which would have had bad effects, inventions or no inventions. But even when this allowance is made, the residue of hardship that sprang directly from the new system is very large.

All times of violent change in industry are times of hardship; it may be lasting or it may be temporary, but it is certain. Now the distinctive mark of the period of industrial history that, roughly speaking, covers the reign of George III. is sudden and unexpected change. The iron industry leaves the woodland counties of Surrey, Sussex, and Hampshire, and finds a new home in the Midlands, Yorkshire, and South Wales, where coal and lime are plentiful and cheap. The woollen manufactures of the eastern counties decay and are superseded by those of the north. The domestic industries of spinning and weaving, almost universal in agricultural districts at the beginning of the period, have at the end nearly disappeared. Manufacturing towns increase in population with astonishing rapidity, and even mere mushroom villages in the north suddenly find themselves more populous than southern cities that can boast a history stretching back for hundreds of years. The whole weight of the population of England is shifting. Hitherto the north had been poor, sparsely populated, ignorant, reactionary. By 1820 it is becoming rich, crowded, vigorous in thought and enterprise, progressive in political ideas.

Here is the bright side of the change; yet none the less there was a darker one. To find that we must look where the furnaces were going out of blast in the south; or where spinners who in East Anglia had been earning 8*d*. a day in 1760, were forty years later making but 4½*d*.; or again in the cottages all over England where the hand-wheels and hand-looms were becoming less in number and very much less profitable. We must not, in all these cases, ascribe the result to the direct influence of the inventions. East Anglian industry was showing symptoms of decay even before the advent of machinery left it hopelessly behind in a contest where water-power and steam-power decided the victory. The domestic industries of woollen-spinning and weaving remained comparatively unaffected until 1800, for the new inventions in spinning applied at first to cotton and not to wool. But sooner or later the competition of machinery against handwork made itself felt, and a hopeless struggle on the part of the hand-worker only became worse if it proved to be long.

Man is of all kinds of baggage the most difficult to be moved. Economists, especially the earlier economists, were apt to be heedless of this fact. Man is classified as "labour", and that is represented as "flowing" where there is a demand for labour. Even now when railways have made it comparatively easy and cheap to go from end to end of the country, and when newspapers give abundant information as to where labour is wanted, how hardly, slowly, reluctantly does labour "flow"! It is the viscous, tardy movement of lava rather than the mobile dash of water. "Labour" is the aggregation of labourers, but in most cases the labourer is not a unit. He is married and has a family to hinder his movements. If he has grown-up sons and daughters, they have occupations which they will have no wish to desert because the head of the family finds work slack near home, and thinks he could do better elsewhere. If he goes, either the home must be broken up or their employments sacrificed. Friends, associations, and that innate dislike of change which grows stronger as age advances, all combine to reduce labour to creeping rather than flowing.

If this is so in our own day, the case was still stronger in the last century when there were no railways, and the only mode of journeying available for the labouring class was on foot, when hardly a man in a village or country town had ever been twenty miles from it, when there were few wanderers to make familiar the idea of leaving home in search of work, and little news of them when they had gone.[1] It is not difficult to see that there is a considerable breach between the glib explanation that labour left without occupation in one district naturally flowed into another, and the seemingly hopeless difficulties and discouragements which met the artisan in the attempt to pursue after his vanishing industry. He might be fortunate enough to over-

---

[1] Apart from the high rates of postage, almost prohibitive to the labouring classes, it must be remembered that the arts of reading and writing were generally unknown.

take it; but on the other hand he might find that under the competition of machinery it had disappeared altogether, and that he himself would be reduced to try another means of earning a living.

To judge of the amount of distress caused by this change in employment, it is necessary to see what opportunities offered for those whose industry was slipping from them to enter another trade. The artisan is always prone to regard labour-saving machinery with jealousy; if a machine enables one man to do the work of three, then the readiest conclusion is that two men are thrown out of work by it. This conclusion, of course, is not necessarily true. It may be that the trade may so expand owing to the new machinery and the cheapness it brings, that there is room for all the old hands and perhaps others. Labour-saving machinery may injure the artisan in industries which do not admit of much expansion, but not in industries that can develop easily. On the whole, the industries affected by the new inventions were of the second class; industries, that is, capable of great extension. A sixtyfold increase in the import of cotton, a tenfold increase in the Yorkshire clothing trade, a twentyfold increase in the output of pig-iron, a sevenfold increase in the total volume of export, a fivefold increase in imports between the years 1740 and 1815, must be set side by side with the fact that the population had hardly doubled; and it is plain that the new inventions brought so vast an expansion in trade that we should seem to be justified in concluding that there was plenty of demand for labour, plenty of opportunity for those who were thrown out from one trade to enter another.

This conclusion, however, requires two important qualifications. There was a great demand for labour, but much of it was for the labour of women and children; to this point we shall have to return; and secondly, the demand was great at first, but diminished as time went on. So long as the new machinery was of such a kind that, while enormously increasing the power of each worker, it still required to be worked by hand labour, no great harm was done. This was the "Golden Age" in the cotton trade alluded to by Radcliffe, when all branches of the industry were active and prosperous. Indeed, the cotton trade continued to employ an increasing quantity of labour; whereas in 1760 it had employed 50,000 hands, by 1833 the number had risen to 1,500,000.

But when the steam-engine came to displace hand-power, and men found that by its aid many jennies and mules could be worked together, labour, especially adult labour, began to find it hard to get employment. This difficulty was further increased when the power-loom became an effective instrument. Many years passed after its invention before this efficiency was reached. Yet when it was reached, the rapidity with which the loom spread and the changes it brought with it were amazing. While in 1813 there were 2400 power-looms in use, in 1820 there were 14,150, and as these machines needed comparatively little attention—a girl and a boy of fifteen looking after four of them, and doing nine times the work one skilled weaver had been able to do with the hand-loom—it is plain that the power-loom displaced more labour than any other invention of the time. But the shearing-frames raised almost as great opposition; indeed no machinery was adapted for use in woollen industries without causing resentment. Cotton had grown up side by side with machinery; workers in it were not able to look back on an earlier and, to them, Arcadian age, ere simplicity had been dispelled at the profane touch of the inventor; it had hardly known a domestic stage; it was young and flexible. But the woollen business, in its early days the spoilt child among English industries, had now grown old and set in its habits, hostile to change, intolerant of novelty; what is more, it was very widely diffused, so that while one district alone was affected by inventions in the cotton industry, the whole of England was agitated by alterations in wool: the interests threatened were wider, the number of wage-earners thrown out of work far greater. Here indeed the Industrial Revolution hit hard. Yet the hardships caused by displacement of labour, and by the vain endeavour of hand-workers to compete with machinery, wide-spread and real as they were, were not the worst feature of the times. Such things had occurred before and must occur in every progressive state of society, even as times of war, and scarcity, and political unrest must occur with all the misery they bring in their train. And when such changes are completed, when peace and plenty return and the political horizon clears, past ills are forgotten in present prosperity, and the country at large is once more contented.

But the greatest evils of the Industrial Revolution, those which have left a permanent effect in the embittered relations between class and class, the distrust between masters and workmen, and the dissatisfaction with law and social order so common in our day, were the direct result of oppression and bad laws. A great wrong was done, partly through greed, partly through ignorance, a wrong so bitterly felt and bitterly resented that not all the prosperity which England has enjoyed in the last sixty years, not all the concessions which the law has enjoined and the employers have yielded, have been able to bring back a good understanding between Labour and Capital, or alter the poor man's fixed idea that he is being exploited for the benefit of the rich. For the oppression the manufacturers, the political economists, and the apathy of public opinion are each in a way responsible; the bad laws were the outcome of an unwise, but in the main honest, attempt to lighten the hard lot of the working-class.

The opening for oppression was through the factory door. When once artisans were massed inside, there was an end of working or leaving off as a man felt disposed; there was an end of allowing for the weak or the children. In the mill all worked alike; while the machinery went on, human hands had to go on also. It is easy to see that the latter might be sadly overdriven if the hours were too long; but no hours are too long for machinery, and the manufacturer's temptation was to keep his untiring giant at work as long as possible. Here, then, is the injury that Machinery and Power inflicted, not so by themselves, but by what they made possible. To use power and machinery artisans gathered in factories, and these factories might become oppressive almost beyond description. They might be virtual prisons where men and children toiled long hours and snatched a scanty sleep amid bad air and foul smells, working till the unending work developed disease and deformity. Gain prompted the manufacturer to begin early and stop late; if the artisan would not work, then it was not difficult to fill his place; to idle was to starve; to wander from one mill to another meant a change of employer, but not necessarily a change in condition. To overdrive labour thus was both easy and tempting; and the only checks that might have been effective, current opinion and the law, did nothing to interfere. At first indeed they both inclined to favour the strong against the weak. Hence, as we shall see, the evils which we have imagined possible became actual; nay more, the reality went in some respects even beyond the imagination.

We have already seen something of the tangle in which the Mercantilist protective policy had ended, when the original ideas had been abandoned, and a mass of duties, bounties, regulations, and restrictions left in their place. The man from whom this complicated state of things received its death-blow was Adam Smith. It is true that the death was lingering. Protection was sturdy and died hard. But after the publication of the *Wealth of Nations* in 1778, it was moribund. To the book itself it will be necessary to recur; at this stage all that need be done is to notice the principle on which Adam Smith refuted the Mercantilist arguments. The Mercantilists had cried out for this or that restriction in order to benefit this or that trade; but Adam Smith held that trade should be left free to go where and how it would; that so it would discover how it could go best, and having found that course it would hold to it; that on the principle of the division of labour each man would be best employed in doing what he could do best, and that his own interest would lead him to do it; and therefore that all restrictions which interfered in the liberty of trade were not only useless, but injurious. In short, he argued that if freedom was granted to the individual to follow his own interest, he would by doing so advance also the interest of the community, that "Man's Self-love is God's Providence".[2] Adam Smith's victory over the Mercantilist policy was slow in coming, but he made a complete and speedy conquest over the minds of those who thought and wrote about economic problems, those who would now be called Political Economists.

The fascination of his work, the simplicity and clearness which came from his plan of separating economics from politics, and isolating the study of wealth from other matters that were entangled with it, gave an enormous impulse to the study of economics; but the economists, revelling in the new

---

[2] A. Toynbee, in his *Industrial Revolution*, p. 11, uses this phrase to summarize the doctrine as developed by followers of Adam Smith.

simplicity, soon began to carry simplicity too far. If the problem of how best to forward industrial prosperity and the growth of wealth was to be solved by the simple plan of giving play to the individual, by allowing each man to do what he pleased, then it followed that all interference whatsoever was wrong. Hence came the doctrine of *laissez-faire*, "let men do as they please"; and with this weapon the economist countered all proposals that Government should interfere in industrial concerns, and answered that such action would be wrong, for each individual in a state of liberty would, by following his own interests, advance the welfare of the whole. Thus Malthus wrote: "By making the passion of self-love beyond comparison stronger than the passion of benevolence, the more ignorant are led to pursue the general happiness, an end they would have totally failed to attain if the ruling principle of their conduct had been benevolence". It is not hard to imagine that, with the sight of children dragging to and fro from their twelve or thirteen hours' toil in a factory daily before his eyes, the ordinary benevolent man came to think that political economy, with its guiding star "a passion of self-love", must be a hard-hearted science, and that there must be something wrong somewhere in its conclusions.

The fact is that there was mutual misunderstanding. Adam Smith and his followers, tired of the trammels of Mercantilist restrictions, had cried out for liberty and free competition as a remedy. But the liberty and free competition which came with the Industrial Revolution, and was welcomed by the economists, was in part a sham. There was "freedom" indeed between master and man, but it was freedom for power to compete with weakness; the cry of *laissez-faire* merely protested against any interference with the liberty of oppression. The blame for the misunderstanding lies with both sides. The economists, and in chief Ricardo, developed an intensely abstract science, based upon assumptions which were convenient for their purpose but not true; assumptions that the conditions of competition were equal, that man was "economic man", a creature following solely his selfish interest in getting wealth, and always capable of doing so; and they did not make it clear to everyone what these assumptions were. Those who listened to the economists, and quoted and repeated their doctrines, did so again without any word of warning that these doctrines were based upon abstractions, and were not necessarily true to the actual conditions of life. And, further, they went beyond their teachers, and assumed a sacredness, an inviolability for the so-called "laws" which the new science proclaimed. Workmen combining to obtain a rise in their wages were denounced by amateur economists in much the same terms as if they were combining to break the Ten Commandments. Harsh as the abstract political economy of Ricardo and his school seemed to the working-man and the philanthropist, it was made to appear far harder by the glibness with which it was applied, or rather misapplied, to industrial troubles. It is no wonder that the science was hated as a new weapon in the armoury of the master, and that traces of this hatred still show themselves in the suspicion and dislike with which most educated artisans still regard the conclusions of political economy.

This idea of *laissez-faire*, that all was going well in spite of all appearances to the contrary, prevailed for a time over the uneasiness caused by the condition of the factory hands. By degrees, however, under the stern logic of facts, apathy gave place to concern, and easy content to anxiety. One glimpse into the factories had been given in 1802, when Sir Robert Peel called the attention of Parliament to the miserable condition of apprentices in cotton mills. It appeared that parish authorities, anxious to relieve their ratepayers of the charge of pauper children, had been in the habit of sending off these luckless children to be apprenticed in mills; once in the mill they were worked like slaves, and housed and fed worse, for a slave is, after all, property, and if he dies there is a loss, but other apprentices could easily be found to fill empty places. Peel's Act restricted the hours of work for apprentices to twelve hours a day exclusive of meals, and made some regulations about education. Then the veil was dropped again, and little more was done. It was not till the report of the Commissioners on the Factory Bill of 1832 that the country realized what was happening, nearly two generations of miserable beings having in the meantime literally "gone through the mill", many of them in hopeless toil and unknown suffering.

It would be easy to quote from that report terrible stories of neglect, over-work, and brutality, especially to children, but it would not be fair to take them as specimens of what was normal. Michael Sadler, who was at the head of the Committee, was fighting with the fury of a fanatic on behalf of the artisans, and the evidence which he called cannot be said to give anything but the worst side. Some of it broke down under subsequent cross-examination. Much of it was shown to be old and bear reference to what had happened thirty or forty years before; instances of what took place in the small mills, especially in those driven by water, where the power was intermittent and the hours in consequence desperately long, were set out as if they were typical of all mills; the manufacturers were not given the chance of bringing rebutting evidence. Still, even when all allowances are made, even when we base our estimate on the more sober evidence and reports collected by the travelling commissioners in 1833, a sufficiently serious state of things was disclosed. In Scotland and the north of England the hours in general were twelve, not including the stop for dinner, and thirteen or fourteen hours were by no means rare. Even this might be exceeded when the mills were making up lost time. "I have worked", said one witness, "till 12 p.m. last summer; we began at 6. I told book-keeper I did not like to work so late; he said I mote." No proper opportunity was given for meals; the stop for dinner was usually forty minutes, but cleaning up machinery had generally to be done during it; no time was given for breakfast or tea—"We took it as we could, a bite and a run, sometimes not able to eat it from its being so covered with dust". This was hard enough for men, but it was not they alone who suffered. At their heels were dragged women and children, the latter often hardly out of the nursery. Though the majority of the children were nine years old or over, it was not uncommon to find in the mills children of six years of age; there were many under seven, and still more under eight. It was inhuman to compel such children to endure the long hours, yet they had to endure them; a child of fourteen who wished to stop at 8 in the course of a 16½-hours day was compelled to go on under threat of dismissal. "I have seen them", said another witness, "fall asleep, and they have been performing their work with their hands while they were asleep after the 'billy' had stopped. I have stood and looked at them for two minutes going through the operation of piecening fast asleep." Punishment, such as strapping, or, in worse cases, sousing in water, was not infrequently used to keep the children awake, though the practice was less common than it had been. "Ever since Sadler started the agitation of this question, masters have not suffered their foremen to go such lengths as they used to do." It was not, indeed, usually the foremen or overlookers who did the beating, but the slubbers and spinners, who were assisted at their work by children placed under them; and the masters cannot be altogether excused if through ignorance or carelessness such practices were allowed to go on. Again, although the long hours did not always cause physical injury, yet weakness and deformity could often be traced to the long straining of immature bodies over monotonous occupations. A witness from Keighley, in reply to the question, "You have stated that about eight of the thirty boys who worked with you in that mill were deformed; have you remarked that other children in other mills were similarly deformed?" replied, "Yes, in Keighley you could find wagon-loads";[3] and medical evidence went to show that so bold a statement was not without some grounds of justification.

The Commissioners of 1833 were able to show that all was not equally dark; that the evils were principally in the older mills, especially those under small masters and those using water-power; that many of the newer mills owned by the large capitalists were well conducted and the workers contented. Yet the existing state of things could not be justified by proving that all masters did not treat men and children as slaves; that such treatment was possible, and in some cases actual, was of itself enough reason for the interference of Parliament. Again, it is not necessary to attempt to apportion the share of the blame between capitalists and workmen. The fact that the most oppression occurred in the small mills, where the master usually worked himself, and might therefore have been expected to have felt some sympathy with fellow-workers, suggests what has indeed been demonstrated again in later experiences, that industries carried on at home[4] are liable to the worst

---

[3] This is from the Committee of 1832. The other quotations are from the Report of 1833.

[4] E.g. nailmaking, and the cheap tailoring and dressmaking trades.

abuses, the longest hours, the most insanitary conditions, and the lowest pay—a fact that should place us on our guard against regarding the large capitalist as the tyrant of industry. Nor can the workers themselves be entirely absolved. Here and there a man was found who refused to let his children suffer as he had suffered himself, but the majority were greedy for the additional wage which their children earned, and callous about the suffering involved in earning it; and so the children were sent on the same road that their fathers and mothers had travelled before them, and went to the mills before they were ten years old.

Enough has been said to show that *laissez-faire*, the leaving of the poor and weak to make their bargain with the mill-owner, meant that in many cases they used their liberty to sell themselves and their children into slavery. Morally, they may be blamed, but practically it is hard to see what else could have been expected. Being themselves easily reduced to absolute want, to struggle with the mill-owners must have seemed to them hopeless. Current opinion as expressed by the political economists gave them cold comfort; the law, far from helping them, stood in their way, for until the repeal of the Combination Acts in 1825 it was an offence, visited with severe penalties, for workmen to combine for the purpose of getting higher wages. And it must further be remembered that the parents themselves having been factory children in their own day, had grown up uneducated and careless. Indeed, the worst feature about the whole system is its cumulative nature. Ignorant and brutalized parents had children in nature like themselves, and even misery grew to be reckoned among them as something to be acquiesced in, rather than remedied. Things were going rapidly from bad to worse, and the entire race of artisans seemed to be sinking into complete degradation.

Unfortunately the harshness and recklessness of some employers was not the only evil which made the latter days of the Industrial Revolution so injurious. Almost as much suffering came from a policy which was suggested by hasty and ill-considered benevolence.

The English Poor-law, as settled by the act of 1601, had recognized that the burden of the poor was one that should fall on the community, and it had further drawn a valuable distinction between the aged and impotent poor who were not able to earn their own living and were therefore fit objects for charitable relief, and the able-bodied poor who were capable of work, and had not the same claim as the others. These might be idle for two reasons, either because they were so by inclination, or because they could actually find no work to do. For the idle the Elizabethan system provided punishment, or at any rate such a degree of discomfort as would act as a deterrent; finding work for the unemployed was recommended, but it was a difficult task. Indeed, though we are familiar enough with the "workhouses" in which employment of this sort was to be given, the word itself has changed its meaning, and is only a house where a certain quantity of disagreeable work is set as a deterrent.

During the 180 years that elapsed between the

Poor-law of 1601 and Gilbert's Act of 1782, three measures call for notice. The Law of Settlement of 1662 had almost reduced the working-classes to servitude by providing that persons coming from strange parishes, though not seeking charity or support from the parish to which they came, might be sent back again to their homes to prevent them from eventually becoming chargeable to their new parish. This act made it practically impossible for a working-man to take the chance of getting work or better pay away from home; it prevented labour from going where it was required; and though modified by later statutes, its action was always oppressive. An act of 1691, providing that a register should be kept of paupers and of the relief given them, and prohibiting the giving of any other relief except by the authority of a justice or by order of the Bench at Quarter Sessions, is worth notice because, though intended to make the giving of relief methodical, it opened the door to later abuses by setting aside the authority of the overseers in favour of the Justices. The third act, that of 1722, allowed parishes to join in unions to build houses for the reception of the indigent, and ordered "that no poor who refused to be lodged and kept in such houses should be entitled to ask or receive parochial relief". This "Workhouse Test", by restricting relief to the form known as "indoor relief", had satisfactory results, not only in reducing the rates, but also the number of applicants. "Lazy people, rather than submit to the workhouse, were content to throw off the mask and maintain themselves." In spite of the increase in population, the rates were less in 1750 than they had been in 1698.[5]

Although this reduction was partly due to the active administration of the Law of Settlement, and was therefore achieved at the expense of binding out pauper apprentices, pulling down cottages, and making it hard for labourers to leave their homes in search of better wages, yet upon the whole things were going fairly well, and this in spite of somewhat confused methods, and a want of uniformity and incorporation. But most of the main principles were sound. The right of the indigent to relief was recognized; the duty of providing it was cast on the community, with the wholesome addition that each locality should be responsible for its own paupers; and, finally, the condition of those in receipt of relief was made less comfortable and less desirable than that of the man who maintained himself. Unfortunately this state of affairs was not destined to last.

An ominous sign of what was coming was furnished by the leap upwards taken by the rates. For the first fifty years of the eighteenth century these were almost stationary. Between 1750 and 1784 they tripled in amount; even taking into account the increase in population, the rise in rates was six times as great. We have already seen some of the causes which were throwing people out of work, temporarily or permanently. But of more effect than all these was the rise in prices as compared with wages. Corn, meat, butter, and all agricultural produce had risen in price and continued to

[5] £689,000 (1750) as against £819,000 in 1698.

rise. Taxation for war purposes made other necessaries dearer also. Near the larger towns, indeed, agricultural labourers were not so badly off; yet in remote districts their condition was miserable. Arthur Young found wages, which within twenty miles of London stood at 10*s.* 9*d.* a-week, falling to 6*s.* 3*d.*, 5*s.* 2½*d.*, and even 4*s.* 6*d.* in Lancashire. While at the present day a quarter of wheat would cost a Gloucestershire labourer the wages of between two and three weeks' labour, in 1772 it represented ten weeks' labour. And although wheat bread was less universally the food of the country than it is now, yet rye bread and barley bread were becoming unpopular and much less used. In whatever way indeed we regard it, the fact is clear. Wages were in many cases insufficient to maintain the worker.

The Elizabethan system had provided for such a difficulty by the Act of Apprentices; according to this the Justices were to fix such wages in their districts as seemed to them reasonable, taking into consideration the price of living. Had this act been in operation at the end of the eighteenth century, it is plain that the Justices would have raised wages in proportion to the rise in corn. But the act had long[6] become a dead letter. In our own times we should look to combination to solve the difficulty; but this was almost as much of the future as the assessments of the Justices were of the past.

[6] How long, it is difficult to say. An assessment made in Lancashire in 1725 was published in 1795 as a historical curiosity; there were assessments in Shropshire in 1739. On the other hand, many contend that the assessments, though occasionally made, were never common, or much attended to even from the first.

Combination in the form of Trade-unions was indeed beginning; tailors, wool-combers, frame-knitters, cutlers, silk-weavers, and many others had Unions as early as 1750. But so far as these attempted to raise wages, their action was a breach of the law, and consequently they could only act secretly and cautiously. In short, neither the old system nor the new was able to raise wages as was required; and in the meanwhile sentimental opinion was stirred by the misery around it, and demanded that something should be done. Like many other hasty and ill-considered benevolent actions, this something turned out to be the worst thing that could have been done, for it was nothing less than the giving of relief or "allowances" to supplement wages. The curious inefficiency of legislation to do good compared with its boundless power of doing harm is a matter of common remark. No better example of this can be found than in the story of the Allowance system.

Two events mark the beginning of this. The first is Gilbert's Act of 1782, which with some wise provisions mingled some incredibly foolish ones; such as, for example, forbidding the admission of the able-bodied poor into the workhouse, declaring that work should be found for the poor near their homes, supplementing wages from the rates, and increasing the power of the justices to interfere in granting relief. The second event was a direct consequence of the first. In 1795 some Berkshire justices, meeting in Quarter Sessions at Speenhamland, declared that the state of the poor required more assistance than had been given to them; and that if farmers and others would not increase the pay of their labourers, they would make an allowance, based on the price of bread, to every family in proportion to its numbers.[7] The alacrity with which this policy was followed over the country has gained for this declaration the name of the "Speenhamland Act of Parliament".

Before proceeding to the actual results of this disastrous measure, it is well to understand clearly what it implied. To begin with, it abandoned all idea of deterring the indigent from pauperism; the workhouse test was given up; the pauper was to be made as comfortable as the industrious. Nay, more, if allowances were to be given to supplement wages, then he who was lazy and earned least might receive most. The more idle, extravagant, thriftless he was, the more he obtained. If he married improvidently and had a large family, this was no burden to him, for an allowance was made for each child. His difficulties were, in short, relieved without a moment's thought of whether they were of his own making or not. On the other hand, industrious and honest labour was punished. If a man, by hard work, prudence, and economy managed to keep himself without help from the rates, not only did he have the mortification of seeing his idle companions as well off as he, in spite

[7] The date is worth notice, for it was just at this time that the competition of the inventions adapted into the woollen industries began to be felt in the agricultural districts where weaving and spinning had helped to eke out wages which were of themselves insufficient. When these bye-industries were collapsing, it was reasonable that the justices should think that something must be done by way of compensation. This may serve to explain the justices taking action, but it does not in any way prove that the particular form of action which they took was wise.

of their idleness, but he had himself to contribute to the rates which supported them. They were enabled to live idle by his toil. Consequently all stimulus to labour was removed. "Why", he would argue, "should I work for them? I have but to be idle myself and the rates will support me." Thus English labour was pauperized wholesale. Not only were the lazy and vicious encouraged at the expense of the industrious, but the workers of the next generation were bred paupers from the very beginning. The self-respecting labourer, who was too proud to go on the rates, could often not afford to marry at all. It was only the paupers who could marry and bring up children in comfort. When we couple with this the physical and moral degradation which we have already seen going on in the factories, we may understand that there is some reason in the theory that English labour is not what it was in the eighteenth century, because during the first thirty years of the nineteenth century the whole tendency of legislation and industrial conditions was to encourage the bad at the expense of the good, and then to go further and make the worst of material which was bad from its very beginning.

To the labourer the allowance system was debasing and demoralizing, but the bad effects did not stop there. When the principle of supplementing wages from the rates was admitted, employers were relieved from the duty of paying their men properly. While the price of food and necessaries had risen, wages had lagged behind; in many employments, both in agriculture and manufacture, men did not earn enough to keep themselves and their families in a condition of decency. The true remedy was that wages should be raised. But it was impossible to bring the necessity home to employers when once allowances were given from the rates. Consequently the obligation which should have lain on employers was shifted from their shoulders on to the nation at large; that is to say, it rested upon property-holders of all descriptions, many of whom were not employers of labour at all, and were therefore unjustly burdened.

In every way the change in the administration of poor relief, begun by Gilbert's Act and the Berkshire justices, was bad. It was demoralizing to labourer and to employer. It was fearfully costly. Rates rose higher and higher; by 1817 they reached the enormous figure of £7,870,801 in a population of 11,000,000. They became so heavy that land actually began to go out of cultivation. At Cholesbury in Buckinghamshire, the rates, which in 1801 had stood at £10, 11s., reached £367 in 1832. At this stage the whole land was offered to the assembled poor, but they declined the offer, preferring to have it worked for their advantage on the old system. This was an exceptional case; but if poor relief had continued to be given in the same way, the same thing would have become common all over England. And meanwhile, in spite of all this lavish expenditure, no one was satisfied or contented, not even the paupers, who, from being "lazy and imperious", speedily became violent. At Bancliffe the paupers obliged the overseer to withdraw by threatening to drown him; nor was such a proceeding without parallel elsewhere. In self-defence landlords pulled down cottages which might harbour paupers, and even resorted to frauds of all kinds to prevent their labourers getting a settlement. And hardest of all was the fate of the honest and self-supporting labourer, who was often turned out to make room for paupers, whom it was cheaper to employ than to relieve.

The picture of the early years of the nineteenth century is a dark one. We may well compare the glory that was being won in the struggle against Napoleon with the misery at home. With the mass of our working-class underfed and underpaid, ill-housed, uneducated, without hope and without prospects, overworked even from early childhood, and finally degraded morally by the offer of poor relief, it is hardly a matter for surprise that discontent was rife, that men vapoured about revolution, that ricks flared in the country, that frames and machinery were broken in the towns, that manufacturers were assaulted and in some cases shot, that troops were called out, and rioters hanged. Grave as was the state of affairs, the evils were in the main the fruit of folly or neglect on the part of the nation and those who shaped its policy, and consequently, when wiser courses were adopted, the evils in their most acute form gradually disappeared. But much of the injury was permanent, and still shows its deep-rooted effects in modern industrial difficulties.

CHAPTER XVIII.

REMEDIES BY LEGISLATION.

The mistakes in policy which aggravated the distress that naturally accompanied the Industrial Revolution, as distress always accompanies any sudden and great change, were very dissimilar in character. The neglect which permitted the evils of the factory system to go on unchecked for so long was new: it was the fruit of the novel ideas of liberty and of the doctrines of the economists; the folly which made bread dear by taxing foreign corn was, on the other hand, old: it came from the survival of the old Mercantile ideas; the degrading Allowance system had its origin in kind-heartedness and sentimental charity, entirely misapplied, but none the less genuine. It is of remarkable, nay, almost of unique, interest, to find the ideas of advanced reform, of the accumulated wisdom of the past, and of humanity and benevolence apparently competing to see which could injure the nation most; and it is hardly of less interest to trace the measures by which the mischief was eventually abated.

Two of these three reforms were the result of a series of measures, and require to be treated in some detail. But the third, the reform in the Poor-law, can be dismissed shortly. The remedy, indeed, was plain; the damage had been wrought by the allowances, by departing from the older and wiser plan which had discouraged outdoor relief, or indeed any sentimental liberality in relieving the indigent. The Report of the Commissioners who inquired into the existing state of the Poor-law,[1] stated that the relief fund was applied to purposes opposed to the letter, and still more to the spirit, of the law, and destructive to the morals of the indigent and to the welfare of all, and this general statement was so completely justified by the mass of confusion, waste, favouritism, and mismanagement revealed, that there was no hesitation in carrying out a speedy reform. In its first principle the new act[2] returned to the old system. Relief to the able-bodied, except in workhouses, was declared illegal. In addition to this, parishes were to be grouped in Unions, and arrangements were made for ensuring economy and uniformity of treatment; the law of settlement was so restricted as to be almost abolished, while the control of the whole was given to a Board of Poor-law Commissioners, who could issue regulations, examine and audit accounts, and, by their inspectors, keep in touch with the local authorities, the guardians. The results of the new measure were immediate and satisfactory. The rates fell at once by a quarter, and in proportion to the numbers of the population, have never again approached the figures of 1834. The percentage of paupers to the total population has fallen from 7·5 to less than half that number; and in spite of the increase of population, while the actual number of those in receipt of indoor relief is about the same now as it was in 1841, outdoor relief has decreased very considerably. It is true that there have been complaints against the present

---

[1] Issued in 1834. [2] The Poor-law Amendment Act of 1834.

system. In 1839 feeling ran so high against the Poor-law Commissioners that it seemed likely that Parliament would dissolve that body, but on cooler reflection the excellence of the work done was admitted, and the Board continued until its absorption into the Local Government Board in 1871. In spite of all that has been done there are still inconsistencies and defects, both in what the Poor-law does, and in what it leaves undone. There is still a good deal of outdoor relief given to the able-bodied poor, in cases of sickness or temporary disablement, so much so that the workhouses contain few able-bodied paupers; most of the inmates are old, or unfitted for work in some other way; thus the disagreeableness of the "house" acts most on the class for whom it is least intended. The regulations about the vagrant class, the "casuals", are ineffective to reduce their numbers. And, finally, the new Poor-law has done nothing to solve that part of the great problem which applies to those who are willing to work yet cannot find work; it draws no distinctions as to whether a man's need is his fault or his misfortune. But in spite of all qualifications the Poor-law Amendment Act remains a striking example of a sound and effective legislative reform.

The story of the movement to Free-trade is sometimes told as if it were all contained in the agitation which ended in the repeal of the Corn-laws in 1846. This is in a way natural. Behind the Corn-laws indeed, Protection found its last shelter; there the last stand was made, and the circumstances of Cobden's attack and Peel's surrender are so dramatic that they are apt to overshadow the interest of everything else. But the abolition of the Corn-laws was, after all, only the culminating point of a long strife, waged between the old ideas and the new; the victory of the Anti-Corn-law League did but finish the work which Adam Smith had begun.

Protection has been defended on all sorts of grounds; we have already seen the justification urged for the Mercantile system, such as the necessity of keeping the country strong, with plenty of money, with men and materials in case of war, and with an adequate corn supply. But when the time arrived for abolition, when the artificial props should be cast aside, the real opposition came from selfish motives, from those who, long protected, now feared that they would be ruined by foreign competition. Before a nation can be converted to Free-trade, manufacturers and land-owners must each be convinced that they will gain more in the long run by the expansion of trade and commerce and the cheapness of goods, than by the duties which protect them. Each party is readier to remove the mote from its brother's eye, than the beam from its own, and more likely to see the advantages to be gained by abolishing the duties which protect the other's trade rather than by sacrificing its own protection, and therefore the resistance must be overcome in detail. So it was in England; protection of manufactures was the first to go, and eventually the manufacturers themselves took the lead in pressing the advantages of Free-trade on the corn growers.

The *Wealth of Nations* soon silenced the supporters

of the older Mercantile school; indeed, the whole system had fallen into a state of such appalling complexity, that any advocate of what was more simple easily convinced a thinking man that some remedy was required. Not only did innumerable duties hamper trade in all directions; not only were industries divided among themselves, some demanding higher duties, while others called for the remission of all taxation on the same articles, spinners being anxious to exclude foreign yarns and weavers to admit them, shipbuilders longing for cheap material from abroad, timber owners protesting against its import; not only were the duties so numerous that a complete understanding of them seemed hopeless, for there were sixty-eight branches of the customs, and some articles paid many different duties;[3] but even so the whole tale of disadvantages was not told. The duties brought in a ridiculously small revenue in proportion to the cost of collecting them. A common topic of discussion in trade pamphlets of the eighteenth century was which of English industries held the second place to wool; cotton, iron, silk, lace-making, each advanced their claims, but an occupation of a less honourable nature had at least as good a title to the place, and that was smuggling. The spectacle of 40,000 persons in the country employed by sea and land in systematically evading the country's laws is a remarkable one, but in the younger Pitt's day this gigantic total was the estimate of a Committee of the House of Commons.

[3] A pound of nutmegs paid nine duties. In some cases the number rose to fourteen.

Pitt had read and appreciated the *Wealth of Nations*, and began the work of simplification; as far as he could, he reduced, classified, and consolidated the multifarious duties. His commercial treaty with France,[4] stipulating for freedom of navigation and commerce in all articles except those specifically excepted, and reducing the duties on many others, was a wise and statesmanlike measure. It set aside the idea that France was our natural enemy; it gave our merchants a wide market close at hand; we exported manufactured goods, and received in exchange wine, oil, brandy, vinegar, articles which we could not produce ourselves, and which therefore it was especially valuable to obtain cheap. Although the treaty found many enemies, it is noticeable that Fox, who led the opposition to it, was careful to disclaim the old Mercantile idea "which deemed exports a gain and imports a loss".

A hole once made in the barriers of Protection, the water flowed in, the flood rose, and bit by bit the old duties crumbled away and disappeared. The new industrial activity which came with the inventions of the eighteenth century showed manufacturers that they had little to fear from foreign competitors, and that, on the contrary, their real danger lay in being starved for want of raw materials, or markets in which to sell their goods. Foreigners could not buy English goods in any quantity, unless Englishmen would take their commodities in exchange; and where protective duties were heavy this could not be done, and the whole national

[4] 1786.

trade was hindered. Thus by degrees the great body of manufacturers became converted to the theory of Free-trade. Little protections were swept away without much outcry; where the trade was large it raised its voice in bitter lamentation. One of the chief features of the Mercantile system had been the Navigation Acts, which had protected British shipping and encouraged British shipbuilders. They had done their work well enough, but the work was now complete, and the only result was to rouse the jealousy of foreigners. So long as the war had lasted British ships had been almost the only ones afloat;[5] but when with the peace this practical monopoly ended, other nations retaliated with similar limitations, and our ships were often forced to make half their voyage, either out or home, in ballast, because they could not get a cargo. America first gained from us a relaxation of our laws in 1814. Eight years later the laws were further modified, and in 1823, Huskisson, Canning's President of the Board of Trade, carried his Reciprocity of Duties Bill, by which the same duties or drawbacks were given to foreign as to British vessels, thus practically ending a system which had begun in Richard II.'s day and had been a guiding principle in our commercial legislation for centuries. The shipbuilders gloomily prophesied ruin for themselves, but they were mistaken, as facts speedily showed, for while the average increase in British shipping for the last 19 years of the old system

---

[5] The French and Dutch carrying trade was almost destroyed by the war. Denmark also became involved and suffered severely. Sweden and the United States were not much affected.

had been 10 per cent, 21 years following on the change saw an increase of 45 per cent.

Other industries were treated in the same way. The silk weavers wished for a reduction in the duties on raw silk and organzine;[6] proprietors of silk mills were ready enough for the first, but objected to the second; the Spitalfields weavers clamoured against any change. Huskisson went further than any of them wished, reduced the duties on raw silk from 5s. 7½d. on foreign produce and 4s. on that from Bengal to 3d., halved the duty on organzine, and provided that two years later foreign-made silks, instead of being entirely prohibited, might be brought in under a duty of 30 per cent *ad valorem*. These proposals were after all for a very modified form of Free-trade, but they caused a panic in the silk industry, many manufacturers finding their only source of comfort in the belief that the two years' delay would leave them time to escape before ruinous foreign competition began; but here again the prophets of evil were false prophets. Ten years later our manufacturers, who had trembled at the thought of French competition, were sending their own goods to France to the value of £60,000 a year. Precisely similar advances were made in the woollen trade when Huskisson reduced the duty on imported wool from 6d. to 1d. per lb., and allowed wool to be exported at the same rate. He was set on for this by both sides; manufacturers approved of cheap wool from abroad, but were afraid that British wool would be sent abroad; British wool-growers, though

[6] Thrown silk.

glad to be able to export when home prices were low, dreaded the competition of foreign wool at home. Yet, as usual, a few years later Huskisson was able to show that both export and import had increased enormously under the stimulus of a reduction in the duty. Where such important industries as shipbuilding, silk and wool, were unable to keep the protection which they had clung to for so long, it was not to be expected that minor industries would be successful. Peel followed up Huskisson's work by sweeping away duties by the hundred. In 1842, out of 1200 articles subject to customs 750 were reduced; duties on raw materials used in manufacture were not to exceed 5 per cent; nor those on partially manufactured articles 12 per cent, nor on completed articles 20 per cent, and by these reductions and abolitions the revenue only lost the paltry sum of £270,000. In 1844 all export duties, and 430 out of 813 duties on raw materials, were given up. Silk, hemp, flax, yarns, furniture woods, manures, ores, drugs, dye-stuffs, and cotton-wool were thus freed from tax; the glass duty was abolished; and further reductions were made in 1845. In fact the general justification of duties was abandoned, and no article could hope to be protected unless it could claim that it was an exception to the usual rule.

Could any article maintain such a claim? Long before 1845 this had been a question hotly debated, for upon the answer depended the existence of the last stronghold of Protection, the Corn-laws. These, too, had been a part of the old theory of National Power as expressed by the Mercantile system, in their time no doubt not unsuitable; but we have more than once been led to notice the ill-effects of policies which survived their day of usefulness; the longer the policy had flourished and the deeper the hold it had taken, so too the period of decay was longer, and the pernicious effects of its decadence more marked. The original idea had been to encourage agriculture, so that there should be a vigorous rural population, and a sufficient supply of home-grain to feed our people; to ensure that the supply should not fall short even in years of scarcity, it was needful to have a large area under cultivation, and to find a market for the large amount of produce which would be raised under normal conditions—more indeed than could be consumed at home—a bounty on export was given. This policy had been for a long time a marked success. English corn-growing had been remunerative, and the price had been kept fairly steady, rarely falling so low as to throw the farmers in difficulties, nor rising so high as to distress the consumer. This stability in prices was ascribed, and rightly ascribed, to the bounty which encouraged corn-growing for export. But during the last quarter of the eighteenth century the home supply became insufficient. The real reason was the growth in population already mentioned,[7] and this was exaggerated by a succession of poor harvests. The second cause, however, served to mask the first; none the less, though the change was not perceived, it was a fact. From 1766 to 1773 the amount of corn imported equalled the amount ex-

[7] See Chap. XV.

ported. English corn was still enough to feed the home population. The next twenty years saw this position fairly maintained, but from 1792 onward England became definitely a corn-importing country. She could only supply herself in good seasons: an average harvest was insufficient to feed her expanded population, a bad harvest quite inadequate. We enter here upon a period of rapid fluctuations and famine prices, which the war, by making supplies from abroad precarious, accentuated still further.

High prices had led to high rents, and if the prices went down, the rents could not be paid. Hence the end of the war only made general what had been occasional before, namely, that a good harvest meant a loss to the farmer, instead of a gain. Accordingly in 1815 an Act prohibited importation at less than 80*s*. a quarter; this was amended in 1822 to the effect that foreign corn might be imported when the home price was 70*s*. with a duty of 12*s*., which duty was reduced to 5*s*. when the price rose to 80*s*. A third Act in 1828 established a sliding-scale with duties varying gradually from 36*s*. 8*d*. when the home price was 50*s*. to 1*s*. at 73*s*.; but whatever the method of these acts, they all aimed at keeping up the price of corn to what was regarded as a remunerative level for the farmer. Strange as it may seem, it is scarcely an exaggeration to say that the Corn-laws, instead of securing the nation from the risks of agricultural scarcity, had been turned to the less noble task of protecting the corn-grower from the disasters of agricultural prosperity.

Such a step was not taken without protest. Before this many men had come to see that the principle was thoroughly vicious. High prices of corn pressed hardest upon the poor, and Government in legislating thus was making the poor man's lot even harder than it need be. And the object aimed at, namely, benefiting the farmer, and making the realm yield a plentiful supply of corn for itself so as to be independent of the foreigner, was not attained. The farmer's terror was a low price of corn; if corn was plentiful the price would be low, and thus he had no inducement to produce plentifully; while all the time it was the landlords who were pocketing the profit in the shape of high rent. The nation bought its bread unnecessarily dear in order to make still richer a class already rich, namely, the land-owners.

The fact was not difficult to see; poor artisans could see it as plainly as the economists. Among all the riots that marked the early part of the century, the dearness of food was generally found among the rioters' complaints. The inscription "Bread or Blood" placed by the Brandon rioters upon a banner was typical of the attitude of many. But though the fact was plain, the task of providing a remedy was not easy. To break down any long-standing system is hard, and it was particularly difficult in this case, for the landed interest was especially strong in Parliament, and land-owners and farmers were at first alike convinced that free corn meant ruin for them. The days had indeed changed since Adam Smith had written "Country gentlemen and farmers are to their great honour of all people the least subject to the wretched spirit of monopoly ". Manufacturers had now got free from this "wretched spirit" which Adam Smith found so strongly marked in them, but it had left them, only to find a house swept and garnished for itself among the land-owners.

For many years proposals had been made in Parliament to abolish the Corn-laws, but they were always rejected, even somewhat contemptuously. The question did not become serious till the foundation of the Anti-Corn-law League in 1838, under the leadership of Richard Cobden. Cobden's work was twofold; he set the vast resources of the League to work in order to form a party of Anti-Corn-law Leaguers in Parliament by effective registration and canvassing, while by his speeches, delivered all over the country, he convinced his hearers that, so far from the farmers being the better for the Corn-laws, they were injured by them. His speeches appealed both to humanity and to intelligence; he showed how miserable the lives of the agricultural labourers were, how badly they were paid, in what wretched hovels they were housed; he made it plain that the land-owners alone profited by the Corn-laws, that the duty did not keep the price steady, but on the contrary made fluctuations in price even more violent; he exposed all the fallacies behind which the land-owners tried to shelter themselves. The most evident proof of the interest taken in the Anti-Corn-law League is the readiness with which money was subscribed to it. It was in vain, Cobden said, for his opponents to call the League an incendiary and revolutionary body when the people of England subscribed £50,000 to it in one year. Yet in spite of all Cobden's work, and the enthusiastic support which the Free-traders gave him, the work of making an impression on Parliament went on slowly. In 1845 a motion for Free-trade in corn was rejected by 254 to 122. But in that year Cobden was aided by a powerful and altogether unexpected ally. As Bright said, "Famine, against which we had warred, joined us". The potato rot broke out in Ireland; Peel saw no remedy but to open the ports and import corn freely; and he saw, what the League saw too, that the duty once taken off, it would be impossible to reimpose it. Peel's colleagues did not agree with him, and he resigned, but the other side could not form a Government, and in a short time Peel was again in power. In 1846 his proposals were carried. For three years more corn was to be subject to a duty of 10*s*. when the price was under 48*s*., falling to 4*s*. at 53*s*.; when that time was over, all corn was to be admitted at a nominal duty of 1*s*.[8] The victory of the League was won; restriction was removed from the food of the poor, the last great barrier of Protection had been broken down, the last remnant of the old Mercantile system destroyed.

The victory of the Free-traders, which we have been engaged in following, was a triumph of new ideas over a policy which had for a long time been held wise, but which had outlived its period of usefulness, and had become a hindrance to the industrial prosperity of England. The Factory Acts were of different character, for they were designed

---

[8] The 1*s*. duty was abolished in 1869.

to remedy an evil of modern growth, an evil which had sprung up on the removal of old methods. Free-trade in corn was the last step forward in a prolonged movement; the Factory Acts were steps retraced in a movement which had been too hasty. Indeed at first many persons believed that they were steps backward; not progress towards liberty, but a retreat into restriction; and at first sight the opinion seemed reasonable. Modern opinion, indeed, does not accept it, but that is because we have changed our view as to the form that "liberty" in industrial matters should take. The principle which underlies the Factory Acts is that it is the duty of Government to protect the weaker party, and especially women and children, in an industrial bargain for the exchange of labour, in such a way that the stronger shall not use his power oppressively; to prevent either neglect on one hand or recklessness on the other from subjecting the worker to needless risks; and to insist on a certain amount of leisure, of education, and of sanitary precaution. But this was a new principle, and, further, it has shown itself capable of wide expansion. Even now we are not at the end of it, for with appeals for Government interference in strikes, and official or semi-official arbitration in trade disputes, and legislative proposals for an eight-hours day, it is being pressed further and further.

The hardships endured by artisans during the latter part of the Industrial Revolution have been already related. We may sum them up as being due to the change in employment caused by machinery, the inadequate rate of wages, and the excessive hours and insanitary conditions that accompanied the establishment of factories. The first of these was inevitable, but it was of its very nature temporary; when once change ceased artisans adapted themselves to the new conditions; the second was amended partly by combinations among workmen to obtain better wages, which became legal after the repeal of the Combination Acts in 1825, and still more by the increased cheapness brought by Free-trade and the repeal of the Corn-laws; the remedying of the third was the work of the Factory Acts.

The first of these, Peel's Act of 1802, has been already noticed, but it applied to a very small section, only indeed to those parish apprentices who had been bound out by parish authorities in order to get rid of them; the Act did not touch the case of children who went to work with their parents in the factories at six in the morning and worked on and on till seven, eight, or nine at night, with no fixed meal times, and no leisure, no education, and insufficient sleep, stunting their growth and deforming their bodies by long hours in cramped positions. Peel,[9] indeed, made another effort; he demanded an inquiry in 1815, and an Act was passed in 1819 laying down nine as the earliest age for entering a factory, restricting the hours for those between nine and sixteen years old to twelve, exclusive of meal times, and prohibiting night-work. Six years later Hobhouse's Act repeated that of 1819, with additional penalties for breaches of the law, and shortened the hours on Saturdays.

[9] Sir Robert Peel, first baronet, and father of the Prime Minister.

These acts did in reality but little; those of 1819 and 1825 applied to cotton-mills only; that of 1802 to parish apprentices, who were no longer employed, when steam-power brought the mills from the beck-sides back to the towns, where an abundant supply of child-labour could be got. And even where these acts applied they were not enforced with vigour or certainty; visits of inspection were neglected, or the visitors not admitted; the justices who heard the cases were frequently mill-owners, and in sympathy with the offender; the penalties were not deterrent. But a new period was beginning. It was not that the workmen had a much better chance of making themselves heard in the reformed Parliament than before, for after the Reform Bill the power of the moneyed class and the manufacturers in Parliament increased. But the land-owners and the Tory party began to take up the workmen's cause, perhaps a little out of revenge for their defeat over the Reform Bill. If the manufacturers had reformed them, they would retaliate by making the manufacturers set their house in order, and this spirit grew stronger as the manufacturers pressed on the reform which the Tory party dreaded most, namely, free-trade in corn. In fact, as we shall see, one of the greatest of the Factory Acts follows hard upon the heels of the abolition of the Corn-laws.

Not only did the oppressed artisans find allies, but they found leaders. Richard Oastler, nicknamed "the Factory King", began to inflame great meetings in Yorkshire by his eloquent descriptions of the workmen's wrongs. Michael Sadler took up their cause in Parliament, and though his bill failed to pass, he obtained the appointment of the Committee, whose report made it clear, even to the apathetic, that the ills were not imaginary, but real and pressing, and that something must be done to amend them. A still more valuable leader than either Oastler or Sadler was found in Lord Ashley,[10] who took up the cause in the reformed Parliament, when Sadler had lost his seat there. His sympathy, eloquence, and untiring devotion to the cause of all who were oppressed, his courage and steadfastness in the face of opposition from the manufacturers and occasional obloquy from his own side, did more than anything else to convince England of the disgrace which the condition of the factories was to her, and to bring the cause to a successful issue.

Although, as we now know, success lay ahead of the reformers, yet it must have seemed to Ashley and his comrades very far distant, and their progress towards it dishearteningly slow. Another act of Hobhouse's (1831) reduced the week's work for those under eighteen years from seventy-two hours to sixty-nine and prohibited night-work, but this again only applied to the cotton mills. But there were evils in other trades too, especially among the woollen manufacturers of Yorkshire, where the agitation took the firmest hold. Ashley's Ten Hours Bill of 1833 was defeated, and Althorp's Act[11] which the Government brought forward to

---

[10] Afterwards seventh Earl of Shaftesbury.

[11] This act applied to cotton, wool, worsted, hemp, flax, tow, linen mills, and besides prohibiting night work to all under eighteen, fixed 48 hours per week as the limit for those between the ages of nine and thirteen, and 69 per week for those between thirteen and eighteen. There were to be two

take its place was not found satisfactory; it did not go far enough, and its provisions were not well enforced. The manufacturers, however, were defeated in an attempt to repeal part of it in 1837, and in 1842 Ashley, who had sat at the head of a commission on the conditions of labour in the coal-mines, and had discovered a state of affairs still worse than in the factories, was able to carry a bill which forbade boys under ten and women from working underground. As the work which these had done, mainly indeed acting as beasts of burden and dragging trucks laden with coal through low galleries in which the shortest could not stand upright, had now to be done in some other way, the miners did for themselves what they had not done for their womenkind and children, namely, improved the galleries, making them a more reasonable size. The act also forbade the payment of wages in public-houses, and appointed inspectors. It was not indeed complete, and has since been extended, but it did a great deal by excluding women and children from the pits. Meanwhile the movement for the ten-hours day went forward. Peel indeed procured the rejection of Ashley's amendment in favour of this limit in 1844, by a threat of resignation if it was carried, but the act which was passed in that year further reduced the working day for children below thirteen, and included women among the protected persons; times for meals were more closely regulated and work after 4.30 p.m. on Saturdays forbidden; fines were

hours' schooling a day, and two whole and eight half-holidays given in the year.

increased and greater precautions taken against false certificates of age. Even greater was the concession made in 1847 when Fielden's proposal was carried, that from May 1st, 1848, all young persons[12] and women were to work a ten-hours day. As the mill-owners kept their factories open much longer than this, and detained some protected persons at work at some times and others at others, often managing to evade the law by the complexity of their arrangements, a further Act (1850) limited the working day for all young persons and women to the time between 6 a.m. and 6 p.m. in summer, and an hour later in each case in winter, no protected person being allowed to work after 2 p.m. on Saturdays; and the same rule was applied to children in 1853.

These acts (1850 and 1853), though applying only to the textile industries and to persons under the age of eighteen and to women, practically determined the conditions of the English working day. It is true that there have been numerous Factory Acts since, but they have been extensions of the same principle: the day's work which was thought right in the great group of textiles was accepted without much difficulty by the others; where exceptions seemed called for, they have been granted, but they are comparatively rare. Further, it is true that there is no restriction placed by these acts on adult men. But although under previous Factory Acts the number[13] of women and children

---

[12] *I.e.* between the ages of thirteen and eighteen.
[13] "In 1835 there were employed in the textile industry 27,715 boys and 28,378 girls under thirteen years of age; but in 1850 the numbers employed

employed had dwindled, and machinery had taken over much that they had previously done, yet their share of the work was still enough in the textile trades at any rate, to prevent the factories running without them; and so when the protected persons worked from six till six, the men did the same and no more. Lately a decided tendency to do less has appeared; but this is for a different reason; overwork is no longer the plea.

It is not necessary to dwell at length upon the good that has come from the Factory Acts; they have given to the factory boys and girls a chance of growing healthy and strong, and with some education and leisure, instead of living through a joyless, overworked childhood, to reach an age of exhaustion at a time when the powers of the body should be at their height. That is so plain as to need no pointing out. But it is not a little curious to notice how firmly the mischievous idea of *laissez-faire* established itself, and how hard it was to tear up the deep roots. Free-trade in goods was so simple, so easy, so refreshing, after the cumbrous system of Protection, that men argued that free-trade in labour between master and workman must be equally beneficial, and that the Factory Acts were hindrances to such freedom. Statesmen of liberal minds and wide sympathies, Peel, Bright, Cobden, Sir James Graham, Roebuck and Gladstone among them, opposed Ashley; many of them later admitted that they had been mistaken. In-

---

were only 21,137 boys and 19,638 girls" (Von Plener, *English Factory Legislation*). This decrease in number compared with the increase in the trade shows how much children's labour was being dispensed with.

deed the argument as applied to commodities and labour does not really run on the same lines; commodities care not where they go, and most of them can be stocked and suffer little loss of value. But labour is less fluid; it is attached to a home and is not ready to go hither and thither in pursuit of every trifling rise in wage; it cannot be stored; a day's work not done is a day's work lost, and in this sense labour is more perishable than any commodity. And finally it is human; if a manufacturer hold a stock of goods which have become unsaleable the goods must be got rid of; they must go for nothing if no one will buy them at any price; but it is impossible for anyone to advise similar treatment for labour that is unemployed and cannot get employment. Hence modern policy draws a distinction, and while allowing freedom in exchange of commodities aims at ensuring fairness in the exchange of labour.

CHAPTER XIX.

MODERN CONDITIONS: TRADE AND THE FLAG.

With the abolition of the Corn-laws and the definite acceptance of the theory of Free-trade, England parted from the last relic of the old system, and entered upon a new one. To give an account of modern conditions would be beyond the scope of this book. Just as natural landmarks owe their character to being conspicuous from a distance, so landmarks in an industrial progress can only be picked out when we are separated from them by a considerable interval of years; just as the traveller in an unknown and rugged country may be confused about his bearings, may mistake the shoulders of hills for their summits, may fail to grasp whither the streams that he crosses are bound, so among events, the outcome and mutual relations of which are not yet fully realized, events that have not yet passed out of the domain of politics, the historian may easily be led astray. Exploration must precede geography; just as the historian may become the geographer of the land of long ago, so the politician is the explorer of the land of the future. Attempts to shape the work of the former ere the task of the latter is complete must be necessarily unsatisfactory.

But even if it is going too far to form any definite opinions about the eventual outcome of what is taking place before our eyes, we may try to pick out some things which appear to be important when judged in the light of past experience; for if history is to teach us anything, it is to apply the past as a touchstone for the present. Selection will be easier if we bear in mind the broad tendencies of the development which has been traced. Thus we have seen society gradually becoming less complex; the influence of status has declined, the sphere of contract has been enlarged; there has been a gradual relaxation of social ties, a slurring-over of the lines of demarcation between class and class, an increase in the power of passing from one employment to another, a greater possibility of rising in the world, if a man has the ability or energy to force his way. In early days the Church, in which alone education was general, alone possessed the democratic character under which the son of a shoemaker might rise to be pope. As, however, education has successively passed from being the monopoly of clerics into being the possession of the well-to-do, and now has been extended till at present it is not only within the reach of all, but is thrust into their hands, so one great class difference has vanished, and one great obstacle to upward progress has been removed. But while the organization of the workers has become more simple, the industries themselves have become vastly more complex. As the advantages of division of labour in production are more and more recognized, specialization of skill has been carried further and further. Instead of a man knowing and practising two or more trades, as was the case when spinning and weaving were almost invariable among the agricultural population, it is now rare that a man is master of the whole of one trade. The modern tendency is for him to learn one process only. Again, we have seen England develop from a country mainly agricultural into one that is mainly industrial; the town population has grown at the expense of the rural population, and this tendency is becoming more marked with each succeeding year.

These are all tendencies that have been at work more or less steadily for a long period: it is not likely that the future will see any reversal in them. But with other policies that are younger we may entertain a doubt about their permanence. Even in the broad principle of freedom of trade, hesitations occur now and again. To imagine a return to the Corn-laws and the Mercantile system would be of course absurd, but it is open to doubt whether the nation as a whole is not becoming more impressed with the danger of foreign competition, and more ready to consider measures whose avowed object is to foster national industries than it was thirty years ago. Measures such as the Merchandise Marks Act, agitations against foreign sugar bounties, complaints against ship-owners who grant lower rates to foreign shippers than to English, the publication of quantities of statistics designed to show how foreign industries are gaining on us, sometimes in neutral markets, sometimes even in our own, are all indications that there is some uneasiness felt about the permanence of our industrial and commercial supremacy, and that in some cases at least there may be a wiser treatment than that of merely leaving the matter alone. So far as the uneasiness provokes keener energy, greater readiness to take advantage of improvements and new processes, a firmer determination not to be left behind in the race, then it is quite in accord with the key-note of Free-trade, namely, that under it each man will best be alert about his own interests and so promote the interests of all. Indeed, there is need for such watchfulness against the national as well as the individual carelessness which the security of success is apt to breed. It is a matter of common experience that great business houses become great through enterprise and remain great for a time by caution, but if, as often happens, that caution degenerates into timidity or lethargy, they are overtaken by younger and more vigorous houses. So, too, with the great industrial state of the world; she may despise her competitors; she may continue to make things as she has been accustomed to do, without allowing for the changes of fashion or the requirements of new conditions; she may refuse to alter her methods of buying and selling; but she may also awake when too late to find herself supplanted by the ingenuity and elasticity of her rivals, who are content with small profits and willing to make every effort to get a footing. It is possible that English industry and commerce are not sufficiently alive to this danger,[1] and thus the periodical agitations may serve a useful purpose. But there is no doubt whatever that in the minds of many there is another aim beyond this of keeping the nation on the alert, a much wider aim, namely, that of attempting to find some fresh methods whereby legislation and government regulation may again be used to foster national industry and commerce. Whether this party is rising in influence, or is merely the surviving remnant of Protectionists, whether if it grows in numbers it will be successful in any measures it adopts, of what nature these measures will be, are all questions for the future.

And putting on one side the question of whether

[1] For example, many orders are lost through our unfamiliar system of weights and measures, and the refusal to use the more widely spread and more easily understood Metric system; complaints are often made of our want of enterprise in refusing to alter patterns to suit local peculiarities; again insufficient pains are taken to push British goods in foreign countries by agents who speak the people's language. These things have been pointed out frequently in consular reports.

Government regulation can in the future assist in the building up of industries, as we have seen it do in the past, there is no question that the tendency to ask for Government interference in industrial concerns generally is on the increase. Ever since the Reform Bill of 1832 the legislative activity of Parliament has grown, and it goes on growing. Much of this legislation has been social legislation; indeed the original Factory Acts themselves have been so enlarged and extended to cover an enormous field with minute regulations of the relations between employer and employed, that if we were to seek an economic landmark of modern times, we should probably be led to fix upon this very remarkable outburst of philanthropic legislation as distinguishing the later part of the nineteenth century. One effect of this has been that the doctrine of *laissez-faire* as applied to the hiring of labour has been partly abandoned. It is remarkable also that the artisans generally have welcomed such legislation, and are prepared to have more of it; and the political importance of the artisan class has grown, and will probably grow further. If we may draw from the views ordinarily expressed in Trades-union Congresses an idea of what the working-classes would like their representatives to urge in Parliament, it is plain that all the activity of social legislation, all the minuteness of the Factory Acts of the past, would be as nothing with the all-embracing regulation that would follow: a compulsory diminution of the hours of the working day, an interference with the practice of leaving wages to be fixed by competition, a limitation of output, a retaliation of labour upon capital for presumed wrongs, would none of them seem impossible. The inference drawn may be a false one; Trades-union Congresses may represent agitators and faddists, and not the real bulk of opinion; by the time the artisans are strong enough to see their own men put forward their own measures in Parliament, and have a chance of carrying them, their general view may have changed. But the power of the industrial classes in Parliament is growing, and, so far as can be judged at present, they will use that power to enlarge, rather than to diminish, the scope of Government interference in industrial concerns. In the early years of the century economists spoke as if for the future politics and economics were parting company, but recent experience is far from confirming this view.

In another respect also the Government is increasingly called upon to interest itself in commercial questions. Reference has been made already to the share which the old colonial policy, as enforced under the Mercantile system, had in the loss of our American colonies. What happened there has not been without later parallels; Spain too has seen most of her American colonies revolt against her and become independent. There have been many who have held that this would be the end sooner or later of all colonies, but this inference can only be drawn fairly when the method of treating colonies remains the same. England, however, has discarded the old policy and adopted a new one, which offers greater promise of retaining colonial allegiance. Our colonies are no longer regarded as commercial possessions and possible commercial rivals; most have been given as complete liberty in self-government as is consistent with their remaining a part of the British Empire; the idea of profit and loss has been laid aside, and the idea of nationality substituted for it. The new policy has been successful up till now, and, so far as can be judged, bears the appearance of permanence. But whether the bond of union will be drawn closer, by imperial federation, by commercial connections, and by that lessening of physical distance which improvements in navigation and communication are continually bringing about; or whether the small differences which spring from a new climate and a new environment will grow until each colony will wish to become a distinct state, are questions which cannot be answered with confidence. At present the factors that make for union appear to be growing faster than those which make for separation. But the latter, though small, tend to be cumulative in nature, and cannot therefore be neglected. Moreover, we have yet to see what effect a wide-spread maritime war may have upon our colonies.

For in spite of the confidence of the Manchester school that for the future wars would become fewer and fewer, and that commerce and peace would go hand in hand, the progress of events has shown that this confidence was misplaced. The nineteenth century, tempestuous in its childhood, and then peaceful in its youth and manhood, has become quarrelsome in its dotage. The quarrels have not, so far, developed into wars, but the pacific spirit appears to be on the wane. Those who beat their swords into plowshares and their spears into pruning-hooks, have found it wiser to beat them back again; the lamb still finds the wolf an uncomfortable neighbour; not even the strong man armed can be sure of keeping his goods in peace. And the reason of this political uneasiness, resulting in frequent scares, is the jostling of colonial interests. The experience of the eighteenth century should teach us how fruitful a source of war colonial jealousy may be; and Europe has lately seen a violent revival of the desire for colonial expansion. France has not forgotten or forgiven her losses; Germany has entered the field as a new competitor; Russia has steadily pursued the extending of her influence eastwards. Each of these nations has found British claims and British dominions an obstacle to their plans. England has indeed occupied so much that the choice of the others is somewhat restricted, and while they naturally regard us as already possessing too much, popular opinion at home presses our Government not to allow our prospective interests to be threatened, and urges that for each step in advance which our rivals take we should take one also. This game of colonial grab is not to be played without international snarling and growling, especially where boundaries are imperfectly delimited, or where trading rights are granted by savage rulers over ill-defined areas of country. Should war result from these bickerings, it is well to realize that the reason is not the jealousy of race, or the clashing of the needs of national expansion, for the countries where the quarrels arise are not suited for European settlement. With the exception of parts of the plateau of east and south-east Africa, the unoccupied lands fit for European habitation have been seized upon; that they have largely fallen into British hands is another source of jealousy. But West Africa and China, where international colonial and commercial interests are most at cross-purposes, offer no inducements to colonization properly so called; the one has a deadly climate, the other is already filled with an abundant population. Territorial expansion is not in itself the end sought for; it is a means to an end, and that end is the desire to protect or extend trade and commerce. The new competitors feel strongly that trade is likely to follow the flag as it has done in the past; that the best hope of raising up an extended commerce lies in an extended territory. This may be a mistake; it may be possible to pay too dearly for settlements in unhealthy climates, to fail in colonial expansion because the race does not possess the colonial spirit, to imitate British policy without rivalling British success, to wear a lion's skin and yet be after all an ass. But with all our free-trading ideas, England still finds matter for alarm in French, German, and Russian territorial acquisitions, or in the spreading of their spheres of influence, wherever these seem to threaten, not indeed our existing trade, but the opportunities for its extension in the future.

If, then, European nations are going to follow Great Britain in striving after a world-wide commerce, while still adhering to a protective policy as to their own dominions, it is evident that the importance of commercial interests in the determining of international relations is likely to increase rather than to decrease. If the flags of other nations are to be carried further afield, in order to lead their trade thither, then it seems inevitable that British trade will have to go on similar lines. The amount of commercial No-man's land will wane; an exclusive system will be set up in many places where traders of all races hitherto have had an equal chance. It is true that, so far, we are but at the beginning of a fresh period of European extension. It may last long, or it may not. Events may lead to the failure of many of the rival world-empires that appear to be the present object of continental ambition, just as the world-empires of the seventeenth century fell to pieces in the eighteenth century. But so long as the present policy lasts, foreign policy will tend more and more to bear the character of foreign commercial policy, and the first duty of the Government will be to uphold the nation's interests abroad, and secure for its industry and commerce that scope which is necessary for its prosperity. This, indeed, is more than individual traders can do for themselves; and as England has in the past grown rich through her industry and commerce, and strong through her wealth, so there may be in the future the more need of a firm use of the nation's power to maintain the sources of wealth on which that power rests.

INDEX.

Achin, 203.
Acton Burnel, statute of, 80.
Ad pensum, 72.
Ad scalam, 72.
Adventurers, 188, 193, 199.
Aelfric's *Dialogues*, 21.
Agricola, 9.
Agriculture — Roman, 10; Saxon, 20, 21; in Norman times, 27, 28; effect of Black Death, 99, *seq.*; substitution of pasture for arable, 107; stock-and-land leases, 107; beginnings of tenant farmers, 108; enclosures, 136; corn-growing area diminished, 141; corn-growing for export, 157, 338; corn-laws, 158, *seq.*; bad harvests, 184.
Agrarian Revolution, Chap. XVI.; decay of yeomanry, 283; defects of open field, 284, 288; improved methods, 285; stock-breeding, 286; enclosure for arable farming; 291; loss of domestic bye-industry, 293; difficulties of small farmers, 295; political influences, 297.
Aix la Chapelle, 251.
Alexander VI., 191.
Alfred, 22.
Aliens, 49, 84, 85; immigration from Flanders, 91, 209; jealousy of, 92; privileges taken away, 120; tolls, 120; riots against, 211; immigration from Netherlands *temp.* Elizabeth, 212; various arts, 215; Huguenots, 216, *seq.*
Althorp's Act, 346.
Alva, 147, 210.
Amboyna, 205, 247.
American colonies, loss of, 252, 259, 260; grievances of, 258.
Amsterdam, 206; Bank of, 206, 230.
Ancient custom, 79.
Anjou, 87.
Anne, 297.
Annona, 10.
Antwerp, 146, 148.
Apprentices, 127, 130; Act of, 170, 175, 178, 179, 187, 323.

Aquinez, 107.
Aquitaine, 87.
Archangel, 194.
Arcot, 251.
Arkwright, 267.
Armada, 95, 194, 198.
Armed Neutralities, 255.
Armegon, 205.
Ashley, 346.
Asiento, 249.
Assize of Bread and Ale, 77.
Assize of Weights and Measures, 77.
Astbury, 275.
Aulnager, 93, 214.
Aulus Plautius, 9.
Australia, 261.
Auxilia, 15.

Bacon, 200, 274.
Baffin, 193.
Bagehot, 228.
Bailiff, 31.
Bakewell, 285.
Balance of trade, 167.
Balboa, 191.
Ball, 112.
Baltimore, 201.
Bancliffe, 327.
Bank of England, 3; foundation of, 239; opposition to, 240; notes, 241; and funds, 242; of St. George at Genoa, 229, 231; of Amsterdam, 230.
Banking, Chap. XIII.; beginnings of, 228; notes, 229; goldsmiths, 238; joint-stock banks, 241.
Barbados, 201.
Barbary Company, 203.
Barcelona, 190.
Bardi, 232.
Barker, 197.
Barnstaple, 213.
Barton aqueduct, 280.
Bath, 13, 99.
Beauchamp, 36, 38.
Bedfordshire, 141.
Bell, 211, 269.
Benedict Biscop, 24.

Benedict de Hulm, abbey of, 113.
Berkshire, 141, 291.
Bermudas, 201.
Best, 205.
Beverley, 56.
Birmingham, 130, 281.
Black Death, Chap. VI.; arrival, 96; mortality, 98; in East Anglia, 98; in towns, 99; scarcity of labour, 99; rise in prices and wages, 102; collision between land-owners and labourers, 105; Statute of Labourers, 105; failure of Parliament, 106; reaction of villein services, 110; peasant revolt, 112.
Blake, 206.
Blanching money, 73.
Bleaching, 276.
Boadicea, 14.
Bodmin, 99.
Boke of Surveying, 142.
Bolton, 224.
Bombay, 188, 205.
Bonhomme, 218.
Boon-work, 30.
Bordars, 29.
Borough English, 40.
Boston, 59.
Boston, U.S.A., 201.
Boulton, 265, 272.
Braddock, 251.
Bradford, 28.
Brandywine River, 251.
Brazil, 190.
Breda, declaration of, 248, *n*.
Bretigny, treaty of, 87, 90.
Bridgewater, Duke of, 278.
Bright, 342, 349.
Brindley, 278.
Bristol, 23, 24, 45, 89, 96, 145, 217.
Brittany, 87.   [225.
Bruges, 89, 92, 146.
Buckinghamshire, 141.
Bullionists, 166.
Burburata, 195.
Burgundy, 146.
Burton, 111.
Butlerage, 79.

Cabot, John, 190.
Cabral, 191.
Cacafuego, 197.
Caerleon, 14.
Caesar, 8.
Calais, 87, 89, 96, 120, 187.
Callao, 197.

Calvin, 237.
Cambridge, 23, 113, 291.
Canada, 252.
Canals, 278; Grand Trunk Canal, 279; cost of carriage, 280; canal mania, 280.
Canterbury, 24, 72, 89, 212, 217.
Canynges, William, 156.
Cape Breton, 198, 252.
Cape of Good Hope, 189, 197, 254.
Capital, 44, 169.
Carlisle, 72.
Carron, 271, 272.
Carta Mercatoria, 79, 80, 86.
Cartwright, 269.
Cash-nexus, 300.
Cassel, 92.
Cassivellaunus, 9.
Caursines, 83.
Cavendish, 197.
Cavendish, John de, 113.
Ceylon, 189, 254.
Champion, 142.
Chancellor, 193, 203.
Charles I., 155, 238.
Charles II., 188, 215; and goldsmiths, 238.
Charles the Great, 22.
Chester, 14, 24.
Chichester, 24, 72, 89.
Chideminstre, 37.
Chili, 196.
China, 191.
Cholesbury, 327.
Christopher, 207.
Cirencester, 14, 148.
City companies, 128.
Clement, 275.
Clive, 2, 251.
Clock-making, 218.
Cloth and cloth working, British, 11; alien weavers, 49, 56; imports of fine cloth, 85; Flemish immigrants, 91; worsted, 93; Clothworkers' Company, 128; progress of industry in fifteenth century, 144; varieties, 146; export of, 146; prohibition of import of foreign cloth, 147; Weavers' Act and prohibition of factories, 148; protective policy of Parliament, 156; immigrants from Netherlands, 211; "New Drapery", 212; varieties, 212; in West Riding and West of England, 213; clothiers, 213, 266; application of machinery

INDEX. 363

to, 294, *seq.*; decay of manufacture in East Anglia, 304, 305; "Spoilt child" of English manufactures, 309; duties on wool, 336.
Coal for smelting, 220.
Cobden, 331, 341.
Coinage, Saxon, 63; Norman, 70; fineness of, 71; alterations of, 169, 187; effect of new silver, 172; reform under Elizabeth, 174; under William III., 240.
Colchester, 13, 99, 117, 212.
Colebrookdale, 274.
Collegia, 14.
Colling, 287.
Cologne, 49.
Colonies, Chaps. XI. and XIV.; private effort, 202; second epoch of colonial gains, 245; gains by treaties, 247; list of existing colonies in 1690, 247 *n.*; struggle in India, 251 and 254; in N. America, 251; value of colonies, 256; new colonial system, 261.
Columbus, 190.
Combination Acts, 319.
Commendation, 26.
Committee of trade and plantation, 202.
Commutation, 42, 110.
Compotus, 38.
Connecticut, 201.
Continental system, 254.
Cook, 261.
Cookworthy, 275.
Coote, 221.
Cordilleras, 196.
Corn (see also *Agriculture*), high prices, 302, 340; corn-laws, 331, 337, 339; abolition of, 342; Anti-Corn-law League, 332, 341.
Corpus Christi, 113.
Cort, 273.
Cortez, 191.
Corunna, 198.
Cotters, 29.
Cotton, 224; prohibition of Eastern calicoes, 225; manufacture in England, 268, 254; growth of, 308.
Court rolls, 98.
Courts of assistants, 126.
Coventry, 146.
Craft gilds, 55, 76, 122; becoming exclusive, 124; growth of class differences, 125; livery, 126; apprentices, 127; journeymen, 127; efforts to escape control of, 130;
confiscation of religious property, 131; decadence of, 133.
Crawshay, 274.
Crediton, 213.
Cressy, 94, 96.
Crompton, 268.
Cromwell, 188, 198, 225, 238, 246.
Cuba, 252.
Curia Regis, 65.
Customers, 79.

Damnum emergens, 235.
Danegeld, 24, 64, 65.
Darby, Abraham, 222, 273.
Davis, 193.
Debts, 59.
De Donis, 78.
Defoe, 96.
Demerara, 254.
Deptford, 136.
Derbyshire, 141.
De Ruyter, 206.
Devonshire, 113.
Dialogus de Scaccario, 65.
Dite of Hoscbondrie, 31.
Domesday, 26, 32, 33, 38, 45.
Dominica, 252.
Dorchester, 14.
Dover, 13, 120.
Drake, 188, 195, 207.
Drapers' Company, 126, 146, 147.
Dudley, 220, 221, 222.
Duke of York, 206.
Dupleix, 250.
Durham, 72, 281.
Dyers, 215.

Earthenware, British, 13; progress in eighteenth century, 274.
East Anglia, 97, 145.
East India Company, 188, 202, *seq.*
Eastland merchants, 203.
Edgar, 22.
Edinburgh, 217.
Edward, 22.
Edward I., 47, 73, 76, 78, 80, 82, 83, 86, 111, 232.
Edward II., 86, 89.
Edward III., 7, 71; and commercial policy, 85, *seq.*; and staple, 89; freedom of trade under, 92, 96, 118, 128, 232.
Edward IV. and protection of home industries, 160, 164; wool, 210.
Edward VI., 131, 147; debases coinage, 172; poor-law, 184.

Edward Bonadventure, 194.
Edward the Confessor, 27.
El Dorado, 197.
El Draque, 197.
Elizabeth, 207.
Elizabeth, 7, 140, 144, 155, 156, 158; her legislation, Chap. X., 194; encourages immigrants, 212.
Ely, 23.
Embroidery, 24.
Enclosures, Chap. VIII.; area of, 141; failure to check, 143; Enclosure Acts, 290; progress of enclosures, 292.
Essequibo, 254.
Essex, 113, 141, 291.
Ethelred, 84.
Eumenius, 10.
Evil May Day, 211.
Exchequer, Ch. IV., 48; officials of, 66; payments at, 67; table, 67.
Exeter, 23, 72, 89, 213, 281.
Extensive cultivation, 18.
Extenta, 38.

Factories, long hours, 311; pauper apprentices, 315; commissioners on Factory Bill of 1832, 315; evils in, 316; travelling commissioners of 1833, 318; Factory Acts, 343, *seq.*; opposition to, 349; modern tendencies, 356.
Fairfax, 212.
Fairs: St. Denys, Rouen, Troyes, 22; Winchester, 59.
Ferm of the shire, 67.
Fielden, 348.
Fire of London, 3.
Fitzherbert, 142.
FitzNigel, 65, 74.
Flanders, 49; and weaving, 91; Count of, 210.
Florence, 85.
Florida, 252.
Flying shuttle, 266.
Fort Duquesne, 251.
Fort St. George, 205.
Fox, 193, 334.
Free tenants, 34, 39.
Free-trade, 331, *seq.*, 352.
Frobisher, 192, 207.
Fulham, 217.

Gascony, 49, 85, 87, 155.
Genoa, 190.
Ghent, 92.

Gibraltar, 249.
Gilbert, 198, 207.
Gilbert's Act, 324.
Glasgow, 23, 281, 277.
Glass-making, 219.
Gloucester, 14, 96, 141, 280.
Goldsmiths, 99, 128.
Gott, 270.
Great Harry, 207.
Great Intercourse, 147.
Great Tew, 103.
Gregory X., 233.
Grenada, 252.
Grenville, 199.
Gresham's law, 230.
Grocers' Company, 128.
Guienne, 90.
Guildford, 146.
Guinea Company, 203.
Guisnes, 187.

Halifax, 213.
Ham, 103.
Hansards, 146.
Hanse of London, 84; of Cologne, 85; Teutonic Hanse, 85; towns of the Baltic, 85.
Hanse towns, 49.
Harecastle, 280.
Hargreaves, 267.
Hastings, 24.
Hat-making, 218.
Hawkins, John, 195, *seq.*
Hawkins, William, 191.
Hawkins, William (the younger), 195.
Hayward, 31.
Heacham, 98.
Heathcoat, 270.
Henry I., 49, 71, 72, 74.
Henry II., 47, 51, 65, 71, 74.
Henry III., 70, 88.
Henry IV., 156.
Henry V., 156.
Henry VI., 125, 156, 177.
Henry VII., 70, 130, 149, 155, 171.
Henry VIII., 71, 131, 148, 155, 156, 171, 184; and interest, 237.
Hereford, 141.
Hertfordshire, 113, 141.
Heveringland, 98.
Hickley, 98.
Hide, 34.
Hispaniola, 195.
Hobhouse, 344.
Hore, 191.

Horrocks, 269.
Hosts, 120.
Hudson, 193.
Hudson Bay, 189, 247, 249.
Hull, 117.
Hunstanton, 98.
Huskisson, 335.

Incorporated trades, 181.
Industrial revolution, 180, 301; expansion of trades, 307; evils of, 310.
Inquest of sheriffs, 47.
Inquisitio Comitatus Cantabrigiæ, 134.
Institution books, 98.
Interest, 235.
Interlopers, 203.
Ipswich, 24, 48, 49, 54, 72.
Ireland, 97.
Iron and iron-working, British, 11; Saxon, 24; smelting with coal, 220; in Surrey and Sussex, 221. Iron-smelting with coal, 273; puddling, 273; rolling, 273; in South Wales, 274; iron vessels and bridges, 274; migration of, 304.
Isle of Wight, 142.
Ivan the Terrible, 194.

Jamaica, 188.
James, 193.
James I., 155, 200, 216.
Jamestown, 200.
Java, 197.
Jenny, the, 267.
Jesus, the, 195.
Jews, 54; and usury, 80; position of, 82; expulsion, 83.
John, 40, 48.
Justices of the Peace, 177.
Jutes, 17.

Katharine of Braganza, 188.
Kay, 266.
Keighley, 213, 317.
Kempe, John, 92.
Kendal, 146.
Kent, 8, 113, 141.
Ket, 142.
King, 298.

La Bourdonnais, 250.
Labour, immobility of, 306; women and children's, 308.
Labourers, Statutes of, 104, 117, 139, 176, 181.
Labrador, 191.
Laissez-faire, 313, 314, 315, 355.
Lancashire, 280, 281, 293, 294, 323.

Lancaster, Sir J., 204.
Lane, 199.
Latifundia, 26.
Law merchant, 59.
Leeds, 213, 231.
Leicester, 46, 99, 141.
Leicester, Lord, 287.
Levant Company, 203.
Lewes, 24.
Liber burgus, 48, 54.
Lincoln, 14, 45, 72, 89, 141.
Linen—in Ireland, 222, *seq*.; in Scotland, 223.
Lisbon, 198; treaty of, 248.
Liverpool, 281.
Liverymen, 126.
Locke, 202.
Lombards, 83, 160.
London, 13, 24, 45, 56, 64, 72, 117, 212, 217, 220.
London Company, 200, 203.
Lucca, 85.
Lucrum cessans, 235.
Lynn, 72.

Macadam, 278.
Machinery and Power, Ch. XV.; England first in the field, 265; in weaving, 266; in spinning, 267; power-loom, 269, 308; colour-printing, 269; lace-making, 270; linen, 270; steam-engine, 271, 272; effects of labour-saving machinery, 307.
Mackintosh, 277.
Madras, 205.
Magdalen College, 109.
Magellan, 191.
Magna Carta, 77.
Maine, 87.
Malmesbury Abbey, 148.
Malta, 254.
Malthus, 313.
Manchester, 130, 224, 281.
Manilla, 252.
Manorial System, Ch. II.; origin, 19, 26; end of, 144.
Markets, 49.
Marlborough, 56.
Maroons, 196.
Marseilles, 190.
Mary, 184, 194.
Maryland, 200, 201.
Massachusetts, 201.
Matilda of Flanders, 209.
Maudslay, 275.
Mauritius, 189.

Mayflower, 201.
Melcombe Regis, 96.
Mellor, 293.
Men of the Emperor, 22, 84.
Mercantile System, Ch. IX.; good and bad trades, 151; main objects, 153; shipping, 154; fishing, 156; corn, 158; home industries, 160; and money, 163;. fallacy in, 165; decadence of, 227; old ideas discarded, 334; and American colonies, 258.
Merchandise Marks Act, 353.
Merchant adventurers, 146, 202.
Merchant gilds, 51, *seq.*; and craft gilds, 55; decay of power, 122.
Merthyr Tydvil, 274.
Merton, Statute of, 138.
Mexico, 191.
Miller, 277.
Minden, 3.
Mining—tin, 12; iron, 11, 24; lead, 12; copper, 12; coal, 12, 220, 347; [salt, 226.
Minorca, 249.
Mints, 71.
Molmen, 40.
Moluccas, 197.
Monasteries, 132, 183.
Money, legislation on, 161; direct regulation, 164.
Money economy, 63.
Monk, 206.
Monkwearmouth, 24.
More, 142.
Mortmain, 78.
Moscow, 194.
Muir, 277.
Mule, 268.
Municipia, 14.
Murray, 270, 275.
Muscovy Company, 194, 203.

Napoleon's efforts to destroy English colonial empire, 253; continental system, 254.
Nasmyth, 275.
National Debt, 238.
Natural economy, 63.
Navigation Acts, 152, *seq.*, 188, 206, 246, 335.
"Navvies", 280.
Newcastle, 89, 127, 220, 281.
Newcomen, 271.
New Custom, 79.
New England, 200.
Newfoundland, 189, 191, 198, 249.

New York, 188.
New Zealand, 261.
Nicea, Council of, 233.
Nombre de Dios, 196.
Nootka Sound, 253.
Norfolk, 141, 142, 290, 291.
Northampton, 72.
North-east Passage, 192.
North-west Passage, 192.
Northwich, 225.
Norwich, 23, 45, 72, 89; and Black Death, 98, 117, 212, 217, 281.
Nottingham, 23, 28.
Nova Scotia, 189, 247.
Nova Zembla, 193.

Oastler, 346.
"Oceanic", 190.
Offa, 22.
Oxenham, 197.
Oxford, 23, 56, 72, 141.

Panama, 196.
Paper-making, 218.
Paris, peace of, 189; treaty of (1763).
Parliament, first appearance in commercial legislation, 78.
Pasha, 207.
Peasant revolt, 112, *seq.*, 139.
Peel, 168, 331, 337, 347.
Peel, Sir R. (first baronet), 315.
Pelican, 207.
Pennsylvania, 201.
Peru, 191, 196.
Peruzzi, 232.
Philip II., 194.
Philip of Valois, 210.
Philippine Islands, 191.
Piacenza, 85.
Picts, 17.
Pie Powder, Court of, 59.
Pilgrim Fathers, 200, 201.
Pipe Roll, 73.
Pitt (the younger), 333, 334.
Pizarro, 191.
Plague of 1665, 96.
Plymouth Company, 188, 203.
Poena Conventionalis, 234.
Poictiers, 94.
Political economy, 312; and *laissez-faire*, 313; misunderstandings, 314.
Poll-taxes, 112.
Ponthieu, 87.
Poor-law, 170, 181, *seq.*; prohibition of open beggary, 182; compulsory poor-rate, 184; work to

INDEX. 367

be found, 186; law of settlement, 321; workhouse test, 321; increase in rates, 322, 327; Gilbert's Act, 324; Speenhamland Act, 324; evils of, 325; new poor-law, 330.
Population, growth of, 280.
Portoria, 13.
Posidonius, 12.
Potosi silver-mines, 2, 172.
Pottery. See *Earthenware*.
Power-loom, 265.
Precariæ, 30.
Prices during sixteenth century, 171, [175.
Prisage, 79.
Provost, 31.
Pytheas, 11.

Quia Emptores, 78.
Quit-rents, 44.

Radcliffe, 269, 308.
Raleigh, 197, *seq.*
Red Dragon, 207.
Reeve, 31.
Reform Bill, 95.
Rennie, 278.
Rent, 108; under Mercantile system,
Ricardo, 314. [159.
Richard I., 77, 85.
Richard II. and peasant revolt, 114; and aliens, 119, 126, 160; and shipping, 154; corn-growing, 157; and money, 164, 177.
Richard III., 211.
Rio de la Hacha, 195.
Roads, 277.
Roberts, Lewis, 224.
Rochester, 24, 72.
Roe, 205.
Roebuck, 222, 271, 273.
Roger of Estra, 47.
Roger of Salisbury, 72.
Roman invasion, 9; roads, 9; villas, 9; corn-growing, 10; peace, 14; taxation, 14; withdrawal from Britain, 20; Roman law on slaves,
Rouen, 22. [41.
Rule of war of 1753, 257.
Ryswick, treaty of, 247.

Sadler, 316.
Sailcloth, 218.
St. Albans, 9, 14, 23, 98.
St. Denys, 22.
St. Domingo, 188.
St. Edmunds, 23, 59, 178.
St. Ives, 59.

St. Kitts, 189, 249.
St. Lucia, 189.
St. Ninian, 23.
St. Thomas Aquinas, 61.
Salt, 13, 21, 38; brine-salt makers, 225; rock-salt, 225.
Sandwich, 24, 212, 217.
Saxons, Ch. I.; invasion of, 17.
Scapula, 9.
Sceattas, 63.
Scot and lot, 48.
Scotland, 97.
Scots, 17.
Senegal, 252.
Seneschal, 31.
Seneschaucie, 31.
Several, 141.
Shaftesbury, 202.
Sheep-farming. See *Wool.*
Sheffield, 130, 281.
Shields, 225.
Shropshire, 141.
Silchester, 14.
Silk-workers, 216, *seq.*; duties, 336.
Silver from America, 158, 163, 172.
Simon de Montfort, 95.
Slaves, 19, 29.
Smeaton, 271, 278.
Smith, Adam, 311; and freedom of trade, 312, 334, 340.
Smith, Henry, 139.
Smith, John, 200.
Smuggling, 333.
Socmen, 34.
Somerset, Duke of, 148, 212.
Southampton, 24; merchant gild at, 51, 76, 212, 217, 225.
South Sea Company, 238.
Southwark, 212.
Sovereignty of the sea, 90.
Speenhamland, 324.
Spenser, 114.
Spice Islands, 191, 254.
Spitalfields, 217, 336.
Squirrel, 199, 207.
Stafford, 281.
Staple, 88, *seq.*
Starre, 113.
Statuta Civitatis Londoniæ, 80.
Steelyard, 85, 120, 202.
Stephen, 33.
Stock-and-land leases, 107.
Stourbridge, 59.
Strafford, 223.
Stretton Baskerville, 138.
Stump, 148.

Sturtevant, 221.
Suetonius Paullinus, 9.
Suffolk, 113, 141.
Surat, 205.
Swan, 207.

Tacitus, 17.
Tally, 69.
Tangiers, 138.
Taunton, 213.
Telford, 278.
Tennant, 277.
"Thalassic", 190.
Thetford, 113.
Thorne, 191.
Three-field system, 20, 27, *seq*.; defects of, 284.
Tison, 191.
Tiverton, 213.
Tobago, 189, 252.
Tomkins, 287.
Torrington, 213.
Towns, Ch. III. and VII.; Roman, 13; Saxon dislike of, 23; growth of, 23; under manorial and royal control, 46; gain freedom, 48; corporate responsibility, 48; maintenance of liberties, 49; and merchant gilds, 51; progress of, 54; townsmen and foreigners, 75; exclusive privileges diminished, 87; affected by Black Death, 117; recovery of privileges under Richard II., 119, 123; decay of corporate towns, 131.
Townshend, 285.
Toynbee, 312.
Trial of the Pyx, 73.
Tributum, 14.
Trinity House, 156.
Troyes, 22.
Tull, 285.
Twyford, Thos., 138.

Usury, 232, *seq*.
Utrecht, treaty of, 189, 249.

Valparaiso, 197.
Van Tromp, 206.
Vasco da Gama, 190.
Venetians, 160.
Venice, 190.
Vera Cruz, 196.
Vermuÿden, 216.
Versailles, peace of, 255.
Vespasian, 9.
Vigo, 198.

Villeinage, 29; reaction owing to Black Death, 110; eviction of villeins, 140; villeinage extinct, [144.
Virgate, 29.
Virginia, 199.
Vortigern, 17.

Wakefield, 213.
Wales, 97.
Walsingham, 97.
Walter of Henley, 31.
Wandsworth, 218.
Wareham, 24.
Waterloo, 95.
Water-twist, 267.
Watt, 271, 272.
Wealth of Nations, 311, 332.
Weavers. See *Cloth*.
Weavers' Act, 148.
Wedgewood, 276, 279.
Week-work, 30.
Westminster, 65, 89; first statute of, 79.
White, 199.
Whitworth, 275.
Wilkinson, 272, 274.
William I., 27, 44, 50.
William III., 239.
Willoughby, 193.
Winchcombe, John, 148.
Winchester, 24, 45, 56, 59, 64, 72, 89; Statute of, 79.
Wine-trade, 90.
Wolfe, 2.
Wolsey, 211.
Wool (see also *Cloth*) exports to Flanders, 88; increase of sheep-farming, 107, Ch. VIII.; enclosures and depopulation, 136; export of, 146; destruction of Flemish manufactures, 210; Spanish wool, 210.
Worcestershire, 141.
Worsley, 278.
Wrawe, 113.
Wroxeter, 14.
Wycliff, 112.

Yardland, 29.
Yarmouth, 79.
Yeomen's guilds, 128.
York, 13, 14, 23, 45, 131.
Yorkshire, 113, 141, 280, 281.
Young, 277, 289, 290, 292, 298, 323.
Ypres, 92.

Zosimus, 10.

www.ingramcontent.com/pod-product-compliance
Lightning Source LLC
Chambersburg PA
CBHW031418230426
43668CB00007B/350